Reshma Ruia is an award-winning author and poet. Her first novel, *Something Black in the Lentil Soup*, was described in the *Sunday Times* as 'a gem of straight-faced comedy'. She has published a poetry collection, *A Dinner Party in the Home Counties*, and a short story collection, *Mrs Pinto Drives to Happiness*; her work has appeared in international anthologies and journals, and she has had work commissioned by the BBC. She is the co-founder of The Whole Kahani – a writers' collective of British South Asian writers. Born in India and brought up in Rome, her writing explores the preoccupations of those who possess a multiple sense of belonging.

STILL LIVES

RESHMA RUIA

SPEAKING
TIGER

SPEAKING TIGER BOOKS LLP
125A, Ground Floor, Shahpur Jat, near Asiad Village,
New Delhi 110049

First published by Renard Press Ltd in 2022
First published in India by Speaking Tiger in 2024

Cover design by Will Dady

ISBN: 978-93-5447-893-2

10 9 8 7 6 5 4 3 2 1

Printed at Chaman Enterprises, New Delhi

CONTENTS

STILL LIVES

FOR THOSE WHO ARE LOST
AND CALL MANCHESTER HOME

We are most alive when we're in love.
JOHN UPDIKE

1

BIRTHDAY WISHES

I turn fifty-five this year.

'You're getting on, old man,' Gupta says when I meet him for a drink after work. He sips his orange juice through a straw like a girl.

I look at his grey lips sucking in the juice. 'There are things I'd still like to do,' I say.

'Like what? Don't tell me you're still banging on about becoming a...' – his mouth contorts as he says in a mock French accent – 'a couturier?'

I push the bowl of peanuts towards him and shrug.

It's early evening and the Victoria in Chorlton isn't busy. A boy in a black biker jacket stands fiddling with the shiny buttons of the jukebox by the door, and the woman behind the bar is polishing beer glasses. Her bright pink lipstick is too young for her face. There's music playing, but it's new stuff, full of banging drums.

I finish my Budweiser and get up to buy another. When I come back, Gupta is still waiting for an answer. He's an accountant. He likes to get to the bottom of things.

'Maybe Geeta is throwing you a surprise party?' His eyes stay fixed on my face.

'Fat chance,' I say. 'I'll be lucky if she remembers. Anyway, it's no big deal. It's only a birthday.'

'Tell you what,' he says. 'Forget having a party. Be a rebel and go to Hertz, hire a fancy American car – a silver Lincoln or a Cadillac – and drive up to Scotland. Take a break from the bloody business. Run away from the family. There'll be plenty of Scotch, and I've heard the lasses in Edinburgh are bonnie.' He clears his throat and grins.

He's in a good mood because it's a Thursday, which means he'll soon be going home to have sex with his wife.

* * *

Driving home, I overtake a hearse on the M56. There are blurred faces inside the cars that follow. The rain hits the windows, smudges their features and streaks down their cheeks, like a clown's tears. I think of Gupta's words. I think of my twenty-five-year-old self, who left Bombay ready to start a new life in America. I'd only stopped in Manchester for a few days to see an old school friend – Gupta – who was studying accountancy at Manchester Poly.

'Stay a bit longer?' he suggested when it was almost time for me to catch a plane to America. We were sat at a bus stop eating our fish and chips, our fingers stinking of vinegar, waiting for the 215 to take us to Levenshulme to Gupta's rented one-bedroom flat. 'Manchester's small. It'll be easy to make money here. To hell with America!' he said, cocking a finger to the sky. His eyes were lonely, but he had swagger in those days.

I stared at the clouds and the dull brown huddle of buildings around, and thought, He's right. It would be easy to shine in such a small place.

'Tell you what, I'll stay for a bit,' I said, slapping him on the back. I'd make a few quid and then move on, I said.

Those early days. We were like brothers, Gupta and I, sharing rooms in Levenshulme, whining about the cold and the thin English girls with their bony thighs who giggled at our accents but let us squeeze their breasts at the Bellevue cinema.

Manchester was a mistake. I should've carried on to America, got proper training in high-tech design, then moved to France.

'Why do you want to mess around in America?' Father had asked me. 'It's a godless place. Stay here. Bombay is booming, beta. Even McDonalds is opening a branch in Juhu.'

But I'd made up my mind. 'I want to try my luck in America,' I said. I had received a scholarship offer to study textile printing at Delaware college. Over there, anything was possible. India was a dead-end street, strangled by red tape and babus begging for bribes. America was the future, with its shiny, germ-free, dirt-free cities. I thought of my job as a shipping clerk in Wadia & Sons, and told Father I was sick of running errands, answering phones and preparing endless cups of chai for the department.

Father jabbed his finger against my chest. 'You've got a soft Indian brain; it won't work in America. They will fry you alive, son.'

He was sixty, an old man, and I was his only child. I understood his desperation, so I kept quiet and let him rant. Mother would've backed me, told me I was right, but she was dead.

We stood in the queue at the State Bank of India. I watched him draw out his savings. Eight thousand rupees for a one-way ticket to New York via Doha with a longer stop in Manchester. Travel didn't come cheap in those days.

'I'll come back rich and famous,' I promised him, slipping the notes into my wallet.

Father just kept shaking his head, his eyes hazy with tears. The day I left he broke a coconut for good luck and handed me a silver coin with Goddess Lakshmi imprinted on it. I must still have it somewhere. 'At least try and be sad,' he said.

But breaking the journey in Manchester and staying with Gupta was a mistake. I got caught there, stuck in the business of buying and selling second-rate frocks. America became just a name on a map.

* * *

Turning fifty-five *is* a big deal. It needs acknowledgement.

So one day, instead of going through unsold stock at my warehouse, I visit a personalised registration plate dealer in Stockport and buy a personal number plate for my car: PK 1. It has a nice ring to it. It says I'm a Somebody. I have to outbid a Paul Kennedy by two thousand quid. I don't tell Geeta how much it cost; I say it's a birthday present from a grateful customer in Ireland.

'The Irish are just like the Indians, don't you think – so kind and big-hearted,' she says. 'But there was no need for such a showy birthday present. You're not a child.' Her hands dip in and out of a big Pyrex bowl of flour as she speaks.

I'd like her to go outside and admire the car with the new number plate, but she stays put.

'Later. Maybe later,' she says. 'I'm busy baking bread.' She waves her flour-covered hands proudly.

'What's wrong with Warburtons bread?' I ask.

I know she'll make a mess in the kitchen, and the bread will burn or stay dense and uncooked in the middle. She's always been a lousy cook.

'Amar wants to try home-made bread instead. Miss Connor was going on and on in class about the wonderful smell of home baking.' Geeta scratches her nose and the flour settles like chalk dust on her nose and chin.

'Good luck, Delia Smith,' I say. 'Just make sure you don't burn the kitchen down.'

I walk out of the kitchen and go outside to check my shiny new number plate, already screwed on to the second-hand Mercedes. In my excitement, I almost knock next door, but then I remember Mr Peters is English, and doesn't like being disturbed.

* * *

Ten years ago, I took out a big mortgage and shifted from Longsight, with its noisy West Indian neighbours, to Bloomsbury Close in Timperley, just south of Manchester. The streets are hush-hush here, and the houses have fancy names like 'Fairholme' and 'Chatsworth'. We have British neighbours – proper ones with English as their first language. I give them a bottle of Johnnie Walker Black Label every Christmas. Our new house has a small garden where I keep trying, without much luck, to grow a mango tree.

'I don't like it. It's too far away and too lonely.' That's all Geeta could say when the woman from Bridgfords first showed us the house.

'Far away from what? India?' I asked, as the agent waited on the front step, arms folded, a thin smile on her lips. She'd told us earlier that we'd be the first Asian family in the neighbourhood. 'That's progress, don't you think?' I said with a grin. I pointed out the electric gates and the garage to Geeta. 'What more do you want? We'd even have an en suite. No more going down the corridor at night searching for the loo.'

Geeta still shook her head. 'It's too big – I do love the gates, but I'll miss…' She hesitated before saying she'd miss Mrs Ahmed, our neighbour in Longsight. They did their weekly shop in Rusholme together, and always stopped for a gossip and a samosa at Pundit's afterwards.

'We're moving here for Amar,' I reminded her. 'There are better schools in this area. He will get more attention at Willows Grammar school if he's lucky enough to get in. And you can invite Mrs Ahmed here. Show off the en suite.' Once I brought our son into the equation, she agreed straight away.

The first time Gupta came around for dinner in our new house, his mouth hung slack in envy. 'Lucky bastard,' he whispered. His eyes were like hamsters, running across everything. 'You've landed on your feet, all right, PK. A detached house in Timperley, pukka English neighbours and just ten minutes to the motorway.'

Mrs Ahmed dropped in a few times, too. Geeta switched on all the lights, flung open the doors and showed her the en suite and the Italian black leather sofa from Arighi Bianchi in the lounge, her eyes flashing with pride. Mrs Ahmed soon stopped coming.

'People are so busy these days,' Geeta said with a shrug. 'It is this country. It gives you no time to breathe. Everyone is just huffing and puffing, puffing and huffing. She has no time for me any more.' Her lips trembled as she said this.

* * *

One day, soon after I bought my number plate, an invite arrives.

BEN LAWTON REQUESTS THE PLEASURE OF YOUR COMPANY
AT A GOLFING DINNER AT MOWBRAY HALL

'Why have they invited you?' Geeta says. 'You don't even play golf.'

'Why shouldn't they invite me? I was their biggest account for ten years. You should know this.'

She looks at the stiff, cream-coloured invite as though it were a bomb. 'A whole weekend? What do they think, you're just sitting around doing nothing?'

It's a Wednesday morning and I'm sitting around doing nothing, in no hurry to leave for work. Geeta, dressed in her weekday uniform of a blue velour tracksuit, is slicing an apple, head bent low and mouth open in concentration. Breadcrumbs cling to her top.

'Are there any mangoes?' I ask. They are my favourite fruit.

'No Alphonso mangoes this year, only the sour Pakistani ones. I didn't bother buying them. There's drought in Gujarat – at least, that's what Zee TV said,' she says without looking up. 'Ravi won't get them till next month.'

Ravi is the Indian grocery store in Rusholme where Geeta does her weekly shop on her way back from the temple.

'Besides, Amar likes apples,' she says, smacking my hand as I lean forward to grab a slice. The slices are neatly arranged in a semicircle on the plate.

I check the cuckoo clock above the sideboard. The hour and minute hands have gone missing over the years, lost in our many house moves. Only the bird remains, chirping out the time in a sickly, syrupy tune. I want to replace it with a digital clock, but Geeta won't let me.

'How come Amar's not left for school?' I ask, knowing her excuses will be ready.

'He's not feeling well,' Geeta says. She gets up to fill the kettle. 'Poor thing. He's got a terrible headache, so I told him to take the day off.'

'Second time he's done this. Last week it was a toothache. He's nearly fifteen, not some old codger.' I say this loudly so Geeta can hear me above the hissing kettle.

'Calm down – he's only a kid,' she says, buttering a slice of toast and pushing the plate towards me.

I look at the invite again and check the dress code.

'I'll need a new suit. The one from Debenhams is looking a bit shabby.'

'What's the point wasting money on a new suit just for two days? I'll get your brown one dry-cleaned and we'll buy another one in the January sales,' Geeta says.

The tracksuit bottoms are too tight on her. Her hips flare out as she bends down to open the sideboard where she stores her Haldiram snacks. She pulls out a Tupperware, grabs a fistful of salted cashew nuts and shoves them in her mouth. The salt leaves a faint silver dusting on her lips.

I catch my reflection in the kitchen window and suck in my stomach, run a quick hand through my hair, slap my jawline. It is still firm, and I have a full head of hair. It's going grey, but I'm in good shape for a mostly sedentary Indian fifty-five-year-old man. Geeta's different; there she sits, quietly giving up on herself, letting the careless pounds weigh down her five-foot frame year after year. Her once wide-open and alert eyes are now small and heavy, hooded with fatigue. Her mouth is set in a thin, anxious line. I want to help her, but I don't quite know how.

* * *

Geeta mentions my invite to her older sister Lopa, who is in Bombay. She phones dutifully every Sunday at 8 p.m. Indian Standard Time. There are letters, too, that she writes – maybe once a month – where she can gush about the misery and glory of her English life.

'Yes, didi, the business is doing well…' she says that day, glancing at me. I turn the newspaper page so she won't think I'm eavesdropping. 'Yes… he's so busy with all the orders… not so cold in Manchester now… he's been invited to an exclusive dinner at the Mowbray Hall.'

The way she says it, you'd think Mowbray was a household name in Bombay, like Buckingham Palace or Harrods. I like the little white lies Geeta feeds her didi about the business doing well. I wish I could believe them myself as I drive up to my warehouse in Grotton day after day, year after year.

A few days before the golf do, I nip into Moss Bros on King Street and treat myself to a new Italian suit with a crimson silk lining. I want to look successful. Back at work, I ring Ben, my accountant at Coopers, the one responsible for the invite.

'Glad you can make it, PK,' he says. 'What's your handicap these days?'

'I haven't played for some time, but it's in single figures.' I make sure Margaret, my secretary, doesn't hear me. I haven't touched a golf club in years, and she knows. But she's in the corridor making photocopies. I'd moved the stationery cupboard and the photocopier there on her advice. It stops the girls pilfering little things like staplers and printing paper.

'I've got some bankers coming up for the weekend,' Ben continues. He knew I was looking to buy some Italian cloth-cutting machines. 'Someone quite important is coming too,' he adds after a pause.

'Prince Charles?' I joke, but there's a dull ache at the pit of my stomach. Bankers mean numbers, which means doing sums, showing profit and loss margins, explaining why my sales figures are quietly tumbling down like a house of playing cards.

Ben laughs. 'Not quite. But someone who might be more useful to you – Cedric Solomon, schedule permitting, of course.' His voice turns reverential.

'How did you manage to rope Cedric Solomon in?' I sit up straight and say Cedric's name loud enough for Margaret to hear.

Cedric is the god of my rag-trade universe. He had swooped into Manchester from nowhere and was busy swallowing up the high street, buying businesses that were teetering on failure and loss-making labels that were still on the shelf past their sell-by date. He polished them, baptised them with sexy new names, and kerching! I hated his appetite and his guts.

'Cedric and I were at school together,' Ben says. 'He's doing it as a favour really. He's a busy man, you know.'

I put the phone down and turn to Margaret, who's now standing by my chair, holding invoices for me to sign. 'Cedric Solomon is coming to the golf do,' I say.

'That's nice.' Her guarded voice gives away nothing. 'You could talk to him about the denim jackets. We over-ordered. He might want to buy the excess stock off us?' She pulls a hanky from her rolled-up M&S sweater sleeve and blows her nose. The damp walls of the warehouse have given her a year-round sniffle.

'I've been trying to fix a meeting with him for years.' I light my first cigarette of the day. 'Just imagine – what if Cedric likes our stuff… who knows what might happen! We could even crack JCPenney and sell in America – he has enough contacts there.'

I shut my eyes and think of the possibilities. America. It's where I should've been right from the start. Americans loved value for money, and my clothes were just that – Italian flair at Chinese prices. All I needed was a backer, someone like Cedric Solomon who'd put up the funds for the stock. And once the stock was gone, I could wrap up this business and go back to my first love, designing clothes – proper clothes that carried the style and cut of masters like Yves St Laurent and Pierre Cardin. Who knows, I could even have an atelier in Paris.

Solomon was shrewd. He'd take a chance on an old pro like me. I've worked in fashion long enough – not the glossy French sort like Dior or Chanel, which is what I really wanted, but the cheap, cash-and-carry variety, specialising in rip-offs of designer gear. I call it my Homage Line. A service to Joe Public. I alter a pocket here, a zip there, and sell it wholesale to retailers – mainly small-time shop keepers – who sell it on to the customer.

I became a hit at the right time: women were reading magazines and watching films and spending more on clothes. They wanted to look like film stars. They couldn't get to St Tropez, but they could wear an LBD to a Salford pub and play at being Audrey Hepburn for a night.

Three years after moving to Manchester, I took out a loan from the Bank of Baroda and expanded the business for a song, soon getting the hang of selling skirts and T-shirts to punters hungry for cheap stuff from the Far East, long before the likes of Primark and Peacocks. I was the first to do it, no question about it, flicking through magazines like *Vogue* for ideas and kitting out the masses on the cheap. They were the golden days. The phone never stopped ringing. The faxes never stopped rolling. The air stank of money.

'I told you we'd be all right,' I said to Geeta after an enquiry came from Mrs Shrimpton, the chief buyer at BHS. She'd nodded happily, her fingers busy knitting booties, her body apple-round with our first child.

I sent Father a photograph of the warehouse, along with a newspaper cutting from *The Grotton Evening News*. There I was, right on the centre page, standing proud in front of the red-brick two-storey warehouse. I was 'the new face of immigration in England – an employer bringing jobs to deprived areas, not a scrounger on social benefits.'

'Don't tempt fate,' Father wrote back in his simple villager's English. 'Luck is like fruit: leave it hanging on the tree too long, it will ripen and rot before your eyes.'

He was right.

At fifty-five, the tide's turned. I own a warehouse the size of two football pitches, but most of it lies shrouded in darkness, musty with unsold stock. New-generation Asians and Jews working out of sweatshops on Cheetham Hill are busy churning out tatty copies off the catwalk. They are always a step ahead, with their websites and smooth-talking salesmen.

Entire weeks pass before the phone rings with an order, and when they do, it's always a tiny one from places like Doncaster and Belfast – places I wouldn't even spit at before.

'Why should the girls break their backs over twelve wraparound skirts for a family store in Bognor Regis?' I say to Margaret, but she's a trooper who won't give up the fight, going around the warehouse switching off lights, sending off for Italian brochures, doing all that she can to keep Malik Textiles from sinking.

Each day I watch the girls leave the warehouse on the dot at five. The days of overtime and last-minute orders are gone. My world is changing. The profit margins on my dresses are shrinking, the big chains are going direct to China and Bangladesh and the local market is crowded with competitors, smarter and younger, snapping at my heels.

'Malik Textiles is no longer the leader of the pack,' I tell Margaret after my chat with Ben.

'What can you do? It's the way of the world...' she says, shaking her head slowly from side to side like a wise Buddha. Margaret's from Scotland. They're used to expecting the worst.

I could tell Geeta all this, but I don't. She has worries of her own. I can read them in the lines that score her forehead like cuts from a knife.

* * *

This summer was particularly bad. Manchester rains chased away the sun yet again. I sit at my desk, surrounded by two container loads of unsold cotton frocks. There are days I want to set a match to the whole damn warehouse and run away to some far-off place.

I phoned my father the day we lost our biggest account.

A ten-year partnership ended in a two-line fax from the head buyer at Croakhams. I found out they were going direct and opening a warehouse in Guangzhou.

'Don't fool yourself into thinking things will get better,' Father rasped over the phone. 'They just tick-tock along until one day you wake up and the whole thing explodes in your face. Boom – just like a bomb.'

'Is that all you can say?'

'I told you, you should never have left Bombay. You should have been here for my old age. It's the gods punishing you now for abandoning your country and your father.'

I slammed the phone down.

He died a month later. A sudden heart attack felled him near his flat in Bombay. A passer-by found my number in his pocket.

* * *

'Here, come closer. Give me a hug, at least,' I whisper to Geeta that night. Talking to Ben has made me hopeful. I slip an arm around her waist, my fingers sinking into the softness, trying to find a spark somewhere between my wandering hand and her slumbering flesh.

'I don't know why you're bothering with this trip,' Geeta says, moving to her side of the bed. 'You won't be there to watch Amar play his match.'

'Something good will come out of it. I can feel it. I can network and make some new contacts. Who knows, I might even be able to start designing again.' I smile into the darkness.

'What's the point? I've seen your wonderful designs. They're too…' She frowns, struggling to find the right word. 'They're too airy-fairy. They're not meant for normal women. Just stick to what you know best. At least it pays the bills.'

I want to tell her that perhaps there's more to life than just paying bills. That although we are growing old there's still enough time left to fulfil our dreams, even dream new ones. I turn to her, but she is asleep.

I dream of Mother that night. I dream of her dying days when, too frail to come out of her room, she called out my name from her bed. I was young and selfish, too caught up in my world to care.

'Come, son, tell me about college.' She wanted me to sit with her and tell her about my day. Did I like economics? Just how many girls were running after her handsome son? I pretended not to hear as I sat cleaning my cricket bat or putting Brylcreem in my hair.

I hated the hospital smell of her room and the thin, skeletal feel of her fingers that tried to curl round mine.

The day she died, the windows of her room were wide open. The cawing of crows crowded the silence. Mother's body lay rigid in bed, a blue checked blanket pulled up to her chin. I stood by the door, watching as Father knelt on the floor, his head clumsily resting on her pillow, his knees splayed out beneath him. He held her hand. It was the only time I saw them touch.

Dear Lopa didi,

Hope the monsoons start soon in Bombay. Did Jijaji's shop get burgled again? The mango season must be in full swing. Poor PK – he wanted to eat one today, but of course I didn't have any. You know how he loves them. He's worried these days. Walks around like an old man, which I suppose he is. It was his birthday last week. He's fifty-five! I even baked him a cake. He thought I was baking bread. Unfortunately I didn't get the oven setting right, so it was a bit undercooked. Never mind – we still ate it. He went and bought himself a personal number plate for his car. God knows how much it must have cost. You didn't ring to wish him happiness. Maybe you were busy. One piece of good news is that he's been invited to an important golfing weekend. He is going to meet people who may help with the business. Let's see. People promise you the world and then laugh and say they were just kidding. I hope PK doesn't get too disappointed – it's not good for his health, all this worrying.

Any plans of coming to Manchester? I will ask again, but I know it's not as simple as that – how can you leave the kids, your in-laws and Jijaji and just catch the Air India flight.

Look after yourself, and I will write again soon.

Lots of hugs to the kids,

Geeta

2

A BANK HOLIDAY DRIVE

It's a May bank holiday, and I'm home with the family. I watch Geeta move about the kitchen. She wants me to put up some shelves in the garage. To store her pickle jars, she says.

'Why don't you keep them in the fridge like a normal person?' I say.

Geeta stops slicing onions and gives me a look. The onions have made her eyes red-rimmed and watery. Every now and then her arm goes up and she wipes away the onion tears with the sleeve of her tracksuit top.

'They won't fit in the fridge. They're the jumbo-sized ones I bought from Costco last week. They were on offer – six for only six pounds ninety-nine. I just had to get them!' she announces proudly, like she's won the lottery.

Everything about Geeta is jumbo-sized these days: the food she piles on to her plate; the clothes she wears; the grocery bags she brings home, crammed with two-for-one offers.

'I'll fix the shelves after lunch,' I say, and go back to reading the *Daily Mail*.

Amar sits at the kitchen table, listening to our bickering. He's pretending to do his maths homework. His tongue sticks out in concentration and his eyes are heavy-lidded with sleep. His cheeks, round and smooth like a girl's, gently puff out as he chews the end of his pencil.

'Amar's starting to look a lot like you, Geeta,' I say. I don't mean it as a compliment. I stopped believing long ago that my son will one day grow into some strapping six-footer with a jaw line that sends girls into a swoon.

'You think so?' Geeta stares at him, her eyes brimming with love, knife hovering over the chopping board, smiling as though I'd reminded her of something pleasant. 'He has definitely gone towards my side – look at those cheeks and eyes, just like his nanaji.'

'And the double chin and the tummy's definitely yours,' I almost add – but I don't. It would be cruel.

* * *

I should be grateful that I have a son. I remember the day Amar was born. A Sunday afternoon. I was setting off for the pub. It was the final game of the season – Manchester United were playing Chelsea. I was almost out of the door when Geeta's waters broke. She slid to the floor, legs folding under her, her head hitting the corner of the IKEA chest as she fell. A thin stream of colourless fluid trickled down her leg, staining the front of her white nightie.

'Please, God, please don't let me lose this one!' she whispered, her fingers holding her belly like a protective net.

'We don't need God. We need a bloody doctor, Geeta,' I shouted, throwing a towel on the back seat of the car and bundling her in.

'Don't use the good towels – they're for guests. Use the old one from our bathroom!' Typical Geeta – practical even while on the verge of death.

She sat clumsily in the car, knees pushed up against her belly, moaning softly as I jumped through red lights all the way to St Mary's hospital. Sunday wasn't a good day for dying or giving birth, but at least the car park was empty.

The locum, Dr Adebayo, a Nigerian man with a caring smile, took charge of the delivery.

'Now, Mamma, just you stay calm,' he said, as he spread Geeta's legs with his small, feminine hands. All these years later I still haven't forgotten the doctor's turquoise ring, the way it glinted on his little finger, and how taken I was by this trivial, absurd detail.

'Can't we get an English doctor? Or at least a lady doctor?' Geeta pleaded with me, her face scrunched, small and frightened.

The labour lasted eight hours, and I didn't let go of her hand even once.

'A baby boy!' Dr Adebayo announced, tugging at the stethoscope that hung limp around his neck like a garland. His forehead was hot and shiny. 'Happy, Mamma? You see, I'm not so bad.' He raised his eyebrow and wagged a finger at Geeta.

Faint with relief, I rushed out of the ward, found the nearest off-licence and bought a bottle of Bollinger champagne to thank the doctor, demanding that the sales assistant wound a bright red ribbon around its neck.

'I'm a father – a father at last! Don't you get it?' I shouted at the woman at the cash register, but she couldn't care less.

'The baby's a little on the small side,' Dr Adebayo said, when I handed him the bottle as a thank-you. He drew the white plastic curtain around Geeta's bed, snapped open his briefcase and slipped the bottle inside, just as the midwife arrived to check the baby's heartbeat.

'He only weighs five pounds, but he'll live. He'll live,' Dr Adebayo repeated, patting Geeta's cheek. His blue ring shone like a bolt of colour against her sucked-in, washed-out face.

'He's breathing? Make sure he's breathing!' Geeta said, tugging at my arm, her eyes fixed on the tiny towel-wrapped bundle the nurse was holding. The doctor gave her a wink.

'Don't worry, Mamma, he'll live to be a hundred!'

'He's a gift from God,' Geeta said when we were finally alone, with the baby lying like a floppy rag doll against her breast. Geeta's eyes were shut, her hands clasped together and pointing towards the hospital ceiling, as though God had set up home there and would shake her hand and say, 'Well done you, you've produced a living child at last!'

It was the first pregnancy she'd carried full term and not lost.

I was afraid to touch the tiny, twig-like limbs and the face with its blunt, blurred features. I was worried that the pressure of my fingertips would dent and bruise the baby's blue-brown skin. How taken was I with this small creature then, little knowing what lay ahead of us – the exam failures, the continual illness, the tendency to shrug and slouch through life. All that lay waiting for us. But that Sunday, holding my newborn child in my arms, I saw him like a gift from God, like Geeta said.

And although the promise of those early days has faded through the years, I can never forget the drama of Amar's birth. A wave of love leaps up inside me as I remember this. Maybe it isn't too late. I can still turn Amar into something special.

'Let's have a party for your birthday this year, Amar.' I lean forward to ruffle his thick head of hair. At least he's inherited something from me.

Amar stops his pencil-chewing and looks at me, his eyes shining.

'Fifteen's a big age,' I say. 'And we've never really had a proper party for you.'

'Can we go to Blackpool? Can we take the whole class?' he says.

'Why the whole class? Why not just one or two of your closest friends?'

'Because then they'll like me and want to be my friends.'

Geeta listens while she stirs ground almonds into his milk.

'That's going to cost a lot of money, Amar,' she says, handing him the milk. The rides are expensive, and we'll have to hire a minibus. It'll easily come to five hundred pounds.'

I know she wants me to overrule her, to say, What the hell, it doesn't matter, we'll take the whole class – money isn't an issue when it's your only child who arrived after three miscarriages.

But I stay quiet. I'd sacked four girls from the hemming floor just the previous week, and it hadn't been easy. One of them had worked for me for nearly six years. Margaret gave them the news at lunch, telling them the business needed to restructure. She used the right words, but they still cried as they picked up their kettles and rolled up their David Beckham posters. They left without saying goodbye. It's not a good feeling to live with.

'Can I at least take one friend? Please, Daddy? Please! A new girl has just joined our class. She's very nice.' Amar's voice goes high.

'We'll go as a family, just the three of us. Make a day trip of it,' I say.

'Let's ask the Guptas to come along. I'll make potato cutlets and get a roast chicken, and some Coke.' Geeta is smiling now. The deep-set frown on her forehead disappears momentarily.

These are happy times, family times, I tell myself as I sit with my family, planning Amar's birthday. But my eyes keep going back to Geeta, to her untidy ponytail and her tracksuit, to where bleach has made a funny white patch on the sleeve.

When exactly did she become this way? When did the woman in chiffon saris and ironed satin petticoats disappear inside the person hiding in shapeless box-cut clothes and Adidas trainers? It was as though, in leaving Bombay, Geeta had left behind her old self, like a snake shedding its skin.

The rain stops. Through the kitchen window I see Mr Peters, our next-door neighbour, out in his garden, bending low over his rose bushes, gardening shears in hand.

'Shall we go for a spin? Go up to the Lakes, Geeta? It's been a long time.' The suggestion comes out unexpectedly, surprising me.

'I've got work.' Geeta points to the pile of laundry on the ironing board and sighs. 'These are your shirts for next week.'

'We went all the time when Amar was young. What was the name of that ice-cream place he loved?'

'Marcello's,' Geeta says straight away. 'It was just across the road from the lake, next to the chip shop.' She has the memory of an elephant where Amar is concerned. 'Amar's favourite was mint-chocolate-chip.' A soft, faraway expression clouds her eyes. She looks at Amar. 'You got a tummy ache. Remember that, Amar? You ate too quickly.'

'Why don't you go, Mum? Go for a spin with Dad?' Amar says. He doesn't want to come along. He wants to stay behind and catch up on his schoolwork.

'It'll be a good outing, Mum. You've not been out all week.' He likes it when we go out together, leaving him alone with the television and the packets of Walkers and chocolate bourbons.

'All right, all right, we'll go,' Geeta says, putting the clothes back in the laundry basket. 'But we'll have to be back by dinner time. I don't like you driving in the dark.'

'Of course we'll be back,' I say. 'Why do you have to make a drama out of everything?'

I put the *Daily Mail* down on the table. The news isn't good. Cedric Solomon has just bought out another competitor in Leicester. I read the article twice and look carefully at the photograph. Cedric is standing with his wife at some charity dinner, smirking at the camera, one arm thrown carelessly around her shoulder. Lucky bastard. I run my fingers over their picture, my thumb tracing the outline of his wife's mouth. Was she always smiling? Was life that good?

* * *

Leaving Geeta to finish her chores, I light a cigarette and go into the garden to check on my mango tree. There are brown blotches on the branches. The wet weather isn't doing it much good. Mr Peters spots me over the low hedge and waves. I wish he'd come nearer the hedge so we could chat about his wife – I'd heard she'd been diagnosed with cancer. But he carries on with his gardening.

'The English are so bloody uptight,' I say to Geeta when she comes over to stand by my side. I point out the brown patches on the mango tree.

'It probably needs a strong pesticide,' Geeta says.

We stand watching Mr Peters.

'Poor man,' she says. 'I sent Amar over with some chicken soup for his wife.'

She's done that before, sent over Tupperware filled with paneer and dal.

'It's no fun being old in this country,' she continues. 'Their kids never drop by. I bet they've not had a hot meal in years. Can you imagine Amar ever doing that to us?' she says. 'I'll just go and pack some alu-chutney sandwiches for our trip. We can have a picnic by the lake.'

'Let's just go, Geeta,' I say. 'Why do we have to drag food into everything? There're plenty of restaurants there.'

'OK, calm down! You'll be the first to complain if there are no snacks in the car. I'll just go and put something warmer on.' She goes upstairs to get ready.

It was going to be good for us to be out in the open, getting some fresh air. In the old days, Geeta would sometimes feed the ducks, throwing fistfuls of peanuts to them as they strolled boldly between our legs, until one day a polite warden came over and told us that in England ducks were fed bread, not spicy peanuts.

I go to the utility room to look for my wellies. They are lying dirty in an old Iceland carrier bag behind the mop bucket. I am buffing off the worst of the mud with a brush when Geeta comes in wearing a bright pink sweater over her tracksuit bottoms.

'Why don't you wear some jeans instead?' I suggest.

'I'll be more comfortable in my tracksuit. It's a long drive,' she says, taking the wellies from me. She stands at the sink, rolling up her sweater sleeves. Her gold wedding bangles slide over her Marigold gloves as she washes my wellies.

The rain starts again. The gutter over the garage sputters out a jet of grey water. Mr Peters appears outside the window, buttoned up and warm in his green Barbour jacket and tweed flat cap. He's walking his dog – an ugly black mutt with a stubby tail – which starts barking as it passes our house. Geeta's convinced he's allergic to Indians.

The rain is falling heavily now. Geeta sighs as she looks up from the sponge and wellies to watch the streams of water flowing down the outside of our windows. 'Shall we even bother going now? It'll soon be dark and the sun's not coming out again today.'

I know what she's really thinking: Will Amar be OK left on his own for so long? What I'm thinking is, What will we talk about during the two-hour car journey? Amar? The Guptas? The trip to India she keeps hankering after?

'Why don't we go somewhere nearer?' I suggest. 'What about Dunham Park? That's not so far. The coffee shop there does good carrot cake. We'll be back in no time.'

* * *

The car park is empty except for a red Ford Fiesta that's parked right at the other end near a large bush.

'The rain has kept the crowds away,' I say, reversing the car into the empty slot next to the Fiesta.

Geeta shakes her head. 'Why don't you park nearer the entrance? It would be less of a walk then.'

I turn off the ignition and tell her it's safer to park next to another car. Hooligans from Wythenshawe are always looking for lone cars to break into and steal the radio from.

Loud music booms from the parked Ford. The young couple inside are kissing; the girl has her eyes shut. Her hands stroke the man's back. I glance at Geeta, who lets out a little giggle. She leans forward to get a better look, her head almost touching the dashboard.

We watch without saying a word. The girl suddenly raises her arms, and the man pulls off her white T-shirt. She's wearing a red bra. He eases off the straps, and I see his mouth go down on her breast. I hear a moan. It's Geeta. Her forehead is beaded with sweat. I'm about to say that we should get out of the car when the man spots us.

He turns off the music, rolls down the window and leans over the girl, his mouth twisted in anger. A small, shiny stud glints in his right ear. 'What are you staring at? Bloody Pakis. Get the fuck out!' He has a thick Scouse accent.

There's no other noise but for the rain and the occasional distant sound of car tyres hitting a puddle. My fingers grip the steering wheel, unable to move.

'Don't call us Pakis. We're Indians. Is that understood?' Geeta shouts back, her face alive with anger.

The man says something else, but I don't understand. He curls his fingers in the shape of a gun, takes aim at our heads and shouts, 'Bang, bang! Get lost, scumbags!'

I hear a click. Geeta is locking the car doors. 'Come on, PK. Let's go home. This country's going to the dogs.' She grabs my arm. But I stay frozen, unable to start the car.

The girl stares straight ahead. Her bra is like a frilly collar around her neck. She's made no effort to cover herself.

'Come on, start the car. What are you waiting for? Do you want to be beaten up?'

I start the car, the steering wheel slippery beneath my hands. My foot feels as heavy as a stone as I press it down on the accelerator.

'What's this world coming to?' Geeta says as we drive away. I stay silent. 'Young people these days have no shame. Why can't they do all this nonsense at home?' She wipes her forehead with an old tissue.

We stop at a Pizza Hut on the way home, and Geeta orders her usual: Margherita with extra cheese, extra red onions and extra jalapeños. She gets a medium ham and pineapple for Amar. I order a coffee. I've lost my appetite.

When we get home, Geeta walks in holding the two pizza boxes aloft as though she's returning with a prize.

Amar's standing at the kitchen sink. His shoulders go rigid when he hears us enter.

'What are you doing?' I shout, and go up to him. He's holding a bleach bottle and is trying to prise open the cap. 'Drop that immediately!' I snatch the bottle from his hand. 'This is serious stuff – it's not meant for kids. Geeta, have you seen what he's doing? Don't leave this stuff lying around.'

Amar's bottom lip quivers as he tries to explain he was only trying to see if he could mix it with Ribena and make a new drink. 'Like a chemistry experiment,' he says.

'It's poison, Amar. It can kill you.' Geeta pats him on the cheek. 'Don't do this again, OK?' She kicks off her trainers and sits on the sofa, her legs folded under her. Picking up the remote and switching the channel to her favourite Indian soap, she pats the space beside her. 'Come on – let's sit and have the pizza.'

I'm not sure whether she means me or Amar.

I start flipping through his school notebook.

'You're home early,' Amar says. He's joined his mother on the couch and is helping himself to pizza.

'It was raining heavily,' I say. I ask him about his unfinished homework. He mumbles something about a girl called Alice, who'd rung him for a chat.

I tell Geeta that I'm going to lie down.

'You must've caught a chill,' she says. 'Shall I make you a ginger tea? And some cheese on toast if you don't want pizza?' She's already forgotten the incident in the car park.

'I'll take some paracetamol,' I say, expecting her to come upstairs and talk about what we'd seen, hoping to find, somewhere inside her, a hunger for something bigger and brighter in life. But her eyes are calm and untroubled.

She goes back to her channel hopping and pizza eating.

Amar follows me up to my bedroom, asking if I'm angry with him about his unfinished homework. I shut the door in his face and go into the bathroom, pulling off my newly cleaned, unused wellies.

I flick down the toilet seat cover, light a cigarette and sit, staring at myself in the mirror above the washbasin. I will be sixty one day. My body and mind will start giving up on things. I think of the couple in the car and wonder if they're married. I wonder how sex in a car would feel. I unzip my trousers, slip my hand in, and imagine how sex in a car with someone more glamorous than Geeta would feel.

Dear Lopa didi,

You won't believe what happened the other day. PK decided we should go to the Lakes – the Lake District is just outside Manchester. We used to go there a lot when Amar was little. It's almost as beautiful as Kashmir. Anyway, our plans changed, and we went to a park near our house. It was a miserable day, raining as usual, and a young couple in the car next to us started doing hanky-panky in broad daylight. It was most embarrassing. This kind of thing would never happen in Bombay. But worse than that was that they called us Pakis. We are just one big brown blob to the people here. They lump us all together and can't make out who is Indian, Sri Lankan or Pakistani. Poor PK – he was very upset. He went straight up to the bedroom and slammed the door shut. I wanted to speak to him, but Amar needed me. Instead I ended up scolding Amar. Can you imagine – he was trying to drink a bottle of bleach. That boy has no sense. But maybe he will be a scientist when he grows up. He is so curious, like Einstein.

How is Jijaji? Is he travelling to Ahmedabad a lot for work? I saw on TV there were some riots. Tell him to be careful – the politicians are creating mischief between Muslims and Hindus. And your mother-in-law? Why don't you get a massage lady to sort out her back? You shouldn't be doing it on top of all the other work you do.

Love to the kids,

Geeta

3

LLAMAS IN WOODBRIDGE

I drive to Mowbray Hall on a rainy September afternoon. The drive is long and I wish Geeta was next to me, with a thermos of ginger tea tucked between her plump thighs, and the sharp, tangy smell of her alu-chutney sandwiches filling the car.

Mowbray Hall floats up at the end of a long driveway, shiny and grand, like a Bollywood film set. I stop the car and admire the view. Marble horses spit water from oversized fountains, and the sloping lawns are a billiard-table green. A herd of deer graze in the distance, their silhouettes sharp against the pearl-grey sky. It's so different to the hot, muddy landscape of my early life, where the only view from our Mahalaxmi apartment window was of rusting television antennae pricking the Bombay sky and restless vultures circling over the Parsi cemetery in Kemps Corner.

I park my freshly washed Mercedes and go in, wheeling a five-year-old Samsonite after me. The girl at the reception desk looks up and smiles. A small dark mole sits just below her left eye. She'd be attractive but for that. I don't want her to notice the scratched leather of my suitcase, so I hide it behind my legs. She's wearing a black and white polka-dot blouse and a black skirt that shows off her size-eight waist. Her polyester clothes are definitely made in China or Turkey.

'Prakash Kant Malik,' she says slowly, reading my name carefully as she hands me a badge. My name sounds foreign and wrong in her pink English mouth.

'Don't worry about it. Just call me PK. It's easier,' I say.

A large gilt-framed mirror hangs on the wall behind the girl's head. I pass a hand through my hair, pull my shoulders back and stand tall.

The girl asks me to follow her. Drinks are being served in the Oval Room. Her high heels ring out on the marble floor as we walk past portraits of kings and queens; their little hands clutch their swords and poodles, their mouths stitched tight. They look overdressed and unhappy.

'They look miserable, don't they,' I say softly.

She giggles and slows her pace. 'You're right. They look totally pissed off.'

I've made an impression. I see it in the way she plays with the bow on her blouse.

I hear Gupta's words in my mind, his voice low and vicious: 'A bloody charmer, that's what your husband is,' he'd once said to Geeta. 'The girls fly to him like bees to a honey pot.' I'd made the mistake of inviting him to my office Christmas party, back in the days when my office parties were at the Midland Hotel and I could afford a proper four-course sit-down dinner for everyone, with a disco afterwards that played Abba songs, and fifty-quid Lewis's vouchers for the staff as a bonus. I invited everyone, even the lads who collected the rubbish from the warehouse.

Gupta had sat upright in his chair all night, watching me swing the office girls round the dance floor. He saw them press themselves against me, their big hairdos brushing my face, and he ran to Geeta telling tales, like a snitch.

But Geeta stood up for me. 'Don't be silly,' she said, putting Gupta in his place. 'PK is the boss – he's just doing his job. What can he do if they insist on having a dance?' She'd thrown me a smile and patted her pregnant belly. The smile said, 'I don't care who you dance with. I'm the one who's carrying your baby.'

A full-blown rose, that's what Geeta was in those days, flushed with happiness, ripe with our first-born child, the one who came out stillborn, his body a mess of bone and blood. It was a boy, the nurses told me later.

'Mr PK? Are you all right?' The girl touches my jacket sleeve, and I'm no longer dancing with my staff at the Christmas party. I'm back at Mowbray Hall, cap in hand, begging for a loan from Cedric Solomon.

* * *

A group of men are huddled around the fireplace. The fire's real; it's not like the fire-effect gas one in my lounge that's switched on twice a year, once at Diwali and then again at Christmas. The number of empty bottles on the table and their loud voices tell me they're already merry. I'm glad Geeta isn't with me. This isn't her world – nor mine, for that matter.

Ben spots me. 'Hi, PK! Good to see you. Was the traffic bad? The M6 is a bloody nightmare this time of day.' He's in a navy-blue kilt that's tight around his paunch. I can smell the wine on his breath. We shake hands.

'What's with the kilt?' I say. 'I thought you were from Doncaster?

'My party piece.' He grins. He pushes a drink in my hand. The glass feels warm against my cold skin.

'So, is the big man here?' I ask. 'Is Cedric here?'

'Cedric couldn't make it. A trade delegation... China or something. Gone with the Chancellor,' Ben says. 'He's sent his wife instead, as a consolation prize.' He giggles and dabs at his mouth with his handkerchief, as though getting rid of a stubborn stain.

My mood nosedives on hearing this. I'd missed Amar's football match for no reason. It had taken four calls to the school's PE teacher to ensure he got a place on the team. My eyes scan the room. 'Who are these other geezers?'

'I'll introduce you. I think one of them looks after small businesses,' Ben says, patting the pleats of his kilt.

'My business isn't small,' I remind him as we join the others.

The men are chatting about golf, something to do with fairways and getting a birdie. Their synthetic ties and cheap shiny suits indicate that they are only paid employees. I quietly finger the sleeve of my new cashmere-blend suit with its crimson silk lining. Six hundred quid it had cost me, and I was too proud to ask for a discount.

'What's your handicap?' It's a fellow with ginger hair and a long, thin neck that sticks out of his collar like a javelin.

I don't care what my handicap is. I want to talk business.

'I'm the MD of Malik Textiles,' I say, projecting the name loudly. I want him to recognise it right away.

He looks blank.

'Malik Textiles,' I repeat. 'We supply ladies' dresses to Harrods.' This is not strictly true, but he's not to know that I had only sent samples for their consideration and never got paid for them. I'm tempted to tell him how I'd sent Jane Fonda one of my designs to wear to the Cannes Film Festival. I remember it well. It was a blue velvet gown with hand-stitched Swarovski crystals that we couriered in from Vienna. In the end, she went for a big French name, not a Manchester desi like me. She did write back and say thank you, though.

'Do you work for Cedric Solomon?' he asks.

'Similar line of business, but I have nothing to do with him,' I say. The wine is giving me a headache.

I step outside and ring Geeta to find out whether Amar has scored in the match. It's only the B team, so he's bound to have played well. The phone rings out. I hope Amar hasn't screwed things up. He's been restless all week, even wet his bed. And all because of a stupid football match. I try Geeta's number again and then go back inside to join Ben and start networking. The evening has to go somewhere.

* * *

A woman is talking to Ben. She turns round when I walk in. I see a mouth that is red and ripe, and a pair of light-coloured eyes. She's wearing a close-fitting silk dress with a swirly black and pink pattern.

Ben introduces us. She's Cedric Solomon's wife, and her name is Esther. 'As you know, Cedric's away in China, but Esther kindly agreed to join us.'

'I'm the plus one without the one,' she says, and throws up her hands in mock despair. 'Anyway, I've always wanted to see the gardens here. They were designed by Capability Brown, I believe.' She offers me her hand.

My fingers close around the giant ruby on her right index finger. I want to say something clever, but all I can come up with is a pathetic, 'Just call me PK.' I'm glad my shoes are clean and my suit is new.

'Interesting name,' she says with a smile. 'One day you're going to tell me the story behind it.'

'I saw your photo in the *Daily Mail*,' I hear myself say.

Ben raises an eyebrow and grins. 'Cedric and Esther are always in some newspaper or the other,' he says.

The fur-trimmed cream shawl wrapped lightly around Esther's shoulders slips a little, and I see the heavy curve of her breasts.

'I like your dress. It's Pucci, isn't it? A reworking of their nineteen-fifties bestseller,' I say, ignoring Ben.

Her eyes go wide. 'How observant of you, Mr Malik. I just adore Pucci. It was lying at the back of my wardrobe, all scrunched up like a poor forgotten thing, and I decided to give it a go. And...' – here she pauses and gives me a triumphant smile – 'it still fits.'

'PK's your man if you want to know about the weight and weave, the fall and flow of fabrics,' Ben chuckles. 'Pity he's only peddling T-shirts with Disney logos these days.' He squeezes my shoulder to let me know it's just banter.

I ask Esther if she'd like a drink. She wants champagne.

'How the hell did she end up with Cedric?' I whisper to Ben at the drinks trolley.

'He met her on a flight to Israel. They were sitting next to each other. He lucked out big time.' He lets out a filthy laugh.

I look back at Esther. She's sitting on the arm of a sofa, holding out her nearly empty glass. I notice the strong muscular shape of her thighs beneath her clinging dress.

Esther wants to know if I'm in fashion.

'I sell frocks for a living, just like your husband. Times are tough – but maybe you don't know that?' I say. She's wearing a dress worth hundreds of pounds; would she really be bothered?

She shrugs. 'We don't really discuss work at home. But Cedric works like a dog. He's very good at sniffing out deals.'

'Cedric's always had a nose for business, even at school,' Ben pipes in. 'He was selling sweets and football stickers in Year One.'

He looks at Esther for confirmation. She nods and says how Cedric could sell anything he wanted. 'He could sell condoms to a nun,' she says, and her laugh, big and warm, wraps me like a blanket.

I smile. 'Yes, Cedric's quite a legend in the fashion world.' I say, and change the topic. 'Have you been to India?' I imagine what Esther's answer will be – 'Too many beggars and flies. But I adored the colours!' Isn't that what all Westerners say about India?

But before Esther can speak, Ben takes hold of her elbow and steers her towards the other guests. My eyes follow her. She listens to them, her head nodding and hands flying as she makes a point. Catching my eye, she waves and smiles.

I remember Amar's match, and I slip outside and ring home again. There's still no reply. They've probably gone out for a pizza as a celebration treat. Geeta doesn't believe in holding back when it comes to Amar.

'I thought you'd run away,' Esther says, when I come back inside.

'I was calling home.'

'Don't tell me you're missing your wife?' Her eyes are playful.

A strange kind of heat spreads to the back of my neck, and I look around for some more wine. Two big gulps and my confidence returns. 'So, I was asking if you've been to India?'

'I most certainly have,' she says. 'What a colourful country.' A loose strand of her long hair escapes, clouding her left eye.

She tucks it carefully behind one ear and smoothes it into place with her long fingers. 'I spent nearly three months in Bombay, and I loved every minute of it,' she continues, placing her hand on my arm so I understand just how much she loved India.

'Did you go recently? I've heard the monsoons have been bad these last few years.'

'Oh no, this was years back. I was much younger then. I stayed with my uncle, who was the General Manager at the Taj Hotel. He's retired now. Breeds llamas on a farm in Woodbridge. Can you believe it?'

Her warmth lights up my face like a torch. 'Llamas in Woodbridge!' I say. 'Whatever next? Monkeys in Manchester?'

Everything feels absurd and delightful, and I almost forget why I'm here. We move towards the windows that look out on the brightly lit back lawns.

'Wouldn't it be lovely to go for a stroll beneath the stars,' she says, raising her glass to her lips. It's empty. 'Would you mind topping me up?' she says.

I gaze at her face. In the dimness of the room, I can't work out her age. She could be forty. Maybe fifty. It doesn't matter – she's beautiful. I'm glad Cedric hasn't turned up after all.

Once upon a time Geeta was beautiful too. She wore her hair long and loose. I'd come back from work to find her sitting cross-legged on the sofa, the cassette player playing her favourite Kishore Kumar songs, her petticoat hitched up high around her thighs, her fingers massaging coconut oil into her scalp. She spent the days doing ironing and washing, but she still had kajal on her eyes and her red Avon lipstick on.

Geeta had spirit in those days. That was before the sadness came and settled over her face, like a season that never changed.

I hand Esther a full glass of champagne.

She taps hers against mine. '*Cin cin*, my friend. Were you hoping to make some useful contacts tonight?' She raises her eyebrows and looks at the other men. 'They don't seem to have much to offer, do they? Dull, dull, dull!'

'I wanted to meet your husband,' I say, 'but he's not here.'

'Well, I hope I can make up for that,' she says, swaying slightly. I catch her elbow to steady her.

'We're a disgrace!' she says. 'We should be mingling. Let's go and mingle, PK Malik.'

The sound of my name coming out of her mouth, the way she pulls out each letter slowly, as though unwilling to let it go… I like it.

'I think we should be eating,' I say. 'I don't know about you, Esther Solomon, but I'm starving.' As if on cue, my stomach rumbles.

'Well, don't you get your hopes up.' She comes closer and whispers. 'I can tell you exactly what the menu's going to be tonight. Corn-fed chicken on a bed of wilted spinach, followed by rhubarb crumble *avec petit fours et fromage*!'

I can't help smiling. This woman is fun. The receptionist who had checked me in comes to the door and announces dinner is being served. The only thing I notice about her this time is the mole on her cheek.

'It's been lovely getting to know you,' Esther says. She places her hand on my arm. 'I hope we're sitting next to each other tonight.'

It feels like a promise.

* * *

I'm in my room, in a hurry to get dressed and go down for dinner, when I notice two missed calls from Geeta on my mobile. I ring back. 'How did Amar's football match go?' I was hoping he'd scored a goal.

Geeta ignores my question and says she's called me a couple of times. I tell her reception is poor in the countryside.

'Is Prince Andrew there?' Geeta is a sucker for royalty. She cried for two whole days when Princess Diana died.

'No, the royals don't bother with this petty stuff. It's not a fundraiser – just some bankers and accountants. Boring types.' I check my watch.

'Why did you bother going, then?'

'How many goals did Amar score?' I say, changing the subject. I want her to be quick. I think of the evening ahead, of Esther and me discussing fashion and style. She might even put in a good word about me to Cedric.

'Speak to Amar. He can tell you himself.'

I picture them: Geeta at the kitchen table, a packet of peanuts nearby, the pressure cooker whistling away on the hob, Amar watching television, feet up on the coffee table, biscuit crumbs on his sweatshirt.

He comes on the phone. His high-pitched voice brings back the headache.

'Hi Dad! How is Prince Andrew?'

'How did you play?' I keep my voice bright, light and encouraging.

'Mr Birch is very mean,' Amar says. His voice is a whimper. 'He kept me on the bench the whole time. He didn't let me play even once. Mum kept telling him to put me on, but he wouldn't listen. But anyway, our school won. The other side was useless.'

'What's the good of winning if you didn't even play?' I say.

'It's no big deal, Dad. You know I hate football. And you weren't even there, so it doesn't matter. It wasn't the Olympics, just a stupid little match,' he says. The line goes dead.

Amar has made everything go dark. I slip on my shoes, splash on my Old Spice and go down to the dining hall. My heart feels old and heavy.

* * *

Esther and I sit together, wedged in the far corner of the long dining table between two accountants from Bradford. She leans forward and whispers as I pull up my chair.

'I had Ben move me. I just couldn't bear the thought of sitting next to…' I follow her glance. A man with silver sideburns and a high, sloping forehead waves to us. Esther waves back and turns to me. 'So let's talk fashion. Tell me about your favourite designers.'

Nobody has asked me such questions in a long time. Normally the talk in fashion turns to numbers and the new kid on the block. Very little has to do with its aesthetics. 'I like Yves Saint Laurent. He's classic, but a bit of a rebel. In fact, the black velvet jacket you're wearing, that's one of his, isn't it?'

Esther strokes the velvet-trimmed lapels. 'I've had this for years. I bought this at a sample sale in Chelsea. It was a steal.'

'It's timeless. Few women can carry off such a masculine cut and still look elegant,' I say. I mean it.

The colour rises to her cheeks. 'Tell me something,' she says, and pauses, looking down at her plate, where a small chicken breast floats in soupy green liquid. She dips her little finger in, tastes it and screws up her face. 'I was right about the food, wasn't I? Anyway, why do you know so much about Western fashion and style? Not many Indian men could spot a Saint Laurent tuxedo.'

'I've a passion for beautiful things,' I tell her, hoping I don't come across as some airy-fairy dandy. 'Actually, I blame my mother. We didn't have much money growing up, so she embroidered saris to earn some extra cash. She stitched these amazing flowers and birds on the chiffons and silks… her fingers were like a musician's.' I stop and think of my mother's hands. I've not thought about them for years.

Esther listens intently, her chair angled towards mine, her back turned to the accountant sitting on her left side. 'My mother was like yours,' she says, her voice a low whisper, 'a worshipper of beauty. She would throw dinner parties and dress in fur and pearls. When I was thirteen, she took me to one side and said, "Always remember, Esther, the way to a man's heart is through his eyes. Always look after yourself." She was a wise woman.'

We raise a glass to the memory of our mothers.

* * *

I fall asleep thinking of the lazy curve of Esther's mouth and the way her long fingers closed around my arm when I spoke of my mother. I dream of her hair and her breasts. I wake up late the next morning with the taste of something dying in my mouth and my body covered in sweat.

When I come down, the girl at reception informs me that the golf has been cancelled due to rain. I glance outside. Raindrops slither down the long French windows like a million fat centipedes.

'All the bunkers are flooded.' She shrugs apologetically. Her face is plain in the cold morning light.

I ask about the others. I was looking forward to catching up with Esther. I want to tell her how right she is about the corn-fed chicken and the spinach.

'A few left this morning,' she says. 'I think they are fed up with the weather and didn't want to hang around.'

'Is Ben Lawton still around? And Esther… I mean, Mrs Solomon?'

She checks her computer screen. 'Actually, I believe Mr Lawton left this morning. Ah, yes, I remember now – he had to drive Mrs Solomon back into town.'

'I think I'll head back too,' I say. 'I don't think this rain's going to let up.'

* * *

I come home to find Amar playing his PlayStation and Geeta watching television. Nothing has changed. I help myself to some beer from the fridge and walk over to Amar. 'I'll have a chat with your PE teacher about not picking you to play,' I say.

Amar stays quiet. I know he is lying about Mr Birch leaving him out, but I don't want him to get away with it so easily. I take the PlayStation controller from his hand.

'I bet you never showed up for the game,' I say. 'You spent the day hiding in your room, didn't you?' I turn to Geeta. 'You'll turn him into a mouse, not a man.'

Geeta ignores me and asks if I'm hungry. It's her way of making peace. She makes us some cheese on toast and opens the pickle jar, spooning two fat slivers of mango on to her slice. The oil dyes the bread and the cheese yellow. I close my eyes and imagine Esther offering me the fruit of her smile.

'You came back early – was the golf no good?' She's trying her best to improve my mood.

I tell her the rain put a stop to the golf.

'Did any royalty turn up in the end?'

I shake my head. 'Cedric Solomon's wife was there. She was the closest thing to royalty,' I say, not sure whether she knows who Cedric is.

'Cedric Solomon's wife…' she repeats. 'I thought spouses weren't invited?'

'He couldn't make it, apparently, so he sent her in his place. So, why didn't Amar play?' I say, changing the subject back.

'He had a tummy ache,' Geeta says. She moves to stand behind Amar, a protective hand on his shoulders. 'He had bad cramps all through the night, so we missed the second half of the match and went to the shops instead, and then we stopped by Mrs Ahmed's to say a quick hello.'

'It's always a tummy ache or a headache,' I say. 'There's an excuse to stop him playing every time. Why not at least give it a try?' I say.

'I hate football,' Amar says, snatching the controller back out of my hand.

I walk past him and flick on the lights in the hall. Geeta's frugality means that most of the house is always dark, lights switched off to save electricity.

The chandeliers and marble floors of Mowbray Hall were a part of someone else's life. I was only a spectator. I belong here. I belong to a woman whose hands are always busy in a flurry of cooking, cleaning, ironing. I belong to a child whose only interest is eating and watching television. Somewhere I had made a mistake.

It wasn't always so – in those early years of marriage, Geeta walked through the rooms flicking on the lights and turning the thermostat up till the house glowed like a Diwali candle. 'I want the neighbours to know that we Indians know how to live well,' she would say when I protested about the high bills. 'We may come from a poor country, but we know how to live rich.'

'I wish you wouldn't force him to play football,' Geeta says, following me from room to room like a dog.

'He's a boy. Why wouldn't he like playing football?'

'But he hates sports,' she insists stubbornly. 'He likes art. You know that.'

'And hanging out with you, listening to you gossip with your sister on the phone,' I bite back.

Dear Lopa didi,

How are the kids? You sounded down on the phone last week. Is everything OK? It's been raining here non-stop for the past week. I know you will think I'm lucky, because the rains still haven't come to India. I saw on Zee TV that farmers are committing suicide in Andhra Pradesh. How desperate one would have to be to take one's life and abandon one's family. I tried telling PK this. We should be thankful we have our son, who is healthy and loving. Does it really matter that he doesn't like football? PK went to that fancy palace I was telling you about, and he came back in a foul mood. I think he wanted to make some business connections, but nothing happened. No royalty – not even Prince Andrew showed up. The whole trip was a flop. Anyway, I must go now.

Lots of love,

Geeta

4

THE BEST BAGELS IN TOWN

I meet Gupta at the Victoria the following week. He has bagged the table by the log fire, right beneath the black and white prints on the wall. The prints are the reason we met there – Gupta saw them and swore he recognised Delhi's Connaught Place in them – and having an evening drink there together has become a ritual over the years. We chat about Indian politics, whether Sonia Gandhi can ever become Prime Minister, if the BJP is going to win. For some reason we never seem to talk about British politics.

'Sonia Gandhi? No chance!' Gupta shakes his head. 'She'll always be an Italian, a foreigner. Can you ever imagine an Indian becoming a PM here, in England?' We bang the table and laugh.

Gupta's in a hurry today, checking his watch and tapping his fingers on the table. 'Asha's waiting. The kids are coming home this weekend. We'll need to finish our business before they arrive,' he says, scratching his chin and lowering his eyes. His long, thick, unmanly lashes graze the top of his cheeks, which still carry the faded scars of a bad childhood bout of chicken pox.

Even though he's as old as me, and married just as long, he still has a girlish shyness when he mentions his wife.

'You make it sound like a chore. Sure you're talking about lovemaking?'

I'm on my second pint of Guinness and am feeling a bit giddy-headed.

'No need to spell it out.' He scowls. 'I was reading somewhere that after fifty sex has to be performed weekly, otherwise you start getting ill… the prostate gets clogged.' He looks worried.

I smile at his confession. He's an accountant, after all – even his lovemaking needs a schedule and a reason.

'What about you, PK? How's it going with Geeta these days? Remember your nickname at college? Randy Pandy. You still got it or what?' He gulps down his orange juice and winks.

'Those were the days,' I say. I tell him about the couple in the car park. Gupta tut-tuts and says things were better under Thatcher. The young knew how to behave, and they respected the older generation.

'She was a real man, that Thatcher. She had balls.' He shakes his head. 'Why didn't you report them to the police? That man threatened to kill you. He was a racist.'

I shrug. 'Wouldn't have done any good. They were in love, poor things – probably didn't have a room to hide in. Actually, to be honest, I felt like a trespasser.' I remember the greedy way we'd stared at them. But Geeta…' I tell Gupta how she stood up to them.

'That wife of yours is twenty-four carat gold,' Gupta says. 'Don't ever underestimate her.' He lowers his voice and asks if seeing the couple in action had made us horny.

I look away. 'It made Geeta hungry, all right. She polished off a whole pizza. You're lucky – your kids have flown the nest, all at top universities. You can be lovebirds whenever you want.' This is a dig. Gupta has always bragged about how his kids would end up at Oxford and Cambridge; instead, the son was doing a Mickey Mouse course at Hull and the daughter was repeating her second year at a secretarial college.

Gupta mumbles something about children being albatrosses around one's neck. 'That was a low blow. You should know better, what with Amar being what he is,' he says, and gets up to leave.

I pat his shoulder and stand up too. 'I'm just kidding. Don't get too carried away in the bedroom – you don't want a heart attack at your age. Anyway, there's nothing wrong with Amar. You just wait and see – he'll outshine us all.'

'Very funny, Mr Malik,' he says, picking up his briefcase. It's the same sad one with the fake Burberry stripes he's carried around for years, picked up from Janpath in Delhi for three hundred rupees.

Gupta is upset about my swipe at his kids, so I offer to get him some vanilla slices from Reuben's. He has a sweet tooth, and Reuben's does the best cakes in south Manchester.

His face softens. 'Forget Reuben's – get the ones from Angelino's instead. The women at my office say the cakes are incredible. It's some special flour they import from Europe.'

* * *

The next evening, instead of taking a right turn for Reuben's, I remember Gupta's recommendation and turn left at Goose Green Lane for Angelino's. The shop is tiny, with a blue and white striped awning and a front door plastered with notices about yoga and Pilates classes. The little bell on the door tinkles as I enter, and a plump man with a black kippah covering his head lifts a hand in greeting.

He is busy attending to the two women in front of me. They have shrill, bird-like voices, and one of them has a blue scarf tied over the rollers in her hair.

I check out the different types of bread on the shelves. I can't spot vanilla slices. The women are taking their time, but I'm in no hurry to get home. It had been a hard day at work. The sales figures were in, and I can still hear Margaret tut-tutting into my ear. 'This isn't good, PK. This isn't good.'

The doorbell tinkles and a woman comes in. It's Esther Solomon. She's at the door, an orange shopping bag in her hand. I recognise her immediately.

'Fancy seeing you here!' we say simultaneously, our faces frozen in surprised smiles.

'This is my local,' she says.

'You live close by?' I ask. 'It seems like a nice neighbourhood.'

'Just ten minutes away.'

'A friend suggested I come here. Is it good?'

'Oh yes,' she says. 'They do the best bagels in town. Sweet like mother's milk.'

The two women at the counter finish buying their bread and greet Esther on their way out.

'They go to the same synagogue,' she explains. She pats her hair and moves her shopping bag from one arm to the other.

The man with the kippah has disappeared into the back room, so we continue chatting.

'What happened to you that day at Mowbray Hall?' I ask her. 'You disappeared.'

'Did I leave early?' She frowns, gazing into the distance, as though teasing out a memory. 'Ah yes… I remember.' Her face clears. 'I didn't sleep well. The room was draughty and cold. Ben drove me home – isn't he a sweetie! Anyway, how did the golf go?' She touches my arm, her touch light like a feather.

'It was rained off,' I say. 'I left early too. It was such a corporate affair…' I stop, not knowing what else to say. My hands curl into tight fists in my trouser pockets.

The shopkeeper returns, and greets Esther like an old friend. 'So, Mrs Solomon, the usual today? We have some wonderful pecan pie just in, fresh as morning dew. Shall I pack that too?' he asks, wiping his hands on his white apron. A soft dusting of flour sticks to his fingers.

Esther gives her order. I ask her if she'd recommend the vanilla slices. She says she imagines the pecan pie is much better. 'Vanilla slices are a bit childish – too sweet.'

I shrug and order them anyway. 'I have a childish friend,' I say, with a smile. I get some granary bread too. I want Amar to stop eating his usual sliced white Warburtons.

Esther rummages through her handbag, looking for money to pay. 'Oh no! I've done it again.' She pushes a strand of hair impatiently behind one ear. 'I've left my wallet at home. Stupid, stupid me. I'm always doing this.'

'Here, please, let me – it'd be my pleasure,' I say, paying for her stuff even before she'd asked.

'Thank you so much. What a gentleman. I tell you what – let's have lunch one day. And it'll be on me. My treat! I owe you one,' she says.

The air is bright and tangy with the promise of the coming spring. At home, Geeta would be preparing dinner, emptying the dishwasher and loading the washing machine while Amar moped about, crisp packet in his hand, and here I am, making lunch arrangements with Esther Solomon.

'You don't owe me anything, Esther. But yes, a lunch would be nice,' I reply.

The bakery gets busier, but we linger, the smiles never leaving our faces. Each time the door tinkles open, a sharp gust of wind tugs the hem of Esther's blue woollen dress, lifting it up and showing me her slip.

'My mother would have liked your dress – the embroidery is so delicate,' I say. Small blue paisley motifs run around the neckline and across the pockets.

'It's Italian,' Esther says. 'I picked it up in Florence. Their workmanship is incredible.'

'I'm trying to import a machine that does the same kind of work – a sort of delicate, traditional, hand-stitched look.'

'That sounds lovely,' Esther says, glancing at her watch. 'Oh! I've got to go.'

'So are you serious about this lunch business? How do we go about fixing it? I'll need your number,' I say, in a jokey, offhand way, so she doesn't think I'm being serious. A sharp feeling of dread kicks in as soon as the words leave my mouth. I hope she'll come up with an excuse about her kids or her husband.

'Sure, I mean it,' she says right away. 'Do you want to save my number on your phone?'

I check my pockets, but can't find my mobile. 'Damn, must've left it in the car.'

She laughs. 'You're as scatterbrained as me – I've forgotten my wallet, and you've lost your phone.' She pulls a scrunched-up tissue from her bag. 'Here, turn your back,' she says, and smoothes the paper against my jacket and scribbles down her number. I feel the pressure of her fingers through my jacket. 'Don't forget to call.' And with that she's gone.

I fold the tissue carefully and put it in my pocket. Then I stop by Gupta's house to drop off the vanilla slices.

* * *

Back home, I sneak into the garden to enjoy a smoke near my pride and joy, my mango tree.

'You've bought some new bread,' Geeta shouts through the open patio doors. 'Did you go to another bakery?'

'Yes, I went to Angelino's,' I shout back. 'Gupta's idea – he swears by it.' I could add that I bumped into Cedric Solomon's wife by accident. But I don't. It wouldn't be of interest to Geeta, anyway. It would be different if I'd seen Mrs Ahmed or Gupta's wife – they were the gatekeepers to her world.

I don't call Esther that day, or the next, or even the next. At the end of each day, I carefully transfer the tissue with her number from one trouser pocket to another. Whenever I'm forced to think about how bad the profit margins are at work, my hand dives into my pocket, and I quietly finger the tissue like it's some sort of mascot.

And then, one day, I'm in the bedroom getting ready for work when Geeta holds up the crumpled tissue. 'What's this old rubbish?' she says. 'I was about to throw it away, but then I saw the number on it and thought you might need it?'

All I need to say is, 'Yes, please get rid of it, it's rubbish,' and the story will end – I'd go back to my weekly drink with Gupta, the daily drive to Grotton and the monthly fumble that passed for lovemaking with a sleeping wife. Instead, I grab the tissue from Geeta's hand and pretend it's the number of a sales rep I met at a trade fair the week before. 'He has a lead for a new supplier in

China. Imagine – they're doing stuff with bamboo, turning it into cloth!' I say, speaking rapidly, going into detail that I know will bore her.

'That's clever,' Geeta says. 'How was I to know? It looks like rubbish. Why don't you just get a diary like normal people?' Her face is open and trusting, like a full moon, bright, without a shadow on its surface.

My gaze is drawn to the wall we're standing next to, which is covered in family pictures. A large, almost poster-sized photo, framed in cheap golden plastic, takes pride of place at the centre. It's a holiday snap taken in front of Blackpool Tower. Geeta gazes unsmiling into the camera, her head cocooned inside a shawl, arms folded, while Amar's face, barely visible, peeps out of a big, hooded parka. I stand apart, a cigarette in my hand, staring at something beyond, my mouth twisted into a weird smile. We look miserable. I don't know why Geeta has taken the trouble to develop, frame and display such a sad picture.

She sees me studying the photo. 'It was a wonderful outing,' she says. 'We should go back.'

It's not the memory I have. It was a cold November day; the breeze cut into us like a knife, and Amar wanted to get back home. He wasn't keen on the big rides, so I went on them alone, determined to make the most of the expensive day ticket, shivering on the roller coaster as it hurtled through the air. There I was, caught between heaven and earth, running round the same tired loops again and again, while mother and son spent twenty quid in the games arcade and got sick on candyfloss. Our memories are so different.

'Didn't Amar win something?' I ask Geeta.

She's good with family details – the little milestones that prop up her life. Her eyes narrow.

'Yes, he won that big red Teletubby. I donated it to the school tombola last year. It was a cold day, but we had such fun,' she says.

I nod and leave for work. The folded tissue with Esther's number on sits heavily in my pocket like a piece of burning coal.

* * *

Instead of taking the M60 to work, I head into Manchester. Most of the city is a tangle of scaffolding and diggers. Planners are working in a frenzy to change the city's skyline and history after the IRA bomb. The warehouses near Ancoats and Salford that once thrummed to the sound of machinery are empty husks now. Property developers have moved in, tearing down the old mills, replacing them with residential lofts that cater to young professionals. I find a quiet street next to the City Art Gallery, park up, take out the tissue and dial Esther. She picks up on the third ring.

'Hi Esther! It's me. It's PK. PK Malik. We met the other day at the bakery.'

'Oh, hi! So nice to hear from you.' She sounds vague.

'Sorry I didn't get round to calling you before – been busy at work.' My heart is hammering. 'I don't know if you remember, but we talked about doing lunch together some time?'

'We did?' She's unsure. The line goes quiet, and then her voice floats back, asking if I want to meet for a coffee instead. Some day. I must be busy.

'I'm in town for a meeting, but it got cancelled. I can meet you for lunch today. It's short notice, I know, but do you think you might be free?' I persist. The business of lying, once you acquired a taste for it, Father said, never left your tongue.

Esther wanted to check her diary. I think of Cedric. I think of Geeta. What's wrong with me? I'm about to hang up when she says, 'I have a hairdresser's appointment this afternoon, but I could meet you beforehand. Where are you, anyway?'

I read the sign. 'I'm right outside some art gallery on Mosley Street.'

'I know where you are. Go inside, and I'll meet you in the Pre-Raphaelite room. Give me an hour,' she says.

It's done. Just like that. Our first meeting and the sun bursts through the clouds, streaking the pavements in shots of yellow.

I stay in the car, my hand still holding the mobile where her voice has just left me. I look at the people hurrying about their daily business. They're carefree and smiling. I could be one of them, focused on my work rather than arranging assignations with married women. But, I reason, she isn't just any married woman. Her husband is Cedric Solomon, and friendship with her could only be good for my business. So, in a sense, what I am doing *could* be described as work.

* * *

In the gallery, I drift from room to room. All my years in Manchester, and not once have Geeta and I bothered stepping in. The security guard clears his throat when I touch an old armchair with faded gold flowers woven into the cushion. The design reminds me of my mother, her long fingers holding the needle, like a magician's wand. 'The fabric is brushed brocade,' I want to tell the guard. 'I'm a textiles man. I know such things.'

A school group comes rushing in. The kids look about ten. Their tongues hanging out in excitement, they flop down in front of a picture and get out their pens and paper. The teacher hisses at them in a low voice. The guard yawns, gets up and stretches his arms. I wonder if Amar's ever been here on a school trip. He would like the huge painting with the horses.

I check my watch. Almost an hour has passed. Esther isn't coming. She's changed her mind. She's seen how foolish it all is. And that's perfectly all right too. I can grab a sandwich, get back to work. There's a ton to get through today, anyway. We are both married. Who am I kidding, striking up new friendships at my age?

A hand lightly taps my shoulder. 'Hey, I told you to meet me in front of the Rossetti,' Esther says, breathless from climbing the stairs.

'Good to see you,' I say, extending my hand, unsure of how to greet her.

'It's good to see you too,' she says. Her handshake is firm, her eyes unwavering.

The schoolchildren are sketching. The teacher fiddles with her papers and gives us a look. I know what is on her mind. A man and a woman meeting in the middle of a working day. It means only one thing.

I suggest the museum café for lunch. Esther screws up her nose and says it only got one star in a recent review. 'But sure, let's try it anyway – maybe they've changed the chef.'

We find a table in a corner, next to the kitchen swing doors.

'Found anything you like?' It has taken me all of two minutes to decide, but Esther's reading the menu like it's a sacred text.

'I suppose the safest choice would be soup,' she says with a sigh.

We wait for the waitress to notice us. Esther moves the place mats to the right and then to the left, her eyes distracted by the waitress, who's serving a large group of Japanese tourists at a nearby table.

'Ja, ja, no green tea, ja…' Her voice floats back to us. She sees my raised hand and nods.

'Don't you think the waitresses here should dress in an artier, more creative way? This girl looks as though she's going to a funeral, all this black, and then Doc Martens for shoes…' Esther gives a theatrical shudder. 'Come on, PK, how would you dress them? You have a designer's eye.'

'I think you'll have a better idea than me. You dress impeccably. Do you ever help Cedric with his designing?'

It's polite talk. What I really want her to say is that she's spotted my talent and would gladly fix a meeting with Cedric.

Esther plays with the tassels of the cream and turquoise paisley-patterned shawl knotted around her throat as she considers my question. 'No… no, not really. I don't discuss anything with Cedric. He's got experts who do that kind of thing. I had kids when I was still quite young – they ate up all my time, and now here I am.' She lays her hands flat on the table, as if in surrender. 'Now, it's almost too late to begin.'

She stops as the waitress slaps down a bowl of tomato soup in front of her, and a jacket potato with grated anaemic-looking cheddar cheese lands on my place mat.

'It's never too late to begin again,' I say, and think of Geeta. She always had dreams of being a professional sitar player. The early years of our marriage were filled with the nasal twang of her playing. Sitting quietly on the sofa, I would watch her fingers race between the sitar strings, her eyes shut, mouth slightly open, head swaying to the beat. Ah, the early years.

Then the pregnancies came, striking her down like an illness. Miscarriage after miscarriage, until Amar arrived, with his hunger and his wants. Geeta's sitar moved from the lounge to the kitchen to the utility room, ending up in the garage, hiding behind the discarded barbeque stand and Amar's bicycle.

'Amar's older now. Time to take the sitar out of hibernation,' I tell her every year, around Amar's birthday.

Geeta always looked puzzled, as though I'd mentioned a long-dead relative. 'Who has the time to play music?' she says, going back to her ironing or channel surfing. Esther is right. Sometimes it can be too late.

'I've never set foot in this gallery until today,' I say, changing the topic.

'I practically camped in this gallery when we first moved up from London. It was the only cultural oasis around. Manchester was such a dump then. No restaurants, no Trafford Centre. Only Lewis's or Kendalls for the fancy stuff.' She smiles. 'What about you? How did you kill time when you first moved here from India?'

'I shared a room in Levenshulme with a friend, and then my wife joined me after she got her papers. We moved to Longsight. There was no time for sightseeing or going to museums. We were setting up home, always on the lookout for cheap deals and shops stocking Indian groceries. I live in Timperley now, a much larger house with a garden. And a mango tree.'

'A mango tree?' Esther raises an eyebrow. 'How exciting. Is that to remind you of home?'

'Maybe. My mother liked mangoes,' I say.

My life sounds dull and small, and I have the feeling she doesn't really know the places I am talking about. I've not thought about those years of hardship for some time – moving from two-room rentals to owning a house, the 5 a.m. start at the cash and carry on Cheetham Hill, long bus trips to out-of-town discount stores, the electric and gas meters that gave up on us in the dead of winter. Geeta and I rushed through our youth, skimping and saving, our eyes blindfolded to the beauty around, eating at Wimpy's for a treat, and here I was, sitting in a museum reminiscing about a past that I didn't want to recognise any more.

'I'm glad I came here today. This place has some nice stuff,' I continue quickly. 'I liked the painting with the chariots and the horses. Looked like a scene from that *Ben-Hur* film. Did you ever see it? The one with Charlton Heston?'

'You liked Wagner's *Chariot Race*?' Esther is pleased by my choice. 'I love the movement in that painting too, and the texture of the colours. The horses look as though they're dancing rather than galloping, don't they?'

I hadn't noticed, but I say yes anyway.

We pass the museum gift shop on our way out. 'One minute,' Esther says, and disappears into the shop. She comes out and presses a postcard into my hand. 'This is for you. To remind you of this museum and to tempt you to drop in again.'

The postcard is a print of the horse painting. This is Esther's first gift to me.

* * *

We walk out into a damp Manchester day, and Esther pulls out a small, folding umbrella from her bag. Her voice floats up from beneath the canopy.

'This rain is murder for my hair. It goes all frizzy.'

I say she would look good in any weather. We stand together on a busy street, surrounded by people. Esther peers into a bookshop window.

'I'll try and remember your advice, you know,' she says brightly. 'It is never too late to catch up on life. I might dig out my old drawings and show them to you one day.'

A dimple appears in her left cheek. I hadn't noticed it before. It makes her look girlish.

'And I'll remember your advice about restaurants. The café was dreadful – I'm sorry,' I say. She had left her soup untouched.

'We'll go to Chester next time, to Chez Pierre. It does proper onion soup. The chef's from Lyon,' she says.

'Chester's far,' I say, feeling old. The afternoon suddenly feels flat and aimless.

'Oh, you must try it if you've not eaten there before. Go with your wife. It's just off the M56. Chester's not far.'

An alarm on her mobile goes off. 'I need to go,' she says. 'I'll grab a cab – I left my car at home. Parking in the city is such a hassle, don't you think?'

'My car's parked just around the corner – I can drop you,' I offer.

If Esther notices the bump on the front fender or Amar's biro scribbling on the back seat as I open the door for her, she makes no mention of it. Her dress rides up as she sits down and I notice her legs. She snuggles into her seat, owning her space in a way Geeta never does. Geeta sits upright, the seat belt pulled tied around her stomach, her eyes scanning the road for car pileups and traffic jams.

There isn't much traffic, but I drive slowly. Esther opens her bag and pulls out a packet of Camels. I spot a set of keys, a wallet, a lipstick and a small red tub of Tiger Balm – fragments of another woman's life.

A lorry hurtles past. It is sleek and black with Solomon's name painted on its side in big swirly gold letters. 'That's one of yours,' I say.

She shrugs her shoulders as though it's no big deal. 'Mind if I smoke?' She winds down the window and lights up before I can say yes. I wonder how her tobacco-filled mouth would taste. 'What kind of music do you like?' she asks, bending forward, fiddling with the knobs on the car radio.

'I like music that makes you feel and not think too hard. Neil Diamond, maybe?' I sneak another look at her legs. Her knees are plump and white. 'I'm showing my age here,' I add, laughing. 'Nearly fifty-six... bus-pass material soon.'

'Neil Diamond is my favourite too. His voice is like broken glass. And seriously, you don't look your age.' She states it like a fact, not a compliment.

My mouth goes dry. I turn up the volume.

'Mr Handsome' – that was Geeta's name for me when we first got married. Running her fingers along my jaw, she'd murmur, with wonder in her voice, 'I don't know why you married a simple girl like me. What do you see in me?' Our embraces and words were exaggerated in silence, while the servant slept outside the thin plywood bedroom door, foetal, his snores melting into the chorus of night-time noises – the barking dogs and the police sirens screaming down the Bombay roads.

My hand lightly brushes Esther's thigh as I change gears. 'So sorry,' I say.

The colour rises to her cheeks, but she doesn't say anything.

I drop her at her appointment, watching her as she makes her way across the cobblestones in her four-inch stilettos.

Geeta could never wear such fancy shoes. She prefers practical flat pumps from Clarks, or trainers for shopping, sometimes even with her Indian clothes. I once opened her wardrobe searching for something and found stacks of high-heeled sandals, my gifts to her, lying unworn and new, still wrapped in tissue paper, like babies sleeping in cardboard coffins.

Esther's perfume, her sheer tights and her impractical shoes – they speak to me in a different language.

'Thank you for the lift and… well, I'll see you around,' Esther says just before she leaves.

That's the last I'll see of her, I think, as I head towards the office. It was a pleasant afternoon – a little break from the monotony, nothing else. Unless, of course, she tells Cedric about me. There's no point even mentioning our hurried lunch to Geeta.

5

A PROPER LUNCH

Weeks pass, and then one day I receive a text from Esther.

'I've been thinking about what you said about never giving up. I would love to show you some of my designs.'

Why not show them to your husband? I think, but I'm pleased she has chosen me – clearly she values my designer's eye above Cedric's. We arrange to meet at the French restaurant she mentioned in Chester.

'A proper lunch. You will love their French onion soup,' she texts back.

I cancel an appointment with a customer and meet Esther. It's a sunny Wednesday afternoon, and there isn't much traffic. I make it in good time. The restaurant is on a dead-end street overlooking the Chester racecourse, which is empty, except for a few joggers stretching and the odd dog-walker. Huge ugly billboards advertising insurance and health-care plans for the over-sixties block the view of the Pennines in the distance.

She is waiting near the door, waving to me. 'I wasn't sure you'd find it. It's sort of tucked away. Careful,' she says, pointing to a dead pigeon lying on the kerb outside the restaurant door. Its hard pebble-dark eyes are open.

'Silly question, but do birds have eyelids?' I ask Esther.

She shrugs. 'No idea. I'm not a scientist.'

* * *

Chez Pierre is posh, with red wallpaper and little golden lamps on the tables. There's one other couple in the restaurant besides us.

I try not to think about the bill as the waitress, wearing a white, lace-trimmed apron, leads us to our table. She seems to know Esther.

I look inquisitively at Esther as the waitress walks away. 'I sometimes pop in here with a few friends after the races,' she explains.

I survey the London prices on the menu and decide not to care. How often do I get the chance to take Cedric Solomon's wife to lunch? 'Let's have some champagne,' I say.

'Are we celebrating?' She smiles. Her blue and brown striped Missoni dress hugs her curves, bringing out the brown of her eyes.

I think about complimenting her, but then change my mind. It would sound inappropriate. 'Your designs – I'm looking forward to seeing them,' I say, while turning off my mobile and slipping it back into my pocket.

Esther orders Louis Roederer, calling it 'just the right kind of dry'. This is the life – dining on French food and wine with a woman who knows how to appreciate the finer things in life. The afternoon stretches ahead of me like the red carpet at the Oscars.

The champagne arrives, and I empty the glass in a single gulp. Esther takes delicate sips. Her lips close around the rim of the glass, leaving behind a deep-red lipstick smudge. Her eyes study the tablecloth while I try to make small talk.

'So, where are those designs? Let's have a look.'

She clicks open her handbag and pulls out a rolled sheet of white A4 paper, smoothing out the wrinkles as she lays them flat on the table. The sketches are of evening dresses. Huge, billowing gowns glittering with jewels at the neck and the hem. They're the sort of clothes a child might have drawn – fanciful fairy dresses meant for dreaming about, not wearing. No wonder Cedric doesn't want her help with design.

'What sort of material were you thinking of? Chiffon or silk?' I ask, pretending to be serious.

She shrugs. 'I don't know. They're fantasies really. I haven't really thought about practical stuff like that.'

'Well, the key thing is the fabric,' I say. 'Something substantial that can carry the weight of those rhinestones – maybe velvet?'

'Yes, yes, maybe velvet. Anyway, I haven't thought about such stuff for a long time. It's only because you said you were interested...' Her voice drops and she rolls up the paper again and stuffs it back inside her bag. 'I don't know why I showed them to you. Nothing will come of them. Let's talk about something more interesting. Tell me about you. Everything, from A to Z,' she says, her chin cupped in one hand. The ruby ring on her index finger sparkles in the lamp light.

'I'm flattered, but I thought I told you, I'm in textiles like your husband...'

Esther lifts her hand and stops me.

'Not boring business stuff. I can get that from Cedric. I want to know what makes PK Malik tick – what makes him leap out of bed in the morning, sets his heartbeat racing.' She puts her empty glass down. 'Go on, fire away,' she says.

'Not much makes my heart race these days,' I say, and suggest another bottle.

'Yes, why not. The afternoon's young,' she says, sticking out her chin defiantly.

She looks around for the waitress, while I pick at my plate. I don't really like the duck Esther ordered for me. It's too fancy and creamy, and my appetite's gone. I would have preferred a pasta dish with more robust flavours, like garlic and onion, a bit like the desi-style Italian food Geeta cooks at home.

'Let's talk about you instead. It's far more interesting.' I lean forward. Our faces are close. I can smell the drink on her breath.

Esther tells me about her childhood in north London and the Friday night dinners with the rabbi. She is Jewish. 'One hundred per cent kosher.' She laughs. 'Don't you think Jews and Indians are alike?'

I think of the Jews I know. The only ones I tend to see are the orthodox ones who live at the end of our road. I see them walking to the synagogue on Saturdays, the women wearing expensive hats and the men with kippahs on their heads. They look elegant and aloof – nothing like the muddling, noisy Indians I know.

'We're so similar,' Esther insists. The alcohol has brought colour to her cheeks. 'We have the same obsession with food and family – all those Friday night dinners,' she pauses, and then carries on, 'the same neurosis about being on the margins. Absolute misfits.'

'Do you have many Indian friends?' I ask, puzzled.

'My doctor's Indian – Mr Shah.' She pronounces his name correctly. 'But then, aren't they all doctors?' We laugh. 'And now you. You're my friend, aren't you?' Her voice is anxious.

'Yes, of course we're friends.' I'm not convinced, but I say so anyway. I wonder if meeting me has made her like Indians, and I think of her husband, who supplies most of the high streets in England. I doubt whether he wastes his time on Indians. He is a part of the English establishment, hunting and shooting with the lords and the ladies. There's nothing 'misfit' or 'marginal' about him. I bet he wears a signet ring.

'There's a golf club somewhere in Cheshire that accepts only Jews and Indians,' I say. 'It says "No dogs or English allowed" on the front gates.' It's a weak joke, but she finds it funny.

'Good for them! Why shouldn't we stick together?' Esther says, playing with the bread roll on her side plate. She's barely touched the duck, and we'd forgotten to order the speciality she spoke of, the French onion soup.

Halfway through the second bottle, the champagne makes me bold. 'Have you always had such long hair, Esther?'

She runs a hand through it self-consciously. 'Cedric hates it. He says it makes me look girlish and immature. I should have a well-behaved bob at my age,' she says and laughs.

'I think long hair is a sign of a woman's beauty,' I say.

The couple at the next table look up from their food and glance at us.

'Thank you. I bet your wife's hair is really beautiful.'

'My wife used to have long hair, but it's much shorter now. Easier to look after, I suppose.'

I hadn't wanted Geeta to cut her hair. But she went ahead and did it anyway. 'It's easier to manage in a cold country' – that was her excuse.

'Why does everything have to be practical and easy?' Esther says, playing with her hair, teasing it until it falls forward, covering one side of her face. A few strands get entangled in her pearl earrings. She sighs and pulls them off carelessly, slipping them into her handbag. My eyes follow her movements, lingering on her earlobes, now soft, pink and naked.

A feeling of unease settles inside me. Everything goes quiet. My eyes travel from her earlobes to her cheeks to her mouth. Maybe I should talk about our families. I could mention Amar, the trouble he's having at school. But the timing doesn't seem right.

I suddenly remember Esther spent some time in Bombay. 'It would have been fun to meet in Bombay when we were younger,' I say, wanting a slice of that young Esther, dutifully doing her twenty laps every morning in the pool at the Taj, her long, white arms slicing through the water while a waiter stood holding a glass with freshly squeezed nimbu pani and the palm trees swayed in the breeze.

'You would've hated me then. I was plump and clumsy with dreadful freckles on my nose. But you – I can't ever imagine you being anything but handsome.' Her clear eyes assess me steadily.

This is the second time she's mentioned my appearance. I look away, unsure of what to say or do. Then, just as in a theatre when the lights come on, the bill arrives. The air becomes cold. A waitress stands at our table.

I pull out my wallet, but Esther wants to pay.

'Don't be silly.' I place my hand on hers. Her fingers are as cold as mine. This is where I should say goodbye and end it. But I don't.

I look at my watch. It's already three. Time to slink back into our regular lives again. To go back home to Geeta's dull face and Amar's empty eyes eating up the television.

'Why don't we go somewhere for a quick coffee?' I say. 'There's a Holiday Inn just off junction five.' I don't look at her as I say this.

She thinks about it. 'Let's find a nice little tea shop that does lovely crumbly cakes instead. A herbal tea would clear my head, and Cedric's away in Hong Kong, so I'm in no rush.' She rubs her earlobe, as though rubbing away a bruise, while her other hand reaches for her cigarettes.

She stumbles over a step as we walk out. I steady her, my hand around her elbow. She doesn't pull away. We walk to our cars, passing a dog nosing the dead pigeon we'd seen earlier.

'Poor helpless bird.' She sighs and moves closer. 'Can't we chase the dog away?'

'He can't help it. It's in his nature.' Every word is a loaded bullet. I wait beside Esther's car until she's inside, putting her bag down and smoothing her dress.

'Follow me to the café, PK. I know these country roads pretty well,' she says, rolling down her window.

I don't want to meet her for tea. What we're doing doesn't feel innocent any more. 'Actually, Esther… I've just remembered… I've got to get back to the office – an important meeting. But it was lovely catching up with you. Keep up the good work,' I say, pointing to her handbag. 'Those drawings show a lot of promise. Don't give up.' I wave and walk to my car, and drive away without looking back.

Dear Lopa didi,
I'm glad the monsoons have arrived. At last, some break from the humidity. Sorry to hear that Jijaji's factory in Ahmedabad was looted. I blame the BJPs – they don't want Hindus and Muslims to live together in peace. They're just like the British used to be. Always dividing and ruling.

Things are OK here. I couldn't tell you over the phone because Amar was listening, but PK has suddenly become very caring. He makes me laugh, and he's telling me to grow my hair long again. The other day he pulled out this shoebox from my wardrobe and told me to wear the red stilettos. Just imagine – they were nearly four inches high! I did wear them to please him, but almost twisted my ankle going up the stairs. He wants to take me to a restaurant. A French one. I said, No thank you, we can have perfectly good meals at home. What's the point in trying to act young and waste money? We are middle-aged. Is Jijaji like that too?

I must go now – Amar wants help with his maths homework. Love to the kids. Tell them their masi misses them.

Geeta

6

PARTY TIME

The Guptas are celebrating their twenty-fifth wedding anniversary at the Lee Hung Dragon in Handforth.

'Can we leave early? It will be a boring evening,' I say to Geeta, but she's having none of it.

'They're our best friends, and Amar is invited too. The Patels will be there, and the…' She reels off a list of names. I know them all – small-time businessmen, doctors and accountants, carefully eking out a living in a foreign land. They are good people, but I don't necessarily want to hang out with them.

I know how the evening will go. There'll be lukewarm house wine waiting for us when we arrive, and platters of spring rolls and chilli sauce slapped down on each table. The women will huddle together, dumping their shawls and handbags on the chairs, saving seats for their best friends. Geeta will make sure she finds a chair next to Mrs Gupta, the chief attraction of the evening for her. I'll make my way to the fake marble bar at the end of the room, where the other husbands crowd together for warmth and solidarity. Here I'll find Gupta, keeping a sharp eye on the bar orders.

'Come on, yaar, don't get carried away, it's only an anniversary; let's just stick to the house wine,' he'll say. There'll be a scowl and angry mutterings if someone dares to order something fancier like a vodka and lime.

The evening is just as I have imagined it. Gupta has reserved a table for us – his 'nearest and dearest', as he puts it. I sit down and look around for an empty chair for Amar.

'Let him mingle with the other kids,' Gupta says. 'That's how these youngsters learn how to grow up.'

But Amar isn't mingling. He goes straight to Geeta and perches awkwardly on her lap. From time to time, his hand dives to the centre of the table, and he snatches a fistful of prawn crackers and stuffs them in his mouth. Embarrassed, I look away.

'So, how is business these days, PK, bhai?'

It's Biku Patel. He sells tights – or 'hosiery', as he likes to call it. Small and rotund, with a small finger perpetually fishing out dirt from his ear, he isn't an ideal dining companion, but I'm stuck between him and Gupta, who is busy scribbling something on a piece of paper.

'Business is fine, just fine, Bikuji. Sold a container load of dresses to a store in Belfast. But things could be better. Lot of competition these days…' My voice falters.

'That's good, that's very good.' Biku Patel nods. 'Ever thought of adding to the line? My cousin in Surat has just started a dip-dye factory, and he wants to export. You can send him jeans and dresses and he can dye them any colour.'

'Actually, I am using a factory in Italy for that kind of stuff. It's a small family-run place just outside Milan.'

'Their costs must be high, no? They are in Europe. My cousin, he is using the latest Chinese technology.'

I shake my head. 'The Italians know quality. The Chinese don't have it. They are like robots.'

But Biku Patel won't understand the difference. He sells third-rate polyester tights out of a small, dark cubicle on Thomas Street, opposite a kebab place called Kabana. These tights turn up selling by the kilo for 99p a pair in market stalls around the country. But then again, he's obviously doing something right, because his kids go to private schools and his wife flaunts a big, fat diamond on her ring finger.

'Any plans for going to India soon?' The man sitting next to Biku Patel cranes his neck forward and asks him.

'Going to Gujarat soon, after three long years. I'm taking the family to see the new Swaminarayan temple,' Biku Patel says proudly. His eyes shine.

The man who'd asked the question – I don't recognise him in the shadowy half-light of the restaurant – declares him a lucky man. 'I'm thinking of taking the kids to Orlando. They don't want to go to India. They find it smelly and dirty.' He sighs and turns to me. 'What about you, PK? What are your summer plans?'

'I'd love to see the Colosseum in Rome. I've heard the way the light hits the buildings in Rome, you can't beat it. But not this year.' I shut my eyes and then open them. I'm still in Handforth.

The men give me a strange look, as though I'd proposed a trip to the Playboy Mansion.

The waitress arrives, interrupting our conversation. All eyes turn to the steaming bowls of food.

'Chop suey… tofu in black-bean sauce… mixed veg in garlic… some more spring rolls and rice,' Gupta announces each dish as it is put down. There's no meat, no duck. The duck is the reason Amar has agreed to come to the restaurant.

'I kept it all strictly non-meat – didn't want to offend the vegetarian ladies,' Gupta winks and points to the women whose chit-chat had stopped whilst they focused on eating. But I know he's done it to keep the costs down.

Amar has somehow slipped from Geeta's lap and is slumped down at her feet. He's playing with his shoelaces, an intent look on his face. Geeta keeps feeding him titbits from her plate like a dog.

The food gets eaten, the wine drunk, and just when it feels like the evening can't get any longer, a chocolate cake is wheeled out on a hostess trolley to the front, like a patient ready for surgery. Gupta's kids rush towards it in a flurry of excitement, and with trembling hands light the twenty-five candles on the cake. The lighting takes a while, and we all edge forward in our chairs, taking a good, hard look at the cake.

Two chocolate-coloured figures stand on top of the cake. One is Gupta, holding a pink marzipan briefcase in his hand, and standing next to him, in a blue marzipan sari, is his wife, with a pink mobile phone glued to her ear.

'A very lovely cake for a very lovely couple!' Geeta shouts out, clapping her hands and jumping to her feet. The rest of us join in, setting up a beat. The men are thumping their feet on the floor, crying out, 'Speech! Speech! We want a speech!'

The room feels warm, because Gupta has forced the waitresses to bring in three extra heaters. The sweat shines on the women's faces, glowing under their make-up. I remove my jacket, placing it carefully on the back of my chair. I don't want it mixed up with Biku Patel's glossy black-and-white-checked BHS affair.

'Friends, friends…' Gupta smiles shyly, making his way to the front. 'There is no need for a speech. This is such a small, humble gathering,' he says, pulling out a sheet of paper from his front pocket. He is well prepared. He clears his throat and begins: 'Friends, family, loved ones…' A few men snigger. He ignores them and continues. 'Many years ago, Usha and I left the love and safety of our families and our home in Bombay to come to a cold, unknown land to make our fortune. And this land, this England, became our new home.'

He pauses, takes off his glasses, surveys the room, swallows once or twice and goes back to his speech.

'And look how richly we have been rewarded. I have a house, a brand-new car, a permanent job in an accountancy firm. My children speak with an English accent. Yes, God has been truly kind.'

'He's only a bloody accountant, hardly Rockefeller,' Biku Patel mutters under his breath.

Overcome with emotion, Gupta is ready to sit down when his daughter whispers something in his ear. Gupta resumes his speech. 'Oho, I almost forgot…' He laughs. 'My companion in this golden journey has been my lovely wife, Usha, along with my oldest best friend PK Malik, who has always had a generous heart.'

Geeta looks at me proudly, and Biku Patel thumps me on the back. 'Good man, good man,' he says. 'What exactly did you do?'

'Nothing much,' I say, with a shrug. 'I just gave him money when he needed it.'

I wonder if I should get up and return the compliment, but his wife Usha is already at the front, bending over the cake, knife in hand, an executioner ready to slice off the marzipan heads.

* * *

Geeta is quiet on the way home. There isn't the usual chatter about who said what to whom and why. She makes me stop at a KFC before we reach home, and picks up a tub of chicken drumsticks and a portion of fries for Amar. 'Poor child – he didn't eat a thing. I could hear his stomach rumbling all the way through the evening.'

'But he was scoffing down the spring rolls like there's no tomorrow,' I say.

'I want duck, duck, duck!' Amar shouts out from the back seat. His mouth is full with chicken, so it comes out as 'fuck, fuck, fuck'. I start laughing.

'What's so funny?' Geeta wants to know.

* * *

'The Guptas are so lucky,' she says, later, in the bedroom.

'Why – what do they have that you and I don't?' I ask.

'There is so much love – I mean, just look at the grand party he threw for her.' She sits down heavily on the bed, slowly easing off her bangles. Her wrists are plump, and she winces in pain as the metal bites into the flesh.

'He spent most of the night talking about himself – the kids had to remind him about her! What kind of love is that?' I say. 'And call that a party? He wasn't even serving decent wine or meat!'

But Geeta is in one of her self-pitying moods, and doesn't want to listen. 'I wish we had done something special for our twenty-fifth,' she says.

'We did – we went to London, remember? We stayed at the Hilton. We saw a show, *The Phantom of the Opera*.'

'I know, I know, but it would have been nice to have friends round and...' Her voice fades as she dismisses the memory. She yawns and gets into bed.

I shut the bedroom door and slip upstairs to my study. I call it a study, but it's more like an attic – a small room that can only be reached by pulling down a thin aluminium ladder that usually lies folded against a trapdoor and shakes under my heavy footsteps.

Geeta wants me to convert the garage – build a partition wall through the middle and put in a desk and a portable heater. 'Why do you want to be like a monkey, always scrambling up?' she says.

But the study is my refuge. For wallpaper, I have plastered the walls with pictures of far-off places, beautiful houses and clothes, photos of Chanel and Saint Laurent. Esther's postcard, the one with the dancing horses, is up there too. It's here that I keep my books and magazines on fashion. It's quite a collection now, and every year I have to add a shelf to accommodate the growing library.

'What do you do up there, Dad?' Amar asks. He's too plump and unfit to hoist himself up, and watches me curiously as I slowly disappear through the hole in the ceiling.

'Let him be,' Geeta says. 'That's his kingdom, where he likes to hide his secrets.'

I pass that night flicking through pages of old issues of French fashion magazines. I don't understand the language, but I understand the images. I particularly like the fashion of the early sixties, the geometrical precision of the mini dress, the way colours have a clear, defined tone and borders, no vulgar flutter of frill or lace. And here I am selling just that, railings of frocks with acres of synthetic lace and boho prints, because fashion that year decided it be so.

My eyes go to Esther's postcard. I look at the colours. I want to bring the same richness and tone to my clothes, and the only way I can do so is by printing fabric with my own designs. I don't want to be marooned in ugliness any more.

Dear Lopa didi,

Remember our best friends, the Guptas? You remember Usha came to see you on her last visit to Bombay – I had sent some KitKats and jumpers for the kids with her. Anyway, it was the Guptas' silver wedding anniversary, and they threw a huge glamorous party. It was a Chinese restaurant, and no expense was spared – delicious food, lovely speeches – but PK sat through the evening looking glum, arms folded, acting as though he didn't want to be there. He does that often with our Indian friends. I don't know why he can't make an effort. Anyway, the party reminded me of my own silver anniversary. I really wanted you to come, but airline tickets are so expensive. We went to London and saw a show – I think I told you about it. Actually, our seats were so far back I couldn't see much, but PK had sweetly booked a five-star hotel. London was exciting – so many people, so many bright lights and shops. One day, I promise I will show it to you. The funniest thing was that PK had kept on drinking the wine from the minibar, and he nodded off and slept through the show! He couldn't remember a thing.

Anyway, enough about me. Tell me, has your horrible mother-in-law finally gone to Haridwar? Let's hope she doesn't come back from that ashram!

Love to the kids,

Geeta

7

THIS MAN IS AFTER BEAUTY

Manchester in winter: early morning and the city shudders awake beneath the frosty blanket of cold. People hurry to work, hands buried in pockets, dazed eyes peeping through layers of wool, their breath trailing after them like a plane streaking across the sky, billowing clouds of vapour behind it. But the air is pure, and when the sun shines, its headlight intensity cuts into your skin.

On days such as these it feels good to be alive. I walk in the garden, the cold pinching my cheeks, blood rushing to my head, the sky above me low and brooding, even at nine a.m. My only worry is my mango tree. Its polythene-shrouded head droops in the wind.

Geeta and Amar hate winter. Swaddled in jumpers and thermal socks, they tiptoe around the house, waiting for spring. The radiators hiss non-stop, the curtains are drawn and the beds are piled up with extra duvets and blankets. Amar lies curled up in bed, a hot-water bottle warming his belly. The school phones home, questioning his absence.

'He has a cold. He has stomach cramps. His ears hurt…' Geeta has a ready-made list for such calls. She warms herself with the continuous consumption of fried snacks. At breakfast she fries banana fritters for herself and Amar, while I eat my boiled egg and toast. Her lunch is potato cutlets and puris. Afternoons are devoted to chips and pancakes, and dinners are usually parathas and chicken curries.

'I will never get used to this cold,' she announces at the beginning of September, when the days start to get shorter and the nights longer.

'It's not that bad, Geeta. You're hardly living in Iceland. It could be a lot worse,' I say, trying to raise her spirits.

'I was born in Bombay. We don't understand winter. It's not in our DNA.' She shuts me up.

On days that are particularly icy, I insist that the girls working in the warehouse are supplied with hot chocolate and warm bacon rolls. Margaret wheels out these offerings twice a day, pushing the trolley on to the main landing, her voice booming out, 'Come on, girls, come and fetch your goodies. Santa is in town.'

'You're spoiling them, PK,' she'll say, coming back into the office.

'They'll work better if they're warm and full,' I always reply. But Margaret never approves of my flashes of generosity. Her eyes are always on the bottom line.

A month or two has passed since my lunch with Esther. I'm busy with new ideas for business. From time to time, my eyes fall on her postcard, and my fingers itch to dial her number, but I stop myself. What good would the call do? 'Hi Esther, how is life? How is your husband? Are you going to introduce us? Will he buy my excess stock?' How pathetic would I sound?

* * *

It's another cold winter's day, and I'm in town visiting Graham Scott, my bank manager at Lloyds. It's about a loan for purchasing a digital printer. I have an idea: to take grey cloth, devoid of colour and pattern, and to print it with my own unique design. The fabric will then be sent to Bangladesh, to my supplier, Mr Ali. He will turn the fabric into dresses and skirts based on exciting new designs that I'll come up with for a young market. The American DigiFab printer that would be ideal for doing such a job in-house has an average cost of 150,000 dollars, and my pockets aren't so deep.

'It sounds very complicated; can you explain it again, Mr Malik?' Graham says. He is a quiet, courteous man, with faded yellow teeth that match the faded yellow whites of his eyes.

I try again. 'Most commercial fabric is rotary-screen printed, and each print run is typically several thousand yards. This jacks up both the cost and the time, because you have to prepare a unique set of screens, with each colour in a design needing a separate screen. It means there's not much room left for imagination. But with this printer, with this one-off purchase, I can…' I stop, because Graham's eyes are wandering to his computer screen.

'Go on, do go on.' His mouth opens into a semi-interested semi-smile, which could easily be a yawn.

I press on. 'Now, if I had a digital printer, I could do very small runs of each design, and I have some fantastic ideas in mind… and then it wouldn't take much time to go from this printing stage to finished fabric, because there are no screens to prepare. This allows you to take advantage of current trends, and even change prints or colours mid-season.'

Graham strokes his chin, hums and haws, and says he'll forward the proposal to his boss. It will take time. 'Keep up the good work, Mr Malik. The industry needs visionaries like you. Too much Chinese tat in the shop these days.' He shakes my hand and walks me to the door.

It's late afternoon by then: dead hours that needed filling up. I fish around in my pocket for the car keys. It's too late to go back to work, too early to go home. I'm out on Deansgate, deciding whether to drop into Gupta's offices, which are around the corner, when I feel a hand on my elbow and an excited voice.

It's Esther, and she's with another woman. 'Hey, PK! Why, it's you, isn't it?' Her hands fly up, twin birds in delight. 'What are you doing here? I thought you worked in north Manchester?'

I had a meeting with my bank manager.' I make a face. 'Not very productive. And how about you?'

Esther looks well, wrapped up in a warm, dark coat, the fur butter-soft against her clear skin and glossy brown hair. Dressed in black, her red leather gloves are the only splash of colour, apart from her mouth, which is painted a crimson red.

She introduces her friend. 'Meet Maratha, my very dear school friend. She's visiting me from London. She's an absolute doll, and my for-ever partner in crime!' She sways a little as she says this; they've clearly been drinking. 'Maratha and I have had a very naughty day. We've been ladies who lunch for a long, long time.'

Maratha listens to Esther, tilting her head to one side. She wears a black astrakhan hat that's too big for her head. It slides over her forehead, stopping just before her eyes. Her face beneath is pale and pointed, but she has a full, red mouth like Esther's. She shivers as we stand talking on the pavement, and folds herself deeper into her coat. 'Why don't we go somewhere for a steaming cup of coffee? My bones are freezing. Is it always this cold in Manchester?' she says.

I have my car keys out by now. 'I don't know…' I hesitate.

'Come and have coffee with us,' Esther says. 'You left in such a hurry last time.'

She knows a small coffee shop inside a church, just off St Anne's Square. We take a flight of steps down into the basement. The steps tire Maratha; she's quite breathless, and asks for a glass of water. We sit near a glass cabinet full of cakes and sandwiches. Two big heaters blow hot air into the room.

The café is lit entirely with candles that have been poured into mismatching tea cups and mugs. A large wooden crucifix hangs on the wall, watching us. I feel as though I'm in an underwater cave, with the candlelight throwing wavering shapes and shadows on the walls.

'Your friend introduces me to the most beautiful, unusual places,' I say to Maratha. 'I've been in Manchester most of my life, and I would never have found this.'

'Maybe you should spend more time with her,' says Maratha.

Esther smiles and pulls her chair closer to mine, her head so close I can smell the apple scent of her perfume. She points to the counter. 'Why don't we share a lovely crumbly carrot cake?'

Maratha wants to know what I do for a living.

'I sell dresses,' I say. 'Not very good ones, but they pay the bills. And I've got some ideas.' I tell her about the fabric printer.

Esther nods in agreement.

'You know, PK here, he's so into beauty. So different to Cedric.' She turns to Maratha and laughs. 'Cedric's only ever been interested in numbers, numbers, numbers. Where's the beauty in that? Tell me! But my friend here…' She flings her hand theatrically towards me. 'This man is after beauty.'

Maratha takes off her hat. Her hair is grey and cropped short, and patches of pink skin show through. The brutal haircut doesn't match her face or her elegant clothes. She catches me looking at her.

'This is not a bad hair day; this is cancer,' Maratha says quietly, and looks down at the table. She sits with her head bent, as though waiting for a blessing.

Our drinks arrive. Maratha sips her coffee through a straw. 'Swallowing is difficult. I've become like a baby: only liquids for me. Liquid grapes are the best.' Her eyes twinkle.

Esther breaks the silence. She lowers her voice. 'Maratha's having chemo. And to think – you had such beautiful hair…' Esther sighs, and her eyes glisten.

I pat her hand. I understand death. I only have to shut my eyes for my mother to rise before me.

'Don't worry, Esther, darling. I'm still here. I ain't going anywhere just yet. I'm just greedier now. I want more than my slice of life,' Maratha says, placing her hat carefully back on her head.

Esther leans forward and kisses her cheek. 'You are so right. Here I am, grumbling to you about petty little things that annoy me about Cedric and the kids when…' She pauses. 'Isn't there a grander, more meaningful way of living? What do you think, PK?'

The question stumps me. My head is busy with keeping my business afloat, paying bills and fretting over Amar – and here she is, asking me to reach out for something different. I mumble something appropriate.

The talk moves swiftly on to Maratha's treatment. Esther knows of a holistic clinic in Mexico that specialises in alternative therapies, things like alkaline diets, seaweed wraps and hypnosis. 'They have a high success rate,' she tells Maratha. 'I'm going to send you there, and don't even think about boring things like bills. I'm going to sort it all out.'

'You are lucky to have such a caring friend,' I say to Maratha.

'Esther's heart has always been bigger than her brain,' Maratha replies. 'Once she takes you into her heart, that's it – there's no way out. Nada. You're sentenced for life!'

The women laugh.

It's raining heavily when we leave the café. I stand on the kerb, trying to wave down a cab while the women huddle at my back, standing close together for warmth. A cab stops and they get in.

Esther rolls down the window. Strands of her hair are stuck to her forehead, her mascara runs loose down her cheek from crying and the rain, and the fur around her throat is like a dead animal. 'Thank you for the coffee. My turn next time,' she shouts above the hiss of the running engine and the rain. Maratha raises a pale hand in goodbye, her face lost within the darkness of the cab.

* * *

The house is empty and dark when I return. A scribbled note from Geeta lies on the kitchen table.

'Taken Amar to the doctor.'

I light a cigarette and stand in the dark, my damp coat still on, reflecting on the afternoon. I think about Maratha's words. Gupta, Geeta, me – we're all shuffling towards nothingness. We've lost our appetite for life.

The kitchen lights come on and Geeta comes in, taking off her gloves, a questioning look on her face. 'Why are you sitting in the dark?'

'Why are you still wearing your coat, Dad?' Amar adds, following me to the cloakroom.

'Silly me – I'm getting old, that's all.' I laugh. 'What's wrong with you, anyway?' I feel his forehead. It feels a normal temperature, but he's dragging his feet and his cheeks are sallow.

'He's caught a chill. I'll give him some Calpol now,' Geeta says, reaching for the bottle on the shelf.

'Isn't Calpol for babies?' I say. 'He's fourteen – he's too old for it.'

'I like the taste. It's like a sweetie,' Amar says, smacking his lips. That settles it; he has three teaspoons.

Dinner is on the table: chicken curry and buttered chapattis. Food designed to keep the cold from entering our bones. The ghee floats on top of the chicken and the chapattis are stiff and burnt.

She's made them in a hurry before she left for the doctor's surgery, Geeta explains. 'I can make fresh ones if you want,' she says, eying my plate.

I shake my head.

'You're not eating much.' She scoops up the leftover chicken and tips it into Amar's waiting mouth.

'I had a big slice of carrot cake earlier,' I say. 'And two cups of coffee.'

'That's not like you.' Her eyes narrow. 'You don't like cake.'

'There's always a first time, isn't there,' I say, pushing back my chair and getting up.

Amar sits still at the table, his eyes like a ping-pong ball in action, moving between my face and Geeta's, his hands curled in his lap; only his mouth moves as he chews his food. He speaks up.

'I have a headache, Mum. Can you make me some hot milk?'

In the kerfuffle of preparing the milk and hurrying Amar to bed, then doing the dishes, there is somehow never chance to tell Geeta about my coffee with Esther and her friend.

8

A FOOTBALL MATCH

It's Derby day. United are playing City at Old Trafford, and because they are the cup holders excitement runs high. Ben invites me to the match; a client has stood him up and he has spare seats.

'Bring your kid, bring the wife,' he says. 'It'll be a good day out.'

Instead of Geeta, I take Gupta along. 'Make sure you wear your red scarf,' I remind him.

'And get beaten up by City fans? No, thank you,' he replies. 'I've been called Paki too many times for my liking.'

I pick Gupta up on the way to Old Trafford. Geeta is spending the day with Usha. 'These ladies will be up to no good,' he says, winking at me as he gets into the car. 'They're planning a mega trip to the Trafford Centre. They are going to skin us alive with their spending.' It's a lame joke. We both know our wives are penny-pinchers who cut vouchers out of newspapers and buy vegetables in bulk from Rusholme. But it's still good to maintain the illusion that they're different.

It's not been easy getting Amar to the match. He hates the noise, the snarl of crowds pushing forward, the traffic ramming the roads. He stands on the ramp at the entrance to our section shaking his head. The air stinks of beer and vinegar and men jostle past us, eager to reach their seats. 'I don't want to go, Dad. It's noisy and smelly.' He clings to the railing, his knuckles yellow against the grey metal.

I try to pry his fingers loose, speaking in a low voice while Ben looks on amused. 'Hey, Kiddo, what boy doesn't like footy? Don't make a scene, Amar. This is a big match and we are Uncle Ben's guests.' I pinch his arm and he lets out a yelp. 'We'll get pizza on our way home, and you can stay up late and watch cartoons.'

'Pinkie promise?' He extends his little finger.

I nudge him ahead, holding on to his shoulder. Ben says kids are kids – you never know what has got into them. He offers me a cigarette and I grab it greedily. At least Amar hasn't slumped down on the road like he sometimes does, thrashing his arms and legs, bursting into tears. It's progress of sorts.

The match isn't so great, after all. It's a goalless draw. The crowd are restless, and a murmur becomes a roar when the referee disallows a United goal.

'Bloody offside,' I mutter to Gupta, who agrees that the player is a wanker. Amar sits wedged between us, his eyes intent on his PlayStation. He ducks down and holds his head every time the ball gets kicked in our direction. At half-time I buy everybody hotdogs and beer, and an extra-large lemonade for Amar.

'Don't forget the pizza afterwards, Dad,' Amar says, snatching the paper cup from my hand.

Ben points to the corporate boxes and asks if I've spotted Cedric Solomon. I stare at the glass cubicles, plastered with adverts, but it's too far away to make out any detail.

'That's him, all right, right there with a Chinese bloke,' Ben insists. 'Must be a big shot from Hong Kong. Cedric does a lot of his entertaining here.'

'Who else is with him? Is his wife there? Is Esther there?' I squint hard, trying to put faces on the far-away blobs suspended above us in their glass box.

'Nah,' Ben says dismissively. 'This isn't her kind of place. She's probably having her nails done, or her hair.'

I wonder if Maratha is still in town, and whether Esther is busy with her.

* * *

'The game was rubbish, Mum, and Dad didn't get me a pizza, even though he promised,' Amar says, running into Geeta's arms and burying his head in her lap.

Geeta makes soothing noises. 'Come, I'll take you now,' she says, but Usha has a better idea. She wants us to stay over for dinner – she has some Costco pizzas in the freezer. 'It'll only take a minute to defrost,' she says, rushing into the kitchen.

The Guptas live in Cheadle, in a comfortable semi that's overstuffed with heavy French-style furniture that Gupta bought in an estate sale many years back and cheap knock-offs of Rajasthani dolls and inlaid mirrors from Kashmir. It's nice enough, but it's not quite south Manchester.

'What a shit match. No wonder Alex Ferguson was fuming,' I complain to Gupta as we go into the conservatory that doubles up as their dining room.

His wife hands me a slice of pizza. She has garnished the tomato-sauce topping with chopped chillies and swirly rounds of red onion. I quietly shift them to the side of my plate.

'Who exactly is this Cedric fellow that Ben was pointing out at the match?' Gupta asks, picking at his teeth.

I shrug. 'He's in the rag trade, like me... He's—'

'He's a big shot,' Geeta interrupts me. 'PK is forever reading about him in the newspaper, and it upsets him no end. You should see his face!' She giggles as though she's cracked the world's best joke. The pizza, riddled with chilli bullets, and the endless hours of gossiping all day have made her merry.

'What have you two been up to?' I turn to Gupta's wife, ignoring Geeta's comment.

'Watching TV and snacking, mostly. It was too cold to go out,' she says. Her voice quivers. 'You husbands should be happy. We saved you money by staying in.'

'Don't you have anything better to do?' The words slip out before I can stop them.

'You spent the day watching eleven men kicking a ball. How is that any better?' Geeta replies, her fork pointing at me.

Gupta bursts out laughing. He claps his hands and tilts his chair back so it's resting against the mock Louis XIV sideboard. One wrong move and the family pictures posed so carefully on the sideboard will come crashing down. The pictures are mostly of his son looking plain and bored. He's inherited Gupta's narrow, sloping shoulders and defeated mouth.

'I love it! I love it when the wives get furious. You will have to make it up to Geeta later, PK.' Gupta gives me a lewd wink and circles his finger inside his fist. I tell him to shut up because Amar's still at the table.

'Aren't you going to make up for your rudeness today?' Geeta asks later that night when we're alone in bed. She loosens the string of her petticoat and reaches for my hand. The mattress dips as she moves closer. I smell the onions on her breath, but I do my duty, and it's over all too quickly.

Dear Lopa didi,

Sorry I couldn't phone you last week. I went to the Guptas' for the day. Saw the re-run of the film Bobby *again with Usha. It was playing on Zee. It has to be one of my favourite films. Remember the song, 'Hum, tum ek kamre…'? Those were happy days when we went to see it with Jijaji at the Odeon cinema in Connaught Place. You were both just married, weren't you, living in Delhi in that cute little house on Rouse Avenue next to that famous poet Kavi Naidu. Remember, you were so shy when Jijaji held your hand. He bought us samosas and popcorn in the intermission. I miss those samosas from Bengali Market. Sometimes I wish I had never left India.*

PK took Amar to a football game. It makes me really happy when they spend time together. Doesn't usually happen – mostly he reads the newspaper and gets upset when I ask him about the business. He has many business rivals. Life can be tough here in England, didi. I know you think that I've been handed everything on a plate, but just because I have running hot water and a full fridge 24/7 doesn't make everything rosy. I wish I could show you my life.

Love to the kids,

Geeta

9

A BOLT OF GOLD

A few days after the match I receive a sample of a special fabric from Italy. Signor Rossi and his son Paulo own a textile factory near Lake Como, just outside Milan. We've become friends over the years. I was a regular customer when times were good, buying fabrics in bulk, but my orders have dwindled over the years. I always looked forward to visiting their factory, which was more like an artist's studio. I would hire a car at Milan airport, and drive to the factory through narrow, winding roads, the scent of pine trees strong in my nose, the rear-view mirror flooded with the intense blue of a cloudless sky. Business over, there was always a long lunch at a nearby trattoria, where we ate risotto with forest mushrooms and finished a beautiful bottle of Barolo.

Signor Rossi's speciality is hunting for unusual fabrics and dresses. He attends funerals and flea markets with the same passion, always on the lookout for something unusual, a piece of cloth that glints with gold or a dress that carries the scent of happier times. He takes these back to his workshop and tries to capture the same effect in his fabrics.

'I don't know why people throw things away when they get old. They let go of so much beauty. It is like getting rid of history,' he said to me once.

He sends me a sample from time to time. I am like him, he said one day, a merchant of *bellezza*, of beauty. The sample this time is a five-metre length of dull gold brocade with an antique finish that had come from an old contessa's villa. 'I had to steal it from under the noses of her rascal nephews and nieces,' he wrote in the accompanying note.

I lift it and it's like holding a woman in my arms. I take the bolt of fabric home and show it to Geeta. 'Isn't this beautiful, Geeta!'

'Nice – just like Banarasi silk,' she says, running her fingers over it.

'"Nice"? Just nice?' I look at her incredulously. 'It's fabulous. It reminds me of my mother's wedding sari. Just look at the weave. You can't get this quality any more.'

'Yes, yes.' Geeta's hands absent-mindedly stroke the cloth. 'What happened to your mother's saris, anyway? I bet that aunt of yours pilfered them all.' Twenty-seven years of marriage and she had just remembered my mother's saris. She walks up to the mirror in the hallway and holds the brocade against her cheek. 'It makes my face look dull,' she says, and hands it back.

'It makes it glow.' I correct her.

'What will I do with it? Make a tunic or a sari blouse? But it's too showy. When will I wear it? Send it back and ask for a refund.'

'It's a gift from Signor Rossi – I didn't pay for it,' I say, folding the fabric. I'll take it back to the office and offer it to Margaret, I thought.

Margaret doesn't want it either. 'You could make a dress for Christmas,' I say. 'The girls could run you a nice little frock.'

Margaret spends her Christmases in Blackpool, helping a nephew who runs a B&B. A dress like that would brighten up the drabness of such a Christmas, I think, lend it a touch of frivolity.

'I don't think it's quite right for me, PK. Kind of you to offer, but it needs…' Margaret tucks a pencil behind an ear. She does this when she's thinking hard. 'It needs a woman who sort of floats around, doesn't get her hands dirty…' She gives up. 'You know what I mean.'

I know just the woman who would appreciate such beauty.

* * *

I call Esther. That's how easy it's become: I lift the phone; dial her number. No need to think of an excuse.

'Why don't we meet for lunch? I have something for you,' I say.

'A present?' Esther's voice sounds puzzled. 'But my birthday's not till next week.'

'Perfect timing! Let's celebrate. Is your friend… is Maratha still here? She can join us.'

I'll give Esther the fabric, I think – she will know what to do with it. I don't want it lying around in a dark, damp corner of the warehouse, gathering mildew.

'Maratha's left for Mexico. It took me some time to find the right specialist at the clinic. I made sure she had a room on the ground floor. She can watch the ocean from her bed.' She pauses and then continues. 'You remember she had cancer?'

'Yes, of course. You are a good person, Esther.'

'Rubbish,' she replies. 'You would have done the same. It's hard watching your friend dying in front of you. Makes me want to hurry up and live a little more.' She sighs and then her voice brightens. 'Maratha loved meeting you. Said you were a true gentleman. The way you stood in the rain that day, trying to get us a taxi.'

I brush away her words. 'So when exactly is your birthday?'

'We can't meet on my birthday,' she says straight away. 'It's next Saturday, and Cedric has promised he'll be in town. We may go out to dinner with a couple of friends. Unless you and your wife want to join us?'

'But won't that look strange?' I say. 'I've never met your husband. I need to be properly introduced first.'

'Yes, you're right, that'd be silly, plain silly. Cedric doesn't know you. It'll be awkward. He's a very private person. But I'm curious about this gift…'

'Let's meet on Monday, then. It will be soon after your birthday, and you can tell me a little more about your friend.'

'Monday… Monday… Monday…' She sounds distracted. I imagine her mind racing through her diary. 'Yes, let's have a lovely birthday lunch to brighten the Monday gloom. Do you think this winter is ever going to end, PK, or are we just going to shrivel up and die?'

'Are you always this melodramatic?' I laugh. I enjoy her child-like enthusiasm for life.

A song from an old film floats back to me. It's from an old Raj Kapoor film. I loved it as a teenager, skiving off school to see the matinée. I must have seen it at least five times. And now suddenly it's inside me again, kicking up the dust of memories. I begin whistling the tune: '*Mera joota hai japani*...'

Margaret looks up from her computer and smiles. 'Someone's happy today!'

* * *

Monday arrives. I put on a Burberry tie and a freshly dry-cleaned jacket. Thinking of a suitable place hasn't been easy. In the end, I choose Wings, a Chinese restaurant in a smart part of town that's popular with Manchester United footballers. They came there with their families for dim sum on Sundays. A dozen white dinner plates bearing their signatures hang near the entrance.

Wings looks bleak and empty that Monday afternoon. Most tables are pushed to one wall, and piles of tablecloths lie ready to be laundered after the weekend's excesses. I'm the only customer.

We'll have a leisurely chat about her friend, and once the plates are cleared I will hand her the gift, and, casually, as though it's no big deal, mention that I'd quite like to meet Cedric. A quick meeting, that's all.

I sit in a red velvet booth facing a wall covered with a huge panoramic print of a Hong Kong bay. Carefully inserted within the sailing ships and multi-tiered pagodas are the names of important local businesses. Cedric Solomon, written in a bold black, mock Chinese flourish is right at the centre of these names. I'll make sure I point it out to Esther.

Settled into the booth, the brocade, wrapped in black tissue paper, lying on the seat next to me, I order champagne. We're celebrating a birthday, after all. Maybe a special one – perhaps a fiftieth, although Esther looks younger than Geeta. But most women look younger than Geeta.

'Would you like to order, sir?' The waitress stands at my elbow, pen and paper in hand. I look at my watch. Esther is late – almost an hour late. The champagne in my glass is lukewarm. Defeated bubbles skim its surface. I try Esther's number, but it rings out. I pay for the drink and leave. Only when I'm back in the warehouse, bending over cartons, lifting the skirts, putting them flat on the table, checking for faulty zips and buttons or discolouring, do I remember the brocade. I've left it behind at the restaurant.

10

A HOLIDAY FROM LIFE

She's sorry.

'I hate Mondays, and the cleaner was at home. I had yoga and stuff to catch up on, but actually there's no excuse at all. Will you forgive me? Please?' Esther's text message says.

Another meeting, another weekday, another afternoon. But this time I choose a nondescript hotel just off the M56. I've used the hotel in the past to freshen up on my way back from meetings in the Liverpool area. I'm meeting a customer, a small-town trader who stocks my T-shirts and has been loyal over the years. I'm taking him out to lunch as a thank-you – nothing fancy, just a pizza and some beer at the local Italian.

The Holiday Inn is just a twenty-minute detour from him. My drink with Esther will be quick and efficient. I'll reassure her there are no hard feelings and we can rearrange our meal, maybe get the spouses involved. Making friends with Cedric can only be a good thing, given his contacts and business skill, and I dream of landing a JCPenney contract with his help. It's time Esther introduced me to her husband.

Esther sits in a corner of the lobby, on a large beige leather sofa, almost hidden behind two big potted ferns. She has her coat on, and her gloves.

'Did you find the hotel easily?' I ask, helping her take off her coat. It's a brown suede, Italian, most likely, and belted loosely at the waist.

'Well, how could I miss it? It's such a big, ugly concrete place,' she says.

'It's certainly not the Ritz,' I agree, 'but at least we'll be comfortable here.'

'Comfortable? It's just a cup of coffee, PK. We're not planning on setting up home here, are we?' She laughs. 'If we are, then I'd better get rid of my shoes. They're killing me.'

She sinks back into the sofa and kicks off her shoes. Her stockinged feet look helpless against the gaudy blue carpet with its giant yellow swirl of flowers. The grey jersey dress hugs her body, accentuating her breasts.

My mouth turns dry. 'Let's have some champagne. A belated birthday drink,' I say.

'Yes, that'll be nice. You know, it's always been my favourite drink, even at uni. Miss Moët, that was my nickname.' She chuckles, and reaches out and touches the leaves of the fern. She rubs a leaf between her fingers, smells them and makes a face. 'Can you believe it? It's plastic.'

I look around, hoping to catch a waiter's eye. The lobby is teeming with sales reps in shiny suits and loud ties. An Elvis Presley song blares out of a jukebox somewhere.

'This place is like a railway platform,' Esther says, rubbing her temples delicately, as though she has a headache. She shifts in her seat. A blob of smudged mascara clings to her left cheek like a tear. Her face looks tired under the bright lights of the hotel lobby. Tiny lines crowd around her eyes.

A waitress walks past, clumsily pushing a trolley heaped with clattering cups and saucers. She disappears through a set of swinging doors before I can get her attention.

'What a useless place,' I say.

Esther suddenly sits up straight as though she's remembered something.

'You said you had a present for me. Where is it?' She looks around like a little girl.

I pull out the tissue-wrapped parcel from a plastic bag and lie it across her lap.

'I almost lost it,' I tell her. 'I left it behind in the restaurant – I only remembered when I got back to the office.'

She leans forward. The faint shadow between her breasts becomes clearer.

'This… this is amazingly beautiful,' she says, unwrapping the package slowly to reveal the golden fabric. She drapes it across her shoulder and then presses her cheek against it, closing her eyes. 'Thank you so much, PK. I can get my dressmaker to make me a little cocktail dress. What do you think?'

'Hmm,' I step back to survey her, chin in hand, like a true couturier. It's clearly made for her, lighting up her skin, deepening the colour of her eyes. 'No – how about a long dress instead? Like a gown, but with a sharp, straight silhouette and a slit on the side that shows off your legs,' I suggest.

I pull her up from the sofa and wrap the fabric around her, my hands moving swiftly and then slowly over the contours of her body.

Esther closes her eyes.

'Something like this. Something that shows off your waist.' My voice is hoarse.

'Oh, my waist is rubbish,' she says.

* * *

The waitress returns, her trolley now piled high with soiled glasses and empty bottles. She stops when she sees us, her mouth open, and rocks the trolley back and forth like a pram. The glasses rattle gently.

'We're like a circus act,' Esther says. She hands me back the brocade, smoothes down her dress and picks up her bag.

'Shall we find somewhere a little quieter?' Did I say that, or was it her? I'm not sure.

We stare at each other, and this time we're not smiling or joking.

'What do you mean?' Esther's voice is small and low. I can barely hear her. She holds her handbag tight against her stomach.

'I mean, let's find a room where we can have a drink in peace, and I can tell you all about the cut and the embroidery you're going to have on that beautiful dress of yours.' I smile.

'Unless, of course…' I spread my hands to show there's still a way out. She can get up and leave, think of an excuse. But she remains quiet, and I take her silence as a yes. 'What do you think? Is it a good idea?' I hesitate, giving us both another chance, but she still doesn't say a word. 'I'll check us into a room.'

'I'll just use the ladies'. You go and find us somewhere quiet.' Esther says, unable to look at me. Her eyes are fixed on the plastic fern.

The man at the reception desk has an Eastern European accent. A badge pinned to his jacket lapel declares he can speak Russian, Polish and German. His name is Bernard Muskowitz. He asks if I want a smoking room.

My hands grow cold as I consider his question. Would we be smoking while we talked, or would we be busy doing other things…?

And then suddenly Esther is standing beside me, her expression still and closed. She has retouched her make-up. Her mouth is red and inviting.

'Smoking is fine, and I'll pay cash,' I say quickly. I look around, paranoid. But I don't recognise anyone. 'Can you hurry up, please?' I say.

A smirk in Bernard Muskowitz's eyes tells me he knows. Everything feels like it's in slow motion – the way he pushes a form and a pen with its end chewed towards me, the way my hand falters as I bring it close to the dotted line to sign. I steady my hand as I sign it, and I check us in as Mr and Mrs Brown. It's as simple as that.

'What names did you give?' Esther asks me in the lift. There's another couple, probably American, wearing trench coats and holding maps. The man scowls when he hears her question, while I try not to think of what might happen next.

* * *

We're in room 464: a plain, brown room overlooking the car park. Pictures of the seaside hang on the walls. My bladder feels full, but I'm too embarrassed to go to the bathroom. Esther looks at the bed with its beige and blue striped bedspread. Her mouth goes all funny, the corners dragging down, making her suddenly look old.

'At least there are tea-making facilities,' I point out.

She walks to the window, changes her mind and sits down on the edge of the bed, still holding on to her handbag. Shoulders slumped, she stares at her feet, arms folded across her lap. The bag now sits at her feet like a faithful dog.

'Let's make things a little prettier,' I say, drawing the curtains and switching off the overhead lights. There's a table lamp by the bedside, the same mushroom brown as the walls. I turn it on, and then I go and sit beside her on the bed. 'Are you hungry? Shall I order something?' I ask.

She begins to sob, her hand pressed against her mouth. I put an arm around her, my hand on her chin, tilting up her face so she can see me.

I tell her I've not stopped thinking about her since I met her at Mowbray Hall.

She wipes her tears with the heel of her hand. 'How has this happened?' She's shaking her head. 'Why am I sitting here? I don't even know you.' Her make-up is smudged with her tears, but her face is soft and dreamy in the lamplight.

'I can't explain it either. But we have a connection. An electricity – it was there the first time I saw you. You're beautiful,' I whisper, burying my face in the nape of her neck. Her dress smells of cigarettes and perfume. She gives a long, deep sigh but doesn't push me away.

'It must be fate,' she says. 'We kept running into each other, and then you were so sweet about Maratha, and now this generous gift…' She picks up the brocade from the chair and presses it against her breast. Her voice trails off and she rests her head on my shoulders.

I raise her face so my mouth can find hers, and slowly lift her arms, wrapping them around me. I want to tell her how wonderfully different she feels. I mean, different from Geeta, from my house, from the wretched sameness of things.

'I hope this doesn't end in ugliness,' she says, closing her eyes.

My hands slip beneath her dress to find her. Cold fingers, cold hands, cold skin, slowly turning warm.

* * *

Esther's body is soft and full, like a ripe fruit just before the bloom wears off. The late afternoon sun shining through the drawn curtains makes her skin golden. Making love to her feels like a theft – the shock and pleasure of touching flesh that isn't mine. It is a betrayal. But it also feels like a rebirth, as though someone has taken possession of me and rubbed away the soot and neglect of previous years. I feel jolted awake.

We stay in bed, our shoulders touching, our hands loosely clasped together, smoking cigarettes and watching old black-and-white Hitchcock movies. Esther makes some tea, which we drink from a single cup like an old married couple, my lips tasting the lipstick smudge she's left behind on the cup's rim. Sex makes us hungry, and we order room service – chicken burgers, fries, club sandwiches and more champagne.

It is a holiday from life.

A young Asian waiter knocks and enters the room, bringing in a tray full of food. He averts his eyes from the bed. He can see the jumble of clothes on the floor and can smell the sour-sweet smell of our lovemaking that fills the room like a heavy cloud.

Esther looks through her bag to find him a tip, and only then does he look up and meet my eye, his lip curling in a sneer.

'A toast to us,' Esther says, pouring me a drink. Her face, stripped clean of make-up, looks years younger. I run my fingers again and again through the thick tangle of her hair.

We are dreamy and full of desire, but we don't make plans.

'This has been an accident. A beautiful accident,' Esther says.

'And we're never going to regret it.' I say, wanting to be sure. I only think of Geeta once, when I use the bathroom and see a strand of Esther's long, brown hair in the sink, so different from Geeta's oily black hair.

'Look after yourself,' Esther says when it's time to leave, buttoning her coat and painting on her lipstick.

'Same time, same place next year?' I act flippant. 'Make sure you're wearing your new gold dress and I'm sitting next to you.'

The world waits at the door, waiting to reclaim us. I remember my warehouse in Grotton, the accounts slowly sliding away. I remember her husband, signing his million-pound deals. I remember Amar sitting in front of the television.

'Let's never ever forget this.' I open my arms to hold her one last time.

11

CONFESSION TIME

It's late – very late – by the time I get home.

'What's the matter? Did something happen?' Geeta asks when I walk into the kitchen. The air is alive with her worry.

I refreshed myself in the car so I can be sure I show no sign of the afternoon. I smoked three cigarettes and bought a bottle of Old Spice at an all-night chemist on Kingsway and emptied most of it on my jacket.

'You look very upset. Did you fire someone at work?' Geeta asks, glancing at the cuckoo clock.

'I'm tired. Just tired,' I reply. 'Sorry I'm late. I was meeting clients. Took them out for a bite to eat.'

Geeta wants to know where I've been, and I tell her it was on Deansgate, a new tapas and wine bar she wouldn't know.

She says she tried calling me a couple of times, but my mobile was off. I make a show of taking it out and pressing buttons. 'You're right. The battery's died.'

I walk to the fridge and help myself to some water.

'Well, there's no dinner left. Amar polished off the macaroni cheese. His appetite is so good,' she says proudly.

'I wish you'd control his eating. He's getting tubby.'

She seems puzzled. 'But it's my job to feed him. I'm his mother. And if you're that bothered about his weight, why don't you do something about it – take him to the gym or go for a walk, like English fathers do? You're always so busy with your work.'

'You're right. I'll do something with him this weekend,' I say. 'Go for a jog, if it's not raining.'

Geeta winces as she gets up, and her hands grip the corner of the table. Her knees are giving her trouble, but she isn't doing much about it.

I wait for her to leave the kitchen and go upstairs to bed. I want to go into the garden, smoke my cigarette and share my shame with my mango tree, but she stays standing in the kitchen, watching me finish my glass of water. I feel sorry for her, for the thin, greying plait sleeping on her plump, rounded shoulders, for her tracksuit with its turmeric-stained sleeves, for her kitchen-sink and TV-centred world. I'm sorry that she's married a man like me. A man who turns up at midnight, the smell of another woman on his fingers and on his skin.

'I'm sorry,' I blurt out, and touch her hand. 'I shouldn't have kept you waiting.'

'Don't worry,' she says. 'Business is business. I'm not angry. By the way, I've invited the Guptas over for dinner next week. Is that all right?' She sounds anxious.

'Good idea. They've not been here for a while.'

I wander towards the patio and peer into the dark garden. The dog next door starts barking.

'Why don't you go to bed, Geeta? It's getting late,' I say in a gentle voice. Dutifully, she leaves the room.

Her tread is heavy on the stairs. I hear her pause outside Amar's room and then carry on to our bedroom. My shoulders relax. I push open the patio doors and step outside. The security lights come on as I walk towards the mango tree. I stroke the naked branches, fragile like a child's bones, stripped of flesh.

'My life's changing,' I whisper to the tree, and stand for a while, looking at it in silence.

Geeta is asleep when I finally go upstairs. The happiness I'd felt when making love to Esther disappears the moment my head hits the pillow. I go over what I had just done in a hotel room with a woman who wasn't my wife and an ugly knot settles within me, making me retch. I go to the bathroom and take a long shower, trying to wash away the crime.

A dull moon the colour of a two-pence coin hangs outside the window. I ask its forgiveness, but it stays mute and gives back no solace.

* * *

The Guptas are punctual dinner guests. Gupta boasts that his life runs on BST, British Standard Time, not IST, Indian Shit Time.

'It really is a magnificent house,' he says, opening the lounge door and gazing around.

'We're sitting in the kitchen,' I tell him.

'Let me admire your new plasma TV again. I hope you got it in the Currys sale?' He's smiling, but behind his glasses his eyes are alert and envious.

'You always say the same bullshit,' I say, handing him an orange juice and pouring myself a whisky.

Gupta's wife, Usha, stands next to him. She may have been beautiful once, but now she's just round, her face a soft blur of circular features.

They could be twins, Usha and Geeta. I imagine Gupta making love to her every Thursday – he will do it dutifully, his eyes closed; he probably even counts to ten before coming. There'll be a box of tissues on the bedside table, and salt and vinegar crisps and a box of After Eights for after. Usha is partial to both.

'PK, why the hell are you smiling?' Gupta shakes his head.

Geeta, who is handing around a plate of samosas, joins in the head shaking. 'I don't know what's come over him. He's been in a funny mood since this morning. Maybe he's won the lottery or something. Didn't even go to work till late, just disappeared upstairs into his study,' she says.

The reason for my smile is a text Esther had sent earlier. 'I can't forget you,' it said.

* * *

Over dinner Gupta keeps whining about me being lost in my own world. I let him carry on.

'I mean, you're hardly being a proper host tonight. What's up, man? Had a fight with the missus?'

He gives his wife a playful wink. She ignores him and concentrates on her eating.

'Geeta, you must give me the recipe for this chicken curry,' she says. At least she's enjoying her food, unlike Gupta, who has the thin, sallow face of a man who's spent his life adding up numbers under fluorescent office lights.

Gupta tears his chapatti into neat little triangular pieces, scooping up the dal and chewing methodically.

'Forty times,' he tells us. 'According to yogic principles, that's how many times one must chew one's food.'

He babbles on, while I think of Esther's text and what it means for my life.

'Usha's just been to Bombay. It's her second trip in two years. Isn't she lucky, seeing her family so often?' Geeta says. She's not been back for almost five years.

'PK can't live without you, Geeta. That's the reason he doesn't let you go away,' Gupta says, laughing.

I pretend to laugh at his joke. 'Maybe it is time you visited Lopa in Bombay.' I say, and pour myself more whisky.

Geeta's eyes brighten, and, for a minute, I catch a glimpse of her old carefree self. 'Really? You really mean it?' She looks like she can hardly believe it.

* * *

The women clear away after the meal.

'This is not a man's job – you'll only get in the way,' they say, shooing us out. Gupta and I go outside for a smoke.

'How is Amar these days? Why wasn't he at dinner?' Gupta asks, taking a proffered cigarette. He holds it awkwardly in his hand, like a child holding a pencil.

'He's gone to a friend's house,' I say, and kick a loose pebble off the drive.

Actually, Amar's upstairs, hiding in his bedroom. He doesn't like Gupta. 'He makes my skin creep, Dad. Always asking about my grades and if I'll ever play cricket again,' he had said.

'Amar is Amar. Nothing changes. Anyway, how are things with you? What about the promotion?' I move the conversation on. Gupta has been hankering after a raise at work. He wants a Mercedes like mine.

He says it would be easier to get a promotion if he was called John Smith. 'With a name like Arvind Gupta, what do you expect? They've already pigeonholed me before I open my mouth.' He takes a deep drag of his cigarette and shrugs. 'At least I'll clear my mortgage in two years.'

It's a dark, damp night. A faint drizzle starts up, but we stay outside, standing on the porch, our faces hidden in shadow. Somewhere beneath this same sweep of darkness, Esther is eating and sleeping and undressing.

Gupta inhales his cigarette the wrong way, and starts coughing. 'It's an unhealthy sin,' he says, as I whack him between the shoulders.

'I can think of far worse,' I say, wishing he'd finish his cigarette and go home.

'Yeah, I've done much worse. Once I committed a very serious sin.' He lowers his voice to a whisper. 'I don't think I ever told you, PK, but I cheated on Usha.' He gulps and continues. 'I slept with another woman.'

His confession rings out like an alarm bell. Is he trying to draw me out? Have I given myself away with a chance remark?

'How could you do such a thing?' I say, my voice full of reproach. 'She's a good woman, your Usha.' I pretend to be outraged.

'It was only once,' he says, pulling at my sleeve as he makes his point. 'You know me, PK. I'm more bark than bite.' He throws away his cigarette, grinding out the butt with his shoe.

'When did it happen?'

Our wives are still inside cleaning up, mopping the kitchen floor, drying the dishes, while their husbands stand outside trading betrayals and lies.

'It was nothing serious,' he continues. 'A work do – the office Christmas party. It's always a work do, isn't it?' He laughs. 'I had too much to drink. She was a temp in human resources – the usual. We went back to her flat.'

'What was her name?' I asked. As though it mattered.

'Anne? Mary? Jane? Hell, I can't remember. You know I'm no good with English names. All I can remember is that she had red hair… down there. First time I'd seen that, and it was quite a shock.' He shudders at his confession.

'What about you, PK?' He gives a low laugh. 'I bet you're a dirty dog. Women always have the hots for you.'

'Let's go in – it's getting nippy.' I'm not enjoying the conversation, and yet a part of me wants to brag about Esther. I want to talk about how her body feels in my arms, the way my head starts spinning just thinking about her breasts. I stop before going in; I find I want to know more, after all.

'Did Usha ever find out about your one-night stand?'

Gupta says he'd confessed right away. 'Why do you think I've stopped drinking? She made me give up alcohol. That was my punishment.'

'So no more fooling around for you, eh?' My hand hesitates on the door handle. I want him to say yes, he'd do it again; he would still go after another woman if he fell for her. I want an ally.

'You crazy, or what? It's not worth the hassle! There's always *Playboy* for rainy days.' He grins, but his face under the porch light shows only regret and loneliness.

He burps suddenly and laughs. 'We're turning into a pair of boring old farts, aren't we, PK?' But his loneliness doesn't belong to me. I have Esther.

Dear Lopa didi,

You must have noticed a change in me. I am much happier now. It's all to do with PK. He has become kinder and more considerate. The other day he asked me about my knees and insisted I visit a specialist at Wythenshawe Hospital. He's very busy at work, but he makes a point of apologising about being late. That's all I want – a little recognition. And guess what – the best news of all! He's promised I can come to India soon. Isn't that wonderful? The Guptas were here for dinner and Usha was showing off her new gold bangles that she'd bought in Bombay. I had had enough of her boasting, and PK came to my rescue. Let me know what you would like from Manchester. Send me a list and I'll bring them with me. Send me Jijaji's collar size also. I will get PK to choose some shirts for him. He has very good taste in clothes – after all, he is a top designer.

Lots of love to the kids,

Geeta

12

A CRICKET MATCH

A month passes. I don't call Esther. She doesn't call me. I move on with my life.

Soon it's spring, and the garden starts nudging into life. Squirrels reappear, as do the daffodils. The marmalade orange of the sky lingers longer into the night. Geeta removes the extra duvets and rolls them into large hessian bags that she shoves under the bed.

Some nights there is a knock on the bedroom door and Amar's heavy step approaches, the floorboards creaking under his weight. I sense rather than see his bulky frame bend over Geeta. Loud whispering follows, the blanket is pulled to one side, and soon there's the slow rumbling of the washing machine kicking into life in the kitchen. Amar has wet his bed. Again. Damp bed sheets trembling on the washing line greet me the next morning.

I'm at work when my mobile flashes. It's Esther. The blood rushes to my head on hearing her voice.

'Did I say something wrong?' she asks. 'You didn't answer my text.'

'I didn't know what to say,' I say, lowering my voice and looking at Margaret, but she's busy, her head bent low over the keyboard, the sound of her fingers tapping fill the room.

'The weather's turning – maybe we'll have a fine summer after all,' Esther says, ignoring what I've just said.

I remember her friend Maratha. 'How is your friend doing in Mexico? Is she any better?' I ask.

There's a brief silence before she speaks. 'Maratha is dead. She put up a good fight, but it wasn't enough.'

'Oh, I'm sorry – so sorry. You were close.' The words feel inadequate. I want to be there next to Esther, comforting her. I feel a kinship with her after what had happened between us. And I don't want her to forget it. 'Why don't we meet?' I suggest.

'I shouldn't have sent you that text. It was a mistake. I was just so low, and Cedric was out of town, as usual.' Her voice cracks and rushes on. 'Maybe it's not such a good idea, after all.' Her text saying she couldn't forget me comes back to my mind. Women are like that. Their minds alter like the seasons.

I tell her I can wait till she is ready to meet again.

Work is quiet – it has been for some time. The summer orders aren't pouring in, and the unsold stock is piling up. Manchester is wet and cold, though the shops are flooded with bright bikinis and shorts. What punter will part with their hard-earned cash for summer dresses when warm days seem so far away?

My mobile rings again. It's Gupta. He wants to meet up for a drink after work. He'd been passed over for a promotion again. Some upstart from London has overtaken him, and he needs consoling. But my head is busy with what Esther had said. I don't have the time for his whining.

'Sorry – I'm tied up with work,' I say.

'What's the matter with you? You're always up for a drink.' He's annoyed.

'How about next week?' I say, my eyes fixed on the blue computer screen. I'm on the Chanel website, looking at their next season's fall collection. Plaid and lace are a common theme. Maybe I can introduce it this season by tweaking my existing orders, I think.

Gupta hangs up, and I go back to nudging the mouse up and down the computer mat. The mat carries a Chinese saying: 'A journey of a thousand miles begins with a small step.' I had bought a dozen of these mats from a street hawker in Shanghai to give to the staff as a morale-booster.

Maratha's death upsets me. She had died alone and cold under foreign skies in a foreign bed, slowly, reluctantly giving up on her breath while those closest to her hurried about their daily life. Would that be me one day?

'What's the point in all this, Margaret?' I say, shutting down my computer and turning to her.

'What do you mean? The Dunehelm buyer called yesterday. They've had a shortfall in maxi skirts; their usual supplier let them down. I promised them we've got stock to cover it. About fifty pieces.'

I shake my head. 'I don't mean the business. I mean, what we are all busting our gut for? We'll all end up as fistfuls of ash anyway.'

'I intend to be buried in Dundee. The plot's already paid for,' Margaret says firmly.

I leave work early. I think of sending Esther some flowers with a note of sympathy. But her husband would surely see, and there'd be questions. I slow down as I drive past Bruntwood Park. Spring is coming. The frost is thinning on the grass, and the tree branches are tipped in green. A group of boys play football, two rubbish bins standing in as makeshift goalposts.

A young couple sits on a bench watching them, the boy's arm draped around his girlfriend's neck like a scarf. Would Amar ever get to that stage? I think of his bed-wetting and his school report. I see him frozen as he is for the rest of his life, sitting at home, fiddling with the television remote, the red tartan blanket pulled up to his chin, a packet of hobnobs close at hand.

I can't imagine him smiling at the university gates or holding his own child in his arms. Maybe it's my fault he's turned out this way. I remember the many ways in which I've let him down.

Watching the boys play football in Bruntwood Park brings back a memory that, like a record-player needle stuck in a groove, I keep replaying. My mind runs back to the bright summer's day five years ago.

* * *

Amar had just turned ten. Ian, the club manager of the Bollin Cricket Club, was organising a Fathers vs. sons match one Sunday.

I stood in the garden at home, having a quick smoke before setting off for the match, enjoying the sounds and smell of summer. The air rang with the sound of children's laughter, the smell of barbeques firing up and hosepipes gargling water. All of Manchester was out, making the most of the sunshine – all except Amar and Geeta, of course. They were indoors.

I went inside and turned off the TV, which Amar was sat in front of. 'Why aren't you outside playing?'

'Don't want to,' Amar said, his small fist gripping the remote.

'All boys like playing outside. Why do you have to be different?'

I thought of my childhood. I couldn't wait for school to end so I could make a frenzied dash to the cricket pitch behind the Charminar mosque on Nehru Road. I thought of the sharp, sweet heat of a Bombay summer, my sweaty top licking my back like a dog's tongue, the batting and bowling and screaming that went on and on until the sun nosedived into the sea and Father came looking for me, shaking his fist. 'Come home now, this very minute, you good-for-nothing!'

I wanted Amar to be my long-ago carefree summer self.

'I can't come. Mummy says I've got a cold. I must stay indoors,' he said. So that was his excuse that day.

I felt his forehead with my hand. It was warm. But there again, it was a July afternoon, the heating was on, the windows were closed and the room was stuffy.

'What are you two on about?' Geeta asked when she saw Amar chewing the skin around his thumb. His eyes, twin puddles, were ready to burst. 'You're looking pale,' she said, handing him an old beer glass filled with milk and ground almonds, keeping a firm grip on his chin until the last drop had disappeared from the glass.

'There's a cricket match at the club today, fathers against sons. I'm taking Amar with me,' I said, ready to argue if she put her foot down.

The phone rang. It was Mrs Ahmed. Geeta, distracted by the call, just nodded.

'But I want to watch *The Lion King* – it will be on soon,' Amar insisted, his feet tucked under him, the whites of his eyes pink in the television glow.

'Rubbish! Fresh air will do you good. Come to the club and watch me hit some balls.' I swung my arm and pretended to hit a six. 'Did I tell you I was the captain of my college team in Bombay? We were called the Roaring Lions, and I had the biggest roar.' I crouched down to my knees, lowering myself until I was face to face with him, and pretended to roar.

Amar shrugged. He'd heard the story before. His eyes ran back to the television screen.

'I was good, Amar. The best bowler in town. Even your mum doesn't know that.'

Geeta sat at the kitchen table, busy on the phone, one hand twisting a strand of her long hair into a loop around her finger, the other pressing the telephone receiver to her ear.

'I'm rubbish at cricket,' Amar said, staring at his shoes.

'Well, you won't get any better sitting on your backside inside. It's not hard.' I tried to make it sound simple. But Amar started chewing his nails.

'I hate your club,' he said when I finally got him in the car. 'It's dark and smelly.'

I turned on the car radio to drown out his voice – I still remember the song that came on – 'Yellow Submarine'. It was summer, the start of something good.

'Tell you what, we'll stop by Benny's afterwards, and I'll buy you some football stickers,' I said.

'I don't even collect them,' he sulked. 'Can I have some ice cream instead?'

'Deal.' I high-fived him. 'We'll thrash them, Amar. Show them what the Maliks are made of.' I turned the volume higher, rolled down my window and sang along to the Beatles.

Amar spent the rest of the drive with his head sticking out of the car window, shouting out the number plates of the cars overtaking us. In those days I drove a Ford Mondeo with no personal number plate.

Many years have passed since that summer's day. I've lost touch with most of my cricket mates, apart from Gupta. But back then, every summer saw me at the club. I'd rush home from the warehouse, strip off my jacket and tie, put on my whites and slam the door shut on Geeta's irritated voice.

We were Ian's 'Rainbow Tribe'. There were Bangladeshis, Pakistanis and even an Ethiopian, who was waiting for his asylum papers. We'd pile into the George and Dragon afterwards, drink beer and talk cricket. It was honest fun. And that day felt no different. There was the usual banter with Ian, and Gupta chatted to Amar about *The Lion King*. We argued about the batting and bowling order.

The other kids were Amar's age, but looked smarter and stronger. I tried bringing Amar into the conversation, but all he did was nod, hands in his pockets, staring down at his feet. His shoelaces were undone. The boys won the toss to bowl first, and Gupta and I took up our batting positions. I looked around for Amar, but he wasn't fielding.

'He's a reserve,' Ian shouted. 'Get a move on.'

'They've left him out on purpose,' I said to Gupta. 'They know he's useless.'

He shrugged. His son was in – he didn't care.

'They're bastards, cutting him out like that. But I'll show them,' I said.

Some teenagers were fooling about at the far end, near the gate. I guessed Amar had gone over to them. I started my batting. The ball spun towards me like a spinning top, and I whacked it hard. 'A six,' I crowed, watching it arcing through the air, vanishing into the bushes that marked the boundary between the club and the nearby houses. I turned around to check if Amar had seen me. But he wasn't there.

A sudden, sharp howl came out of the bushes, and then silence, followed by the sound of feet running towards the noise. Gupta's, Ian's, mine.

'I thought I'd hit a dog,' I told Dr Spencer afterwards.

But it wasn't a dog – it was Amar I'd hit. He had been sat in the bushes playing with a pile of stones when the ball soared through the foliage and hit him on the head. He squatted there, slowly rocking back and forth, mouth twisted in a foolish grin of pain, one hand rubbing his forehead. I wish I had held him tight then, brushed away the pain. But all I did was stand still, numb with shock, until it gave way to anger. 'You, stupid, stupid boy! You could've been killed! Why the hell didn't you sit on the bench like Ian told you to?' I said.

Gupta pushed me to one side, crouched low on his knees and spoke kindly to Amar, while Ian ran to the club to get a bag of ice. He'd just completed a St John's Ambulance First Aid course, so he knew the drill. He made Amar stick out his tongue and count his fingers, while I stood by, useless, arms hanging limp, helpless in my anger and fright.

I thought Amar was faking it, or that he'd done it on purpose to show me up and stop my game so he could run back home to his mum.

'What will I tell Geeta?' I asked Gupta as we walked back to our cars. The game and the drink at the pub were called off.

'The truth! What else, you fool? It was a bloody accident. You didn't mean to hurt him,' he said.

'Let's take him to a specialist. The best one in England. Let's take him to London, to Harley Street.' This was Geeta, pulling at my sleeve while we waited at the Parrs Wood Surgery later that afternoon. Her face was restless with worry.

I flicked open my Filofax and saw the week ahead, chock-full of appointments. Those were busy days – business was slowing down, and taking time out was a luxury I couldn't afford.

'But there's a trade fair on in Birmingham. I'm exhibiting there. Let's wait and see what the doctor says. Let's not rush,' I said.

'Dr Spencer will give him Calpol and look at his watch and tell us to go home – that's all he ever does,' Geeta said. She pulled

Amar closer, laying his head clumsily on her shoulder. Her hands ran through his hair, fierce and tender.

'Stop it, Mum!' Amar pulled back, embarrassed in front of the other people waiting in the surgery, who were watching us.

'It's just a bump – no need for an X-ray,' Dr Spencer said, opening his drawer and sticking an 'I am a good boy' sticker on to Amar's checked shirt pocket.

He prescribed Calpol, and Geeta doubled the daily dose of almond milk.

'What about a second opinion?' Geeta challenged him. 'Cricket injuries can be serious.'

Dr Spencer's voice was stiff as he told her that she was welcome to take Amar to London, but he wasn't sure whether it would be covered by the NHS. 'Do you have private insurance?' he asked.

We shook our heads. I told Geeta to trust the doctor. He'd been practising for nearly thirty years. 'It was just a cricket ball – nothing serious,' I kept reassuring her.

'He's had a serious accident, and you don't even want a second opinion!' Geeta complained on days when Amar's headache or tummy bug kept him home from school.

'But he'll fall behind at school if he keeps taking days off,' I would say, trying not to see a connection between the cricket incident and Amar's bed-wetting or headaches.

'What's more important, his grades or his health?' Geeta's eyes cut through me like blades.

It was easier to take Dr Spencer's side. He was English, with an armful of gold-framed certificates on the wall. He knew Amar's body better than we did. He retired soon after, and moved to the Costa del Sol to play golf.

* * *

The teachers called us in when Amar moved to senior school. They told us our son was a below-average student. He needed to try harder.

'Amar hasn't found what he's good at as yet,' said the headmaster. 'But given time, I'm hoping he will blossom.' He looked at me. The two deep vertical lines running down the sides of his nose gave him the sad look of someone who didn't quite believe his own words. 'Time and encouragement, Mr Malik. Our school believes in that. Children are like flowers that need nurturing.' His voice trailed off.

'Do you think some extra tuition after school might help? He could easily be top of the class – he has the potential,' I pleaded, unwilling to believe that my only child could be labelled 'below average'.

The headmaster's sad eyes washed over me. 'I have twenty years' experience in this field, Mr Malik, and I believe your son has special needs. He will, in time, find something he is good at. He can't be rushed.'

'Amar is our only child! How can we give up on him? I don't buy this special-needs bullshit. He's just being lazy, that's all. And you're spoiling him,' I said, turning to Geeta.

'We've not done enough for him. He needs treatment. Let's take him to a specialist', she said.

'He needs to work harder,' I told her again and again.

* * *

That summer was the start of a new kind of darkness.

Geeta's hair – her long, shiny hair, which ran like a waterfall down her back – began falling out. She'd come to me after a shower holding clumps of it in her hand, her eyes wide and bewildered. 'What's happening to me? I tried Amla oil and Keo Karpin, but nothing's working.'

'It's the Manchester water – too much calcium in it. Maybe you need to change your shampoo,' I consoled her, rubbing her back as she sat on the bed, her fingers gripping the bed frame as though it were a precipice she was afraid of falling into.

One day I came home from work and found Geeta ironing in the kitchen, her hair chopped to a chin-length bob.

'What are you staring at?' She pushed a strand of her short hair behind her ear.

'But… I loved your long hair. Why did you cut it?'

'Short hair is more practical. All that hair kept clogging the bathroom sink,' she said, blinking too quickly. Her short hair made her already round cheeks look rounder.

That's when she started eating, too. I'd open a sock drawer and find a packet of chocolate bourbons tucked inside. Empty crisp packets were stowed between old magazine issues.

'Amar's not been the same since the cricket accident,' Geeta said to family and friends. 'If only you had taken him to the right specialists,' she said each time his report card came, 'Amar would be different. He'd be coming top of the class.'

She stored her grievances away like a squirrel collecting nuts, and slowly our love for each other curdled, like milk that had gone sour.

* * *

The weight of these memories drags me down – it pulls me so low that I have to stop in a Tesco car park and lay my head down on the steering wheel.

It's not a day for betrayals. I don't feel like seeing Esther any more.

Dear Lopa didi,

I am so pleased Chintu got into IIT on the Finance and Management course. The entrance exam must be so difficult. He will be able to get a good job at Microsoft or Google in America now. His future will be made. He's got Jijaji's brains, for sure. I wish I could also give you some happy news about Amar. But he remains the same, always bottom of the class. The teachers keep saying he is special needs, but what needs does a child have? Just love and attention. And I'm doing my best to give him that. Sometimes I feel it is because of the cricket injury he got all those years back. It did something to his head. I'm not blaming PK. It was an accident, pure and simple. Can a father ever mean to hurt his son? It's impossible. We should have taken him to a specialist in London, but everything is so expensive in England. Back home, I know you and Jijaji would have used your contacts and got us the best doctor in Bombay, but we are nobodies here. Anyway, you must think I'm grumbling all the time. Life is OK. I tried making bread from scratch recently. It was so easy, just like making chapattis. Are you going to Simla again for the summer holidays? It will be lovely. I don't think we will be going anywhere in the school holidays. PK hasn't mentioned my trip to India again, and I don't like reminding him. Poor man, he has so many business worries.

Love to the kids,

Geeta

13

EVERYONE LAUGHS AT A RICH MAN'S JOKES

But we do meet again.

'Ben's invited us to the Retail Awards dinner at the Midland Hotel next week. Want to go?' I ask Geeta.

It's evening, and we're home watching television – or rather, I'm watching Geeta watch television. A Bollywood soap is on. The mother-in-law, rolling pin in hand, is screaming at her daughter-in-law. Geeta's hand slowly dips inside the bag of Walkers salt and vinegar crisps.

I repeat my question. 'Do you fancy going to the Retail Awards dinner next Tuesday?'

If Geeta doesn't want to come, I could slip away early – maybe even meet Gupta at the pub. I've not seen him for a while.

'Nice of Ben to invite us. He's always doing kind things for us. He invited you to that golf do, and now this. I think I'd like to go – it'll be a change,' Geeta says, her face brightening. 'The food will be good. Make sure you tell them I'm vegetarian.'

Geeta is vegetarian on Tuesdays, and she fasts every second Sunday of the month. It's a private pact she's made with her gods for saving Amar's life. Three miscarriages, one after the other, and then, just when we'd given up hope and Geeta was turning forty, Amar came along. Going meatless was a small price to pay for the miracle of a child in middle age.

'We'll just be going as guests this time. I've not been nominated for anything,' I say. I don't want her to have high hopes. It was a different story years ago, when Malik Textiles was a runner-up in quality and customer service two years running. 'I just hope you don't get bored. There'll be lots of speeches,' I warn her.

She replies that she knows the format – she'd accompanied me all those years back when I'd won an award and mentioned her in my acceptance speech. All I remember of that evening is clutching the framed certificate and my hammering heart. But she's like a magpie, hoarding memories.

* * *

Geeta dresses up for the awards dinner, wearing one of her wedding trousseau saris, rather than her usual shiny black Debenhams trouser suit, which she thinks made her look modern. She's breathing heavily as she comes down the stairs, holding on to the banister for support. Dangling from her ears are long earrings in the shape of tiny paisley flowers. The same flowers encircle her neck. I recognise her jewellery – it once belonged to my mother.

'This is for your wife. Keep it carefully,' Mother had said, not long before she died, pressing the blue velvet box into my hands, her sour, medicinal breath fanning my face.

'There was no need to call a cab. I can drive.' Geeta protests when I tell her I've ordered us a taxi.

She presses down the pleats of her sari with her hands and inspects herself in the hallway mirror. Years of living in tracksuits and comfortable clothing have left her unsure about the delicate craft of tying a sari. I can see the hem of her petticoat peeping clumsily from beneath the orange silk. She sees me watching her. 'Is something wrong?'

'You look great,' I say, hurrying her outside to the waiting cab.

In the taxi, Geeta snaps open her handbag and takes out two cardamoms, popping them into her mouth to refresh her breath. It's an old Bombay habit.

She mentions the car again, but I remind her of how nervous she is of driving on motorways at night. She asks if I've remembered to order her the vegetarian option.

'There's been so much on at work, it slipped my mind, I'm sorry,' I say. I can't see her face in the darkness, but I can sense her disappointment. The darkness feels like a tunnel I'm swimming through to get to the light at the other end. 'Sorry,' I say again.

This evening was meant to be a special treat, and I've gone and ruined it for her.

'Don't worry. I'm sure they'll make me a pasta or something,' she says.

* * *

Ben is waiting in the foyer at the Midland Hotel. The hotel is the only decent five-star in the city, and it's a favourite venue for corporate dos and bar mitzvahs. I've always liked its plush carpeted foyer and the low-slung chandeliers that give it such a decadent air.

'This is where Mr Rolls met Mr Royce and started Rolls Royce,' I tell Geeta as we walk up to Ben. She looks suitably impressed. He wears the same blue-grey tartan he'd worn at Mowbray Hall. I clasp his hand warmly. 'Thanks for inviting us.'

'So, how's business these days?' He squeezes my hand like an old friend.

Although he doesn't manage my account any more – it's been passed on to junior staff – he still likes to be in the know. I give a vague answer and look around, recognising old faces from my early days in the rag trade milling about, looking purposeful and ambitious.

Ben hands me a champagne glass and points out people he feels I ought to know. 'That man there, in the navy pinstripe – he's the regional head of TK Maxx,' he whispers. 'And the bloke standing by the door – that's the chief buyer of Debenhams. Useful chap, worth getting to know. He's partial to Christmas hampers from Harrods, if you get my drift.'

I listen politely. It was a different story in the past – I'd be rushing up to those men, handing out my card, inviting them to dinner. But at fifty-five, ambition is seeping out of me like an ice cube melting in the sun. I want Amar to grow up, change and take charge of Malik Textiles.

I check the seating plan by the door. Ben is on the top table; his company is a big sponsor. We're on table thirty-five, which tells me what I already know – I am lucky to have been invited at all. 'I bet we're near the kitchens,' I whisper to Geeta as we make our way to the back of the room.

The room is a sea of round tables tightly packed together. White lilies on the tables shimmer beneath the bluish-white light of the overhead lights, giving everything a ghostly appearance. Geeta's orange silk sari glitters in the sea of dull black frocks the other women are wearing.

At least my chair faces the stage. Poor Geeta is sitting next to the swinging kitchen doors. The other guests around the table are middle-management types, accountants and lawyers. I try not to look disappointed as I hand out my business card.

Geeta helps herself to the wine. She looks good when she remembers to make an effort. At fifty-two, her cheeks are still plump, and her neck is smooth. Only her forehead gives her age away, little disappointed lines running across it like a race track.

'Having a good time?' I ask her.

She bends forward to hear me, and the fold of her sari pallu slides a little, showing the ripe outline of her breasts beneath the blouse. A bolt of heat travels through me as I try to remember the last time I'd touched them.

'Let's leave early,' I whisper to her. I feel a sudden urge to smother my face against her breasts and lose myself in the warm familiar scent of talcum powder.

The waiter refills her wine glass. She takes small, tentative sips from it, like a bird dipping its beak into a pond. I watch her, pretending she's somebody else's woman. She is different this evening – more desirable with this new way she has of drinking wine and making small talk. She never touches alcohol at home, because of Amar. 'No need to set an example with our bad habits.' That's her standard line. Looking at her now brings back our early married years, when it took just one glass of wine to get her tipsy. We'd rush home from the restaurant, weak with desire, and pause on the front steps, where she'd be fishing for the keys and my hands would be busy unbuttoning her blouse. She'd press her thumb against my mouth, saying, 'Shh, be quiet! We don't want to wake up the neighbours.'

Ben is doing his rounds, pausing at each table, bending low and exchanging pleasantries before quickly moving on. He finds us. 'The guest speaker is Cedric Solomon,' he says, his little blue eyes flashing in excitement.

My heartbeat slows. 'Where is he? I don't see him.' I try to spot the stout, balding figure who shares Esther's life and bed. I've seen enough pictures of him to recognise him straight away. I'm not sure how I'll feel when I see him.

Ben's eyes scan the room. 'The bugger's probably running late. These big shots always do.'

There's a sudden commotion towards the front of the room, just as the food starts to comes out from the kitchens. A couple are noisily making their way to their table. Chairs scrape back, conversations halt, faces look up.

Ben turns to me. 'There they are, the Solomons – making an entrance! You remember his wife, Esther, of course? Striking woman…'

I see a tall woman in a long brocade dress with the neckline slashed low at the throat. It's Esther. She's holding on to her husband's arm, tucking a long strand of hair behind her ear. He whispers something and she smiles.

Cedric Solomon looks good in his expensive dark suit, his sparse grey hair neatly combed behind his ears. His lips are sensual and full. I imagine them feeding on Esther's mouth night after night. I push aside my plate.

Geeta notices. 'What's the matter? You've stopped eating.'

Cedric is on stage now. He's shorter than I'd imagined, with the stocky, broad shoulders of a rugby player.

'Ladies and gentlemen, this is such an honour – for my dear wife, Esther, and I to be invited to the two thousand and...'

I push back my chair and make my way to the gents'. I sit on the toilet for a while, readjust my tie and splash cold water on my face. I check my mobile and think of texting Esther to tell her I'm here.

I return to Geeta's worried face. She says something to the man next to me and swaps seats with him.

'You look ill. Is everything OK?' she says.

'I'm fine! Stop making a fuss,' I snap.

Geeta's lipstick is smudged, and the drink has made her eyes bulge. Her earrings suddenly look garish and cheap. She looks common compared to Esther's grace and poise.

'It's rude to get someone to move. Go back to your own seat,' I say. Geeta's face became small and rigid, and I squeeze her thigh under the table to show I don't really mean it.

The evening is long. Cedric Solomon stays on the stage for some time, telling anecdotes with the down-to-earth humility only the very rich can afford. I move my chair, turning it to an angle from which I have a clear view of Esther's profile.

She's wearing the ruby earrings she'd worn the first time I saw her. I will her to turn and see me, but she's busy chatting to the mayor, an old man who keeps patting the heavy gold ceremonial chains draped around his neck.

His spiel finished, Cedric hands out the awards and joins his wife at the table, bending down to kiss her cheek.

* * *

It's time to leave. I rush towards the hotel entrance. I don't want to come face to face with the Solomons in all their marital glory.

'Why are you walking so fast?' Geeta complains. 'What's the hurry?'

I slow down, waiting for her to catch up. In her rush to keep pace, her sari pleats came undone, and a long piece trails after her on the floor. She stands by my elbow, breathing heavily, as we wait for the cab. A sleek, black limousine is parked in front of the lobby. It's a Rolls, with the number plate 'CEDRIC I'.

'Only a VIP could afford such a fancy car,' Geeta observes. We get into the cab. The rain starts and Geeta shivers, the thin fabric of her sari pulled tight across her hunched shoulders.

* * *

The ride home is long. I keep seeing Esther, her brocade dress lit up like a flame. I'd recognised the fabric, and am worried that Geeta might remember it too.

And what of Cedric? Wouldn't he have questioned Esther about her striking new dress? Or was he so busy counting his cash that he barely had time to notice such things? All these thoughts run through me, along with an insane and almost impossible desire to be with Esther again.

We're almost home when Geeta suddenly says she can't find her handbag. She's frantic with worry. The cabbie slows down, and pulls up at the side of the road. The engine still running, he flicks on the light and turns a bored face to us.

'Check under the seat,' he says.

I bend down and squint at the floor. My knees, stiff from sitting for so long, creak complainingly. I can't find her handbag.

'We have to go back,' Geeta tells the driver. 'The house keys are in it.'

'Can't Amar let us in?'

'I didn't want him to be home alone, so I sent him to stay with the Guptas. He's watching a film with them. They'll drop him back in the morning,' she says.

The cabbie heads back into town.

'I must have left it under my chair. Remember? I swapped seats to come and sit next to you,' Geeta babbles on.

Stupid, stupid woman! I check the taxi meter.

We are hurrying through the hotel lobby when a familiar figure breaks away from a group near the bar and moves towards us. It's Ben. A couple is standing near him. It's Esther, in her brocade dress, holding a drink, and her husband.

I nudge Geeta towards the banqueting hall. 'They'll be still clearing up. Have a good look around for your bag. Make a fuss.'

She dutifully walks on while I join Ben, feeling shabby and unclean in front of the sleek smoothness of the Solomons. My trousers have dusty patches on the knees from kneeling in the taxi.

And this is how I come face to face with Cedric Solomon.

Cedric's eyes assess me. 'Malik Textiles…' He repeats the name. 'I can't say I've heard of the business before. How long have you been going?'

I imagine his head busy doing sums and running through the company's balance sheet.

'I was one of the first in the trade. Our head office is in Grotton, just off the M60.' My voice turns high and squeaky, like a salesman who's desperate to make a sale. We talk about sourcing and the effect of rising cotton prices on my profits. Cedric mentions names – small-time traders I wouldn't have spat at once, but who now have offices in Hong Kong and New York. His every statement stabs into me like a knife, and I'm afraid I'll fall apart. It won't take him long to discover my deception.

Esther stands by his side, one long arm holding a cigarette, her elbow resting on the bar. Her eyes are on the hand holding the cigarette. She's wearing red nail varnish, but she's put it on clumsily, so that splashes of colour bleed into her skin. She brings the cigarette to her mouth and inhales deeply. Her shoulders sag as she blows out the smoke, her long lashes low upon her cheeks.

I want to make love to her.

'PK's an old friend. At one time, his company supplied Harrods and all the top department stores, but he's having a little wobble. Perhaps you guys could meet…' Ben explains to Cedric, who smiles politely in the fixed way people do when they've stopped listening. He fishes out his blackberry. I am yesterday's news, not tomorrow's headline.

Esther tells her husband they should go home. It's getting late. He has an early start the next day. She sounds like any old nagging wife.

I stand straight so she can see that in spite of his Italian suit and his Rolls Royce, Cedric is no match to my six-foot height. I want her to remember the hotel room where we'd both come alive.

Her eyes skim my face and immediately wander off to somewhere behind my shoulder. I turn around to see Geeta walking towards us clutching her cheap, sequined clutch to her chest.

'Thank God I found it,' she says, waving the bag.

'This is Geeta, my wife,' I introduce her to Cedric, but his mobile rings, and he wanders off to the other side of the room.

The barman pulls down the shutter over the bar, and the waitresses came out of the kitchen holding Tesco bags in their hands. The world seems to be closing in on itself, dimming its lights, slowing its heartbeat, leaving just three shadows facing each other: my wife, Esther and me.

'Lovely to meet you, Greta, and…' Esther comes forward, stretching out her hand like a queen granting an audience. She hesitates and catches my eye. 'Lovely to meet your husband, too.'

Geeta describes the adventure of the misplaced bag. 'Whatever you say, the English are honest. The boy who was clearing the table kept the bag with him. He gave it to me right away. I gave him two pounds as a thank-you,' she says.

'Good for you! You made his day.' Esther smiles.

Geeta tried to make small talk, asking Esther if she had heard the main speaker. 'He went on and on, didn't he?' she says.

'Yes, Cedric has a tendency to ramble,' Esther agrees, adding that Cedric is her husband.

Has Esther's accent always been so cut-glass? I grab hold of Geeta's elbow. 'Nice to meet you all,' I say, turning to wave to Ben.

'We're leaving too,' Esther says. 'We have an early flight tomorrow. We're not back till next week. I just can't wait to get back and catch up with my friends.'

I wonder if her words are meant for me.

* * *

Geeta's in the bathroom getting ready for bed. I go over Esther's words. She's travelling again and Cedric is with her. I can't remember where she said they were going – was it New York or LA? These places are little more than Tube stops to her.

The bathroom door opens. Geeta comes out, the dark brown droop of her nipples visible through the transparent peach nightie she's wearing. An M&S price tag dangles from one sleeve.

'Nice nightie,' I say. 'Is it new?' I reach for the switch on the bedside-table lamp.

'I bought two last week. There was a special offer. Only twenty-two pounds. And it can go in the washing machine,' she says.

Instead of going to her side of the bed and falling asleep, something she does every night, Geeta comes over and sits near me. 'It was a nice evening,' she says, her fingers picking at a loose thread in the bedspread.

'A bit dull, if you ask me. At least we found your bag,' I yawn and switch off the light. I sense more questions are coming, and want to be in darkness when they do.

'Amar's sleeping at the Guptas',' she says, moving closer.

'I don't know why he doesn't like them,' I say. 'They're always so kind to him. Gupta's an old codger, but he does have a heart.' I give another big yawn.

'That woman we met tonight… Esther Solomon… She's very beautiful, isn't she?' Geeta's voice is normal, neutral. Not the voice of a woman who suspects her husband.

I stay quiet.

'You know the dress she was wearing… it reminded me of that piece of cloth you brought home.'

'The brocade?' I correct her. 'Oh, I sent it back long ago. It's quite a common design. She could've picked it anywhere.'

'She didn't remember you, even though you'd met her before,' she says.

'I don't think I've met her before… have I?'

'Yes, you have,' Geeta insists. 'She went to Mowbray Hall instead of her husband.'

'Her husband was a right prick,' I say. 'Didn't even say hello to you. And did you see how Ben kept laughing at whatever he said?'

'Everyone laughs at a rich man's jokes. People think being friendly with a rich guy makes them rich too,' Geeta says, taking my hand and stroking my fingers.

'It's late,' I say, and shut my eyes.

'Amar's away,' she repeats, 'and I'm not tired.' The wine at dinner has made her light-headed and bold.

She unbuttons her nightie and places my hand on her breast. I start rubbing her skin mechanically, and feel it turn warm. Her nipple slowly stiffens under my finger.

I sit up and bury my face in the nape of her neck, inhaling deeply the old, familiar smells that once excited my blood, but there's no comfort in her flesh any more. She senses the change in me and gently removes my hand from where it lies on her breast. Limp, unfeeling, dead.

Dear Lopa didi,

Do you remember the old Hollywood actress called Sophia Loren? She was Italian – a very beautiful and sexy lady. Her posters were everywhere during the Italian Film Festival. You must be wondering why I'm asking you this. I met someone the other day who looks like her. A tall and very busty lady. Her skin was like milk. English women have perfect skin. We met her at a business dinner. Poor PK – he used to win such big awards once upon a time, and now we are there just as onlookers. It must have hurt him real bad. You are fortunate that Jijaji's business is expanding into Sri Lanka and Mauritius. You must be a proud wife. This lady I am telling you about is the wife of a big shot. He's also in textiles, but much, much bigger than us. He could be very useful to PK, so I got a bit angry that PK didn't even recognised the lady when I asked him about her. How could anyone forget such a beautiful face? He was very rude to her. This lady was wearing a beautiful dress – it almost looked like a sari. The material was like an antique brocade – something a queen would wear. PK had given me a similar piece of fabric, but it was no good on my skin, and just made my complexion look dark and dull. I gave it back straight away.

What are you wearing for Diwali this year? Are net saris back in fashion? Get a nice blue one with silver embroidery. It will suit you.

Love to the kids,

Geeta

14

SOMEWHERE NICE AND SAFE

The hunger for Esther kicks awake within me. The taste of her mouth. The touch of her flesh. I want it back.

'Can we meet once more? Just once? Somewhere quiet,' I beg her over the phone.

'Manchester is such a small place,' Esther says. 'Do you think we can pull it off?'

'I hope you're not giving up on us now. Our story has only just begun,' I say. A strange fear grips me when I say this. I want a story with her, but I'm afraid of how it'll run. 'I'll find us somewhere nice and safe,' I promise, my voice ripe with longing.

There are a million hotel beds in which to be unfaithful. But Manchester suddenly feels small, crowded, with too many knowing faces and eyes. And then I find the one – quite by chance – scrolling through the computer: the Didsbury Queen, 56 Elm Road. I like the name. It has a romantic ring to it. I call Esther and tell her about it.

'You're such a romantic,' she says, a smile in her voice. 'Seeing you again brought everything back. I was so afraid your wife or Cedric would pick up on it. I had a hard time keeping hold of myself.'

The Didsbury Queen is a small Victorian house conversion that has seen better days. The peeling white pebble-dash and the iron bars on the ground-floor windows tell me it isn't the most romantic venue for a rendezvous, but it's small and anonymous, and there isn't much passing traffic. Most businesses on the road are shut or boarded up, except a funeral parlour. The sign on its window says:

Hades and Sons
Serving the nation 24/7
Except Sundays and Bank Holidays

A young Jamaican man with orange dreadlocks sits at the reception desk, reading the *Daily Mirror*.

'I need a room. Your best one,' I tell him. The room rates are scrawled in chalk on a blackboard. They're cheap – about three-star rates.

'We only take cash – no credit cards,' he says, folding his paper neatly and placing it on the counter. 'TORY MP CAUGHT WITH RENT BOY', the headlines scream. It's a funny world we live in, I think, everyone at it like dogs.

I ask to see the room. What would Esther make of the faded grey carpet of the reception area and the red plastic flowers on the window ledge? The young man opens a drawer and takes out a heavy old-fashioned iron key, dangling on a thick red velvet cord.

'Room six is a deluxe room. It's on the third floor. But there's no lift. You up to it?' He looks at my grey hair and knees pointedly.

'I'll be fine,' I reply, but I'm breathless when we reach the room.

'The bed's clean.' The man nods and points with his chin towards the blue sheets. He goes into the bathroom and flushes the toilet.

'I'll take it,' I say, giving a friendly smile. I want him on my side.

He shrugs, but I can tell he's pleased when I hand him the cash. I say I will stick around for a bit and wait for my wife. The word 'wife' slips out of my mouth so easily. He nods and leaves me to it.

I shut the door, take off my jacket and check myself in the full-length mirror behind the bathroom door. Am I good enough for Esther? The first time didn't count – it was an accident and we got carried away. But this is different. This is deliberate. We're coming to each other with open eyes. One false move and I'll lose her for ever.

I unbutton my shirt, suck in my belly and take a hard look at myself. The thick patch of hair on my chest is grey, but my arms are still muscular. I've not let myself go Gupta's way, soft and flaccid in middle age. I slap some Old Spice on my cheeks and gargle with cold water until the inside of my mouth feels new again. I quickly run a finger around the inside of the sink to make sure it's clean.

'Is it safe?' Esther asks when I phone her. 'Coming to you like a thief in broad daylight?'

'As safe as it'll ever be,' I say.

I check the window. The street is empty. 'No one will ever find us here. Don't let me down,' I say. I tell her to park her car on a side street away from the hotel, and not to give her name at reception.

I ring home. 'I'll be late tonight. I'm going through the next season's stock. Don't wait up,' I say to Geeta, making my plans vague and unclear.

'But isn't your stocktaking in November?' Geeta's worried tone makes things difficult. She's breathing heavily. She's probably rushed downstairs to take the call.

'Some quality stuff has come up, and it needs urgent sorting out. I might even have to work through the night. I've done that before, haven't I,' I say, reminding her of the times when, too tired to drive home, I'd slept on the couch in the showroom.

'Amar's brought a new friend over for a play,' she says, changing the subject. 'It's a girl. An English girl.'

'An English girl? That's good!' I'm pleased. He's brought the occasional Chinese boy home to play before – boys who are timid like him, who sit on the sofa and watch cartoons with him – but never a girl, nor even a regular English boy who'd want to go outside and kick a ball. I go back to the window, peering out for Esther's car.

'Are you listening?'

'I'm still here.'

'I'm not sure about Amar's new friend…' Geeta continues.

'Why not? He's fourteen. Isn't it great he's making some friends?'

'Yes, I suppose it is,' Geeta agrees reluctantly.

She'd have preferred an Indian girl – someone who called her Aunty and offered to make her tea.

'This girl is very rude. She just said "Hi Greta" and then they went upstairs. Couldn't even get my name right. They're in his bedroom now, and they've shut the door.' Her voice is worried.

'They'll be fine,' I say. 'Order them some pizza. Some Domino's. Kids love that.'

'I've made lamb curry, and also some chips, in case she doesn't like Indian food,' says Geeta.

* * *

A red Mini is nudging its way into a space behind my car. It's Esther. She's forgotten my instructions about parking elsewhere.

'Let him have fun. We'll talk later, when I get home,' I promise Geeta, and rush downstairs.

Esther isn't at reception. I find her in the car, her hands on the steering wheel, eyes staring straight ahead. I tap on the window and smile reassuringly. My hands are clammy with sweat. It's the shock of seeing her again, so close and so reachable.

She clicks open her door and steps out. The sleeve of her blue dress brushes against my face. I touch her cheek lightly. Her full red mouth trembles in a half smile.

'Just silly nerves, that's all. I didn't feel like going in by myself and asking for your room number,' she says.

I slip my arm through hers and lightly kiss her on the forehead. It's damp. 'Thank you for coming,' I say.

We walk inside together, but I drop her hand. The Jamaican man is playing on his phone, but he looks up as we walk in and stares at Esther.

'My wife's here now,' I say, nudging Esther towards the staircase.

'Whatever,' he mumbles, and goes back to his screen.

Esther stops on the final step to catch her breath. The sunlight coming through the landing window circles her head like a halo.

'I found this place quickly. I hope it's all right for you,' I say, shutting the door softly behind me.

She doesn't answer.

We're alone together now, but neither of us is sure of what to do.

'We should've had a drink before – met up at a bar or something,' I say, and then instantly feel foolish for saying so.

Esther stands still, arms folded across her chest, and I stay by the door. Neither of us looks at the bed, with its blue and white checked bedspread and two pillows that will soon carry the weight of our bodies.

I go up to Esther and put my arms around her.

'Don't be afraid. Trust me,' I say, and pull her towards me so her body falls against mine. My hands are on her face, lightly massaging her cheek and her nose, pressing her eyelids closed.

'I don't know what to do,' she says. 'I've tried to stop myself falling for you. I know it'll only lead to trouble and more trouble, but still I want to be with you.' She raises her face to me.

'Will you just let me love you?' I say, and unzip her dress. I rub the small of her back till it feels warm.

And this is how, quietly, without too much of a fuss, in room number six of a shabby Manchester hotel, I become someone else.

* * *

Esther gives me a new name that day. I'm her 'mensch'. She says it's Yiddish for 'gentleman'.

'An honourable, upstanding gentleman. That's how I see you,' she says.

I cup the heavy weight of her breasts in my hands and look down at our bodies intertwined in bed.

'There's nothing mensch-like in what I'm doing,' I say, kissing the moist inside of her arm. The sour taste wakes up a memory of hot, humid nights in Bombay when the power went out. Sitting in the darkness on the balcony, while the generator slowly coughed back to life, I fanned myself with a palm-leaf fan scented with the sweet odour of khas khas and promised myself a better future. The taste and smell travels across continents, across years, anchoring me to my past.

Esther lies beside me, one arm behind her head, her hair spread like an untidy cloud on the pillow. Pale stretch marks encircle the sides of her stomach like an unclasped silver belt. Her belly's gentle sag shows she's a mother, but I don't want to think about children.

'I'm off to Israel soon, but I'm just so tired.' She sighs. 'I make a trip at least once a month. It's more out of duty than anything else. You've got to give something back to the mother country. At least, that's what Cedric says. You must do the same – with India, I mean. It's such a poor country.'

I try and bring India alive in my head, the crush of people scrambling on the trains at Victoria, clinging to the open doors of packed trains, the tip-tip of the monsoon rain drowning my sandalled feet, the smell of the moist red earth rising up and wide-eyed children sitting at traffic lights, their folded hands forming a begging bowl. I remember in a flash my mother's head bent over the kitchen hob, frying pakoras while the Doordarshan radio blared out filmi songs. The only India I've carried with me is my mango tree, shivering beneath the Manchester sky.

'I've left India behind,' I tell Esther. Since Father's death I've only gone back once, to sell his flat, close his bank account, carry his ashes in a plastic pouch and feed them to the Ganges river. My passport and my flag is British. Over the years I've become that most exotic of species: a British Indian with more British in him than Indian.

'What exactly are you doing in Israel? Sightseeing? Isn't it dangerous with all the Palestinian problems going on?' Replete with love, I suddenly feel protective of her.

'I'm visiting an orphanage,' she says. 'I'm one of the trustees of the Golda Meir centre for abandoned children. We have quarterly board meetings – long, tedious affairs, always about raising funds.' She stops and makes a face. 'I'm boring you, aren't I?'

Everything about her world is new and exciting. I tell her to continue.

'Maybe next time.' She plays with the thin gold chain around her neck. The Star of David pendant swings dreamily between her breasts.

I like the way Esther says 'next time'. It gives our afternoon, our lovemaking and us a strange kind of legitimacy and future.

'There'll be a next time? You still want to us to meet?' I say, keen to secure a promise.

She lifts my hand to her mouth, kissing each finger slowly, as though memorising their shape and their smell.

'I still remember what Maratha told me before she left for Mexico. I'm merely obeying her orders.' She closes her eyes and recites it like a poem. '"Esther, dear, it is your duty to be happy. You owe it to yourself. You've got just one life – go grab it by the throat." And I've not felt this happy in a long, long time,' she says, opening her eyes.

My life is not going to be the same again. 'What about your husband?' I ask. 'What about Cedric? How can you hide this from him?'

She frowns. 'Cedric won't suspect a thing. He's so tied up with his deals. As long as I'm there for charity functions and dinners and his shirts are ironed and ready, he won't really notice. She pauses and then continues. 'But what about your wife? Your Greta. I'm worried about her. I've heard Indian women can be quite needy. She was clinging to you at the do the other night.'

'She's called Geeta,' I correct her gently. 'She's too busy looking after the house and our son. She's like your Cedric – she takes her responsibilities very seriously.'

We laugh, relieved to think that that maybe things were going to be easy after all.

'Now there's only your business to worry about. How will you find time to meet me?' she asks.

Esther sits on the edge of the bed, her pale, bare back towards me, brushing her hair with slow, deliberate strokes. I wonder what she thinks of me, lying in bed, smoking in the dark, indifferent to the running meter of time. The men in her world are always in a hurry. They have businesses to run, bills to pay, contracts to sign. My hand holding the cigarette feels heavy.

'I'm different to your husband,' I say. 'I'm going to make time for you. Isn't that what you want?'

'Yes, yes, yes, my mensch.' She throws the brush on the floor, climbs back into bed and presses me to her tightly. 'I love the fact that you've got time for me. I love that you're so carefree and so different to all the boring men I know.'

She doesn't know me at all.

15

HAPPINESS CAN BE A KIND OF DEATH

A stubborn nub of sadness lies at the heart of most happiness – a dull ache hinting that darkness is waiting just beyond the reach of the light. I had that feeling the day my mother fell ill. The house was ablaze with Diwali candles, pakoras piled high on plates, fireworks somersaulting through the Bombay sky, various visiting cousins sprawled about, laughing, joking, and in the midst of this, flitting about like a shadow, was my mother. She sat on the sofa, a blanket covering her knees, her cheeks hollowed out with the shade of the afterlife, urging me to eat one more laddu. Her hand clutched a handkerchief, stained by the blood in her spit.

She didn't last a week after that. Dead at forty-five. She was ten years younger than I am now when she died.

My happiness with Esther feels like a kind of death. There's an aftertaste, a bitterness that slowly builds inside me so that, when I wake up in the morning, the first thing I think of isn't a memory of the passion of moments spent together but a guilty awareness that I spent hours away from my home, making love to a woman who isn't my wife.

The mobile rings as I drive home from the hotel one evening. It's Margaret. 'Your wife called,' she says, and nothing more.

'I had stuff to do in town.'

'That's what I thought,' she says. 'I told her you were entertaining clients in town.'

Her tone is neutral. She adds that we've missed the deadline for an order from Ireland.

Margaret is loyal. She's seen me through rain and sun. She knows I know there is no stocktaking this month, nor clients to entertain, but she has my back. I see her at her desk each morning, pen in hand, running red lines through my diary, cancelling appointments and meetings, making space in my life for another woman.

'Mr Ali's coming to see you. Eleven o'clock tomorrow morning. You're not too busy to see him, are you?' she enquires.

'I'll be there. Just make sure you pull out that denim skirt with the faulty zip. I want to show it to him.' I want her to know I am still at the top of my game.

Ali is our main supplier; his job is to stitch our dresses from the samples I send him. I've visited his factory a couple of times – a small building with prefabricated walls, with a well nearby that the workers use to wash when their shift finishes. The factory is in Bilashgunj, a bumpy two-hour drive from Dacca.

I'm still thinking of Ali when I enter the house. Geeta's outside in the garden, hanging out the washing. She sees me and comes in. She has dark circles under her eyes, and she's wearing my dressing gown, rather than her usual tracksuit. The gown trails at her feet. I'm worried she'll trip and fall and break her neck.

'I rang the office,' she says. 'and spoke to Margaret. She said you were in town.'

'What did you want?' I move away, worried she might smell Esther's perfume.

'How was your meeting?' Geeta pronounces the word *meeting* like a foreign word.

'Oh, the usual – boring.' I say, opening the fridge. I'm starving. 'Why the sudden interest in my business? You've never asked before,' I say, pulling out a Tupperware box containing some leftover chicken and rice. 'Can you heat this up for me? I'm hungry.'

'Leave the leftovers – I'll make you something fresh,' she says.

She cracks two eggs into a bowl and starts slicing onions for an omelette. There's something reassuring in the way she moves about the kitchen, putting the kettle on to boil and popping the bread in the toaster, and instead of running upstairs to hide, I stay, watching her cook.

'What's with all the washing?' I ask. She does her washing on Tuesdays normally – I know this much about her world.

'It's Amar,' she says, and hesitates. 'He… he wet the bed again last night. That's two nights in a row.'

'Where is Amar? How come he's gone to bed so early?' I ask, buttering two slices of bread and pushing one towards her. She eats it quickly and puts another one in the toaster.

'His friend, that Alice girl, is a mistake. She's upset him – she's too bossy around him,' she says.

I remember the girl who came round to play. Amar's new friend.

'He has to learn to stand up for himself,' I say. 'He's not a kid any more. Is she nice otherwise, this new friend of his?'

Geeta pours some more tea into my cup. 'She's English. What can you expect?' she answers, as though this summed up everything about her.

'The English *can* be very nice,' I say. I was thinking of the dark scatter of freckles on Esther's right shoulder.

Geeta doesn't answer. She takes her spicy banana wafers from the cupboard and goes over to the television, switching it on, surfing the channels until an Indian film comes on and fills the kitchen with its noise.

'You think inviting the girl home upset Amar? He's not used to socialising,' I press on.

She shrugs. 'I don't know what to do.'

I take a packet of cigarettes from my pocket. They're not my usual Marlboros, they're Esther's. I must have picked up her Camels by mistake. I wonder if Geeta will notice the difference.

She watches me light up and suddenly turns off the TV, a frown on her face. 'Why did you come home so late?'

'I thought I told you the reason,' I say.

She picks up the cigarette box and reads out the health warning, loud and slow, like a child learning to read.

'I wish you wouldn't smoke so much. It's not good for your health.' It's the first time she's ticked me off for my smoking.

'I'll try,' I say. 'But it's not easy. I thought you liked me smoking and drinking. You said it made me look westernised and modern.' I mimic her tone, wanting her to smile, to lift the shadows crowding her eyes.

'I was young and stupid then. What did I know of the world?' she says, and sits down next to me, still holding the packet. 'This is poison, PK. You must stop.'

'Only if you stop eating your banana wafers,' I tease her. 'Look at me!' I want to shout. 'Question me more! Make me stop!'

'You're always after my wafers!' She slaps my leg playfully. 'I'm not going to stop eating them.'

It's almost like the old days – the joking way we'd tease one another, the silly inside jokes, the banter, the carefreeness.

She senses it too, and reminds me about the time we smuggled some whisky into the Bombay flat, hiding it inside a Campa Cola bottle, terrified Father would pick up the smell.

'Yes, yes, I remember now,' I say, my forehead creased in memory. 'The liquor store in Kala Ghoda, next to the bicycle repair shop. The chap who sold us the bottle, you said he looked like Yul Brynner with his shiny bald head. You should ask your sister if the shop is still there. Some things in a city should never change.'

'I've not spoken to her for a few weeks,' Geeta replies, looking away.

We're quiet, lost in our memories. Then Geeta does something she's not done in a long time. She holds my hand, her thumb rubbing against mine, feeling the rough calluses. She keeps holding it until I pull away. 'We'd better get to bed,' I say.

Dear Lopa didi,

Thank you for calling me. I'm not ill and I don't have the flu. I just feel uneasy all the time. I can't put a finger on it. It's not that PK and I are fighting. We were never the type to act lovey-dovey or hold hands – been married too long for that. But when I am cooking or hoovering, I look up and he's sitting in his chair watching me. He opens his mouth and is about to say something and then shakes his head and leaves the room. He is becoming very absent-minded too. Is Jijaji like this too – forgetting his mobile phone, not ringing when he will be late? I suppose men are very different from us. They are dealing with the world, their heads busy. What do I do? Just look after the house and Amar. I'm not paying any bills. I went into the garage yesterday and took out my sitar. I've not played for God knows how many years. Anyway, I tried playing Raag Lalit. I was so happy I could still play it. Amar saw me and asked what kind of guitar it was. He knows nothing about our Indian culture. I only blame myself.

I promise to ring next week.

Love to the kids,

Geeta

16

TOUGH TIMES

Ali is at the warehouse. He tells me our shipment will be delayed by a month.

'That's no good!' I say. 'The new season's stock needs to be in the shops before then.' My voice rises.

Margaret looks up from her desk, her mouth shrinking into a thin line. She doesn't like me shouting at suppliers, and Ali is a favourite. She's had a soft spot for him ever since he gave her a pashmina one Christmas.

Ali wipes his forehead with his handkerchief. He's sweating, although the room is cold and the radiator is off. 'It's labour trouble, Mr PK – you know how the unions are.' He gives a helpless smile, like one brother to another, claiming kinship in a foreign land – two brown brothers in it together.

'No, I don't see how you can let labour affect you. We're talking about Bangladesh, not bloody Sweden.' I take out a cigarette and offer him one. He shakes his head. It's Ramadan.

'Don't underestimate our workers, Mr PK; when they go on strike, they do it one hundred per cent. The whole factory comes to a halt,' he says, pushing back his chair, crossing one plump leg over the other. The red laces of his Nike trainers peep mischievously from beneath his grey pinstriped trousers.

'There must be a reason for the strike. Haven't you paid their wages?'

'Of course I pay their wages, I'm an honest man. Just like you.' His face simpers and then distorts into a scowl. 'It's just a small incident. The workers look for excuses all the time – you know how the labour class is: shirkers, one and all. One of the women got her arm trapped in the machine, and it took a little time to get her free.'

'I hope she's OK?'

'Unfortunately not, Mr PK. She lost her right arm. The ambulance couldn't get there in time. I've had to fire her – she's of no use now with one arm – and the trade unions are not too happy. They say she is the sole breadwinner of her family…' His voice trails off and he scowls again. I've reminded him of something unpleasant.

Margaret's face goes pale. This is the world we live in, I want to tell her. All those shiny frocks hanging in swanky boutiques on Bond Street and on plastic hangers in discount stores – they have something in common. There is a cost – a bloody trail that goes from there to the hovel-like factories in Bangladesh, where empty-bellied women hunch over sewing machines. We know it. The punter pretends not to know it. Who said the world was equal? But it still makes my stomach turn.

Ali's unperturbed eyes show that there's nothing more to say on the subject. I take him to the stockroom and hold up the denim skirt with the faulty zip.

'Look – just look at this,' I say, and yank up the zip. It slides up and then stops abruptly in the middle. Three hundred such skirts sit in the warehouse, all with the same broken zip.

Ali extends one fat finger and touches the zip tenderly, like a doctor examining a wound. He rubs his chin and asks whether one of the girls on the hemming floor may have caused the damage. 'Vandalism. Maybe she wants a raise?' he says, smiling slyly and eyeing my cigarette. I hand him one. He grabs it gratefully. 'It's the tension, Mr PK, that makes me smoke, but I can feel your pain. These skirts, they are no good,' he admits, his face momentarily blurred behind a cloud of cigarette smoke.

'There are three hundred more skirts like this. This is a quality issue. Your crap quality.' I tear open one of the cartons.

Ali raises his hand. 'Please, please, there's no need to be losing your temper.' It's his Korean supplier, he says, who's sold him the defective zips. 'You need to go after Mr Kim.'

'Korea or Timbuktu, I don't really care. You need to replace the whole consignment. I'm not chasing anyone for you,' I say.

'That will take time, Mr PK. I don't know when the strike will end, and cotton prices are also going up. In fact, before I forget, I have to increase the delivery price for any new orders you want to place.' He pulls out a handkerchief from his breast pocket and wipes his face. The handkerchief has his initials embroidered in red.

'Don't use the excuse of cotton prices. Everything takes time with you, strike or no strike,' I snap, but I keep thinking about the accident at his factory. I see the young woman with her arm in the machine, her blood dying the denim skirt she's working on red. I see her children clambering around her, begging for food, while she nurses her dead arm. The fight goes right out of me. 'The injured woman in your factory – are you going to compensate her family?' I have to make sure he is doing the right thing.

Ali is puzzled. 'Come on, Mr PK! We're living in tough times. Who has the money for compensation? You know that yourself. In the past you were placing orders every month – now it's every six months. It's difficult to make money, even for you – don't talk to me about compensating old employees!' He clears his throat and looks at his watch. It's a Swatch, in the same red as his trainers. 'So how about placing some new orders, Mr PK? I've got some wonderful polyester coming in – feels like Italian linen, I swear.'

He's dragged me back to reality. I can't afford to antagonise him – he's my main supplier in Bangladesh. We begin haggling over prices for next year's stock. I mention the weak dollar and manage to squeeze him down by ten pence per dress. This way I can improve our cost margins and still pass on some mark-up to the retailers.

'Shall we go out for dinner later?' I ask, when our business is over and we're waiting outside for his taxi to take him back to his hotel.

'I'm already booked for the evening, Mr PK.' He bends down to tie his laces.

'Who are you going out with?' I've always been his only customer in Manchester, so I'm curious.

'It's Mr Cedric Solomon's people. His sales rep is taking me out to dinner and then to the casino. There's a new one that's just opened in Manchester, I hear?' His dark, liquid eyes look at me for confirmation.

Years ago, Margaret told me to find other factories, have a few more suppliers on the go. 'Don't go putting all your eggs in one basket,' she said. But I ignored her and only kept up with Ali. I liked his style. He was a Man U supporter and smoked Cuban cigars on the sly. But his meeting Solomon's people makes me uneasy.

'I hope you don't discuss the prices we've agreed or the new orders for the next season. He's much bigger, but he's still a competitor,' I remind him.

'No need to be worrying! You're my oldest customer, Mr PK. How can I forget?' He shakes my hand, but he won't meet my eye.

* * *

I check my mobile after Ali leaves. There's a missed call from Esther. The very thought of her lightens everything inside me. I want to call her, but Margaret's desk is next to mine now, since I made the office open plan. 'We want the business to look more modern, more accessible,' I had explained to Margaret. But she's no fool – she knows it was to save costs. I kept cramming the staff into fewer rooms so that large portions of the warehouse now lie shrouded in wretched darkness – a wasteland to which I keep the door shut.

Geeta had once suggested I sell the warehouse and move to smaller premises nearer the city. I should've listened. 'At least you will get some decent money for the land,' she had said. 'Some developer can convert the warehouse into yuppie flats, and you'll save on petrol.'

I'd dismissed her suggestion. What did she know of the real world? 'I will never do such a thing. A laughing stock – is that what you want me to become? Can you imagine Gupta's face if he heard I'd done such a thing? "PK Malik is downsizing because times are tough" – that's what he'd say! The business will pick up again, just you wait and see.' The glint of ambition had shone in my eyes, but Geeta had known better.

I go downstairs to the smart bathroom which is set aside for visitors and call Esther. It's a foreign ringtone, which means she's still in Israel. I could tell her about my worries about Ali and the rising cotton prices, but I don't want to share the smallness of my day-to-day life.

She says she'll be back in a week.

'A week is a long time,' I complain. In my head, I am already in the hotel room, my hands running greedily over her body.

'There's so much red tape to get through out here, and the kids are in a dreadful state. I wish you could see them,' she says. Her voice sounds tired.

I imagine her cradling crying babies in her arms, standing in the middle of a burning, yellow desert while gunfire booms all around. A scene from a CNN report.

'I'm not Florence Nightingale,' she says, laughing off my image. 'I'm just a bored, rich woman trying to do some good. Who knows – I might even come back early. I might be missing somebody.'

I lean back against the green tiles of the bathroom and let her words ride through me.

A face stares back at me from the mirror above the sink. It's carefree and young. It's not the face of someone who's been haggling over prices in a sweatshop. It's the face of a man on the phone with his lover, his mouth unable to stop smiling. I don't recognise that face. But I know it belongs to me.

17

ANYBODY CAN BE HAPPY

Geeta stands in the driveway, her face pressed against the wrought-iron columns of the gate, a prisoner waiting to be let out. It is Amar's parent's evening and I'm late getting home from work. She has made an effort for the meeting, and is wearing some red lipstick and a pair of black polyester trousers that I've not seen before. A sari would have been kinder to her waist, but there's no point in saying this to her.

There are too many red lights on the way to school. Stopping at one, I notice a woman in the Mercedes in front. Her hair is long and brown like Esther's. She's with a man.

'Why have you slowed down?' Geeta asks. 'We'll be late.'

'Too many speed cameras. I don't want any more points.' I drive slowly until the car carrying the brown-haired woman disappears from view.

Miss Connor, Amar's teacher, is also running late. We join the other parents in the refectory. Most of the mums and dads appear younger and happier. I recognise a few from previous years. Geeta goes over to one of the mothers.

'That's Alice's mum,' she says, coming back. 'I said a quick hello.'

'Alice? Who is Alice?' I can't put a face to the name. I shuffle in my seat, looking around. The hall smells of food and my chair is hard and uncomfortable.

'She's Amar's friend – the girl who comes around all the time. Where's your head these days?' Geeta's voice is impatient.

I glance at Alice's mother, a thin, plain woman wearing a blue nurse's uniform, her hands folded in her lap.

'She looks like a proper dragon,' I whisper to Geeta.

'Well, she's a nurse. They have to be strong,' she whispers back.

It's our turn to go in. Miss Connor has well-meaning blue eyes that sparkle behind her red-framed glasses.

'Amar is doing much better now, Mrs Malik,' she says, flicking through the notebook on her desk.

I sneak a look at the book. Rows of names and grades are neatly arranged in columns. I try to see where Amar stands on the list. There is an unbroken row of As and Bs and then a line of straight Ds after his name.

'Did Amar get a D in maths?' I point to the column.

Miss Connor looks guilty. 'Yes, that's him. But I can tell he's tried very hard. He just missed a C grade by a couple of marks.'

The news reassures Geeta. 'Thank you so much,' she says.

But it doesn't satisfy me. 'What about English and history and the rest? Are those all Ds too?' It was the same story. Amar was at the bottom of the class, but he was trying his best. 'Are *you* trying your best with him? Giving him proper attention? These test results clearly show he's not improving,' I challenge her. I don't give a damn about her kind eyes.

'Oh, but Amar's much happier in class now. He's interacting more with the others. And…' Miss Connor triumphantly turns the pages of her notebook and moves it towards me. 'Just look at that,' she says.

Her finger stabs the paper where one lone A glitters like a star in a sea of Cs. Amar got an A in art.

'Art is a girly subject. It won't take him far in life,' I say. 'I want him to do well in maths and science – proper subjects, not airy-fairy ones.' Even as I say this, I think back to my own passion for designing clothes. There's nothing macho or masculine in that, and here I am berating my son for appreciating the finer things in life.

'But Picasso wasn't a girl – and what exactly do you mean by "airy-fairy"?' Miss Connor is in a fighting spirit. She removes her glasses and rubs her eyes. Her pink nail varnish is chipped.

I'm in no mood to appease her. 'What about sport? That's important too. All this skiving PE lessons won't let him shake off his sickliness. Does he play more football, tennis? Get fresh air? I asked about that last time too, remember?'

Miss Connor shifts uncomfortably in her seat and looks at Geeta. 'Poor woman, married to this demanding ogre' – that's what she's thinking.

'Well, Mr Malik, as you well know, Amar's always had a thing about sports, and since his…' She pauses tactfully. Geeta's face remains still and expressionless. Every academic year, Geeta writes a letter to the teachers explaining Amar's head injury that was caused by a careless cricket ball hit by his father. Miss Connor continues, 'Amar doesn't like competitive, rough games, but…' Her voice brightens. 'But, as you can see, he is enjoying his art. He has made a new friend, and the two often go off to the art room at lunchtime and paint together.'

'Is this new friend Alice?' I ask.

'Yes, it is. She joined us last term from Grimsby. They seem to get on all right.' She smiles and gets up. Our time is up.

We're about to leave when Geeta, rummaging through her handbag, fishes out a large packet of roasted cashew nuts. 'For you,' she says, handing it to Miss Connor. 'They are good for health, and they're not too spicy.'

Miss Connor is confused, but then accepts the gift, pushing it clumsily inside her bag, muttering thanks.

* * *

'I'm not happy with this school,' I say to Geeta on the way home. 'Shall we move Amar to a private one?'

'I think Miss Connor is lovely. So helpful. And he's settled now. He likes his routine, so why upset him?'

'We need a better teacher for Amar. He can do better; she's not pushing him hard enough. You saw his D in maths,' I say, not ready to let her off the hook.

'We can get him a tutor. Mrs Ahmed's nephew has just finished a maths degree in Birmingham, and he's looking for a job. He won't be expensive—'

'Geeta, you don't get the point,' I snap, cutting her short. 'Tutors aren't going to help. It's just pouring more money down the drain. Amar doesn't want to do well. He is wasting time painting pictures with this Alice,' I say, spitting out the last word.

'But you like drawing too – you're always sketching women's dresses. What's the big deal, as long as he passes and goes on to the next class?' she asks. 'I'm happy if he is happy.'

I nearly crash the car when I hear this. 'What's the big deal? He should be doing better than us! That's the big deal. We didn't come to England to be happy. We came here to make money. You don't spend your days mopping your front steps so he can be Mr Average. He has to be bigger and brighter than us. He's our only child, and our only chance to shine. Who will take over the business after I'm gone? You or Mrs Ahmed's bloody nephew?'

My words pour over her like hurtful acid. Geeta stares out of the car window, blinking rapidly, as though trying to see through the thick curtain of rain falling over the city. I feel trapped by her silence, by the greyness of the city and the unsmiling, washed-out faces of the other motorists staring straight ahead.

I pull into a MacDonald's car park and stop.

'Why have you stopped here?' Geeta narrows her eyes and tries to read the drive-thru menu on the board. 'I've made dinner. We're having roast chicken, Chinese style, and egg-fried rice.'

Here she is again, worrying away about feeding her family.

'Can we stop talking about food for once?' I snap. 'I want to talk about Amar's future.' I park the car in one of the loading bays and light a cigarette. Geeta starts fidgeting with the seat belt, unlatching it and then latching it again. The clicking sound gives me a headache. 'What do you want from Amar, Geeta? He's fourteen now, he's not a baby any more.'

'I want Amar to be happy, that is all,' she says, clicking open the seat belt.

'Being happy is not enough. Do you understand that? Why do you think the business is in such trouble… because everybody is busy being happy rather than working hard,' I say.

I put my hand on her seat belt to stop her clicking it shut again.

'But are you happy, PK?' she asks.

'We're not talking about me. Anybody can be happy – there is no skill in that. What is important is to become a *someone*.'

Here I am, repeating my father's words. I remember his scorn when he saw me come home after a long day of cricket, my dirty white shirt sticking to me like a second skin. 'It is only hard work that will take you somewhere, not this banging around of balls,' he'd shout, following me into my room, the ceiling fan whirring noisily above our heads, Mother tossing with her sickness in the next room.

'I don't give a damn about exams! I want to enjoy life, be happy. Not be a boring third-rate clerk like you – someone who can't even afford a car!' I shouted back, shaking a fist at him, the blood rushing to my head.

He was jealous of me. My own father was jealous of my youth. He wanted to cripple me with his own disappointments. His mediocrity was the reason I left Bombay. I didn't want to be a part of his small world.

I remember the scene all those years ago in Bombay as I sit in the McDonald's car park in Manchester, shaking a fist at my own wife. I start the car.

'I want you to be stricter with him, Geeta. His GCSEs will soon be around the corner. It's make-or-break time,' I say.

'Are you still talking about him?' she asks, her eyes unblinking and wide. For a moment, for just one moment, I'm afraid she knows about Esther.

'Who else would I be talking about?' I say, rushing on. 'You seem to think Amar's life is my problem, not yours. That he's got his father's business he can swan right into. Well, that's not the case, Geeta. It's a nasty world out there. How long can I protect him from his problems? Who will look after him when we are dead?' I bully her, becoming vicious and spiteful in my fear.

Geeta's face seems shut, solid and impenetrable like a closed door. 'I have never thought of Amar as a problem. He's just... special,' she says slowly, her eyes leaping into life.

A memory comes back when she says this. Amar was little, maybe two. We were renting a semi in Longsight. I was at work, but a meeting was cancelled, so I came home early.

When I got home I was greeted by the radio playing old Hindi film songs that Geeta listened to while ironing. I went into the kitchen, then to our bedroom, but there was no sign of mother or child. I opened the bathroom door and saw them having a bath together. Amar the baby, scrambling on Geeta's naked belly, her face alive, in rapture, while her tender hands soaped his back, and she sang to him, old lullabies from her own childhood.

I'd felt like an intruder that day.

* * *

We come home to find Amar waiting for us at the kitchen table, a plate in front of him. We've come home without stopping off at Pizza Hut for his favourite treat.

'No pizza today?' His bottom lip sticks out, but it's not cute. He just looks fat.

Geeta kisses the top of his head. 'Sorry, darling. We didn't have time. You can have chicken today; I'll get pizza tomorrow.'

'Don't you want to know what your teacher said about you?' I ask him. 'Aren't you curious?'

'Miss Connor was lovely. She said some nice things,' Geeta says quickly.

But I don't want Amar to get away with it. 'You must try harder, Amar,' I say. 'Your grades are very disappointing. Can you at least try for a C in maths next time?'

'I do try, Dad, I try hard, but numbers are so difficult. They give me a headache.' He lowers his head and starts biting his thumb. His double chin looks just like Geeta's.

I open the fridge and take out a beer. I remember Miss Connor mentioning Amar's paintings, so I ask him to show them to me.

He's thrilled. 'You want to see them? Seriously?' He runs up to his bedroom and comes down with three tightly rolled sheets that he unfolds on the kitchen table. Geeta leaves her cooking and comes over to see them too.

The pictures are of a boy and a girl holding hands. In one they are in a park, bathed in light from a big yellow sun, and in the other they were inside a square, orange house. The boy is brown, the girl pink. They're smiling. The colours are bright and full of hope.

I point to the girl. 'Is that supposed to be your friend Alice?'

'Yes, that's her,' Amar says, smiling shyly.

'We met her mum at the school,' I tell him.

'Can Alice come over tomorrow, Mum?' he asks.

'Why doesn't she ever invite you back to her house?' Geeta asks him.

'She can't,' he says. 'Her mum is a nurse, and she works long hours.' He pauses a moment. 'So you like my paintings?' He seems desperate for our approval.

Geeta says he could be the next Picasso if he wanted. She scoops a spoonful of rice from the pan and feeds it to him. They start chatting about the DVDs he wants for his birthday.

The next day I ring Mrs Ahmed's nephew Haroon and call him in for an interview at the warehouse.

Haroon is a timid-looking boy with a wispy beard and an ill-fitting fake leather jacket. I like him, but I don't like his tuition rates. 'You're not cheap for a recent graduate,' I grumble.

'I have a student loan to repay,' he says, apologetically.

'Why don't you get a proper job rather than doing tuition for kids?' I say.

'I've got a PhD in trigonometry from Salford Uni, but it's very difficult to get a job these days. I could try in London, but the cost of living is too high. This is only temporary – I might apply to the NHS next year.' He speaks with an annoying Brummie accent.

'Go easy on Amar,' I tell him. 'He's a bright boy with a lot of potential, but he's not had the easiest childhood…' I trail off.

Haroon nods understandingly, his head bowed. 'I know, Geeta aunty has explained you hit him with a cricket ball. I will be patient.'

'It was an accident.' I emphasise. 'As long as you help him get an A in maths, that's all I want. You see, one day, all this…' I slowly and ceremoniously sweep my arm in front of us to indicate the breadth of the warehouse. 'One day all this will be his. He will grow this into an empire, and people will forget he was the son of a second-class immigrant. He will belong.'

'I will try my best to help him, Uncle.' Haroon pauses and looks around the office. 'You are an inspiration. One of the first Asians to make it big. You should come to Salford Uni and give a talk on how to run a business. I could propose you to the economics department?'

I wave him away. 'I'm nothing. There are many others doing far better than me. You know… Cedric Solomon, for instance. You should ask him. You must have heard of him?' The name sits heavy on my tongue.

Haroon looks puzzled and shakes his head. 'No, never heard of him.'

I don't know why, but his admission makes me happy. I get up and shake his hand. 'You've got the job, young man.'

Once Haroon has left, I imagine the stories Geeta might have spun him about Amar's accident. The careless way I had lobbed the ball, my reluctance to show him to a specialist. All these years later, she's still pointing fingers at me.

Dear Lopa didi,
You can spend a lifetime with someone and feel as though you've known them only for an hour. That's how I feel with PK right now. You should have seen the fuss he kicked up over Amar's grades at the parent's evening. Poor Miss Connor, Amar's teacher, was red with embarrassment. He refuses to be happy or to take pride in Amar. Wouldn't you be delighted if Chintu or Bubbly got an A in art? We had a horrible fight going back home. He looked at me in that mean way he has – his lip curling up. He tried to tell me that we were in this country only to make money. I'm not a fool, I know he's right – why else would anyone leave their home, their family, their life behind? But I told him that being happy is important too. Amar is happy. I can see that when he is painting his pictures and talking with his new friend, the English girl I told you about. Seeing him happy makes me happy. It's that simple. But talking to PK is like shouting at a wall. He doesn't see me. Please ring me soon.

Love,
Geeta

18

A SLOW, QUIET POISON

It could be someone else's life, not mine. I wake up each morning and drive myself to work in my old Mercedes. There it stands, the seat of my empire: a red-brick two-storey warehouse, plonked in a sea of council houses just beyond the M60. The round blue plaque above the front door says it's a Grade II listed building, erected in 1875 by a cotton baron, one Charles Dewsberry. Large windows trap the sunlight, and there's enough space to carry the weight of the spinning and weaving machines. It was a flax mill once, producing 'fine quality linen', and was granted the Royal Warrant some time in the seventies.

I bought the mill on a whim. Mr Dewsberry had made his fortune in Calcutta, on the back of natives handing over their cotton crop, and here was I, the son of such a native, buying it back from the previous owners, who had used it as a dumping ground for out-of-date agricultural equipment. It felt like historical justice of sorts.

Much of the warehouse now lies empty. The entire stock and staff can fit on one floor. Bats have set up home under the eaves, and Margaret tells me she can smell asbestos when the rain is particularly bad. The tarmac is riddled with potholes, but at least the reception area is clean and bright. Fake orchids bloom on the sleek welcome desk, and the screen above the receptionist's head shows a continuous loop of stock markets in New York, London and Tokyo. A Nespresso machine is ever ready to offer visitors espressos, cappuccinos and lattes. Appearances have been kept up.

I get the same ugly feeling each time I enter the warehouse, as though somebody has kicked me in the belly. I pretend to sift through the invoices and credit notes on my desk, aware of Margaret's eyes following me. She's waiting for me to shout an order, fix a meeting, make a phone call.

I joke around with the few girls still left in the warehouse. My favourite joke is about exhibiting at the major convention in Paris.

'This time next year we'll have a stand at the Prêt Apparel, right next to the big boys from London. We'll have cocktails near the Eiffel Tower in the evening and watch the sun set on the Seine,' I say, watching their faces to see if they can sniff the bullshit.

At twelve, Margaret nips out to Kostas, a Cypriot chippy around the corner, and brings me a bacon butty and a mug of strong builder's tea with plenty of milk and sugar.

Esther ticked me off the first time she saw me drinking PG Tips and eating sliced white bread. She recommended Twinings and sourdough. In Esther's world, I'd be sipping champagne, eating organic food and attending charity lunches.

There are days when I waste time flicking through pages of old order ledgers. I've kept them all. 1984 was a good year. There were orders from Debenhams and BHS, and there was even interest from Harrods. The day I delivered my samples to Harrods the head buyer treated me to oysters for lunch, and he pointed out Fayed as he swept through the restaurant like a god, his small figure almost carried aloft between two burly minders.

'Can I get a picture with him?' I asked, puffed up with confidence. But the buyer said Mr Fayed was a very exclusive man. I bought Amar a teddy bear with the Harrods logo emblazoned in big, gold letters across its sweater. Geeta grumbled about the price, as usual. But all that was a long time ago.

* * *

'Malik Textiles – how can I help?' Margaret's voice is too eager as she picks up the phone, pen in hand, order book open.

It's a wrong number. I go back to flicking through the old order books until it is time to meet Esther. I don't make excuses any more. I just get up and leave, but I always make a big show of tidying up my desk, making sure the papers are neatly piled on top of each other.

'See you tomorrow,' Margaret says, not looking up from whatever she's not doing. 'Have a good one.' I'm not sure what she means.

'Have a nice day, PK,' Grace, the receptionist, shouts out as I leave. I had sent her on a Dale Carnegie course, back in the day when the office was flooded with visitors and making a good impression counted. She's hung on to the American plastic politeness. I like that about her – the refusal to go down with the sinking ship.

I'm halfway down the M60 when I realise I've left my wallet behind. I turn back. It's only three o'clock, but the girls from the stitching floor are already at the gate. I wait quietly in the car, engine idling, watching them head towards the George and Dragon across the road.

'The girls left early,' I mention casually to Margaret, who is still sitting at her desk, tongue hanging out, probably pencilling around job vacancies in the Greater Manchester area.

She shrugs. 'There's not much work. There's no point in them hanging around,' she says.

'Are you blaming me for that?' My fingers curl into a fist.

She says I'm too busy being busy to notice things and hands me a letter. It's an enquiry for shrouds from the NHS. A big order – nearly five thousand of them, to be ready for the first of January.

'January is peak time for dying,' Margaret says. 'A lonely Christmas and the cold – it finishes them off. The oldies can't face another year of it.' She kisses the silver cross around her neck and shudders.

'I think we should go for this NHS order, PK. It's a big volume, and it will be a foot in the door. If we get it they might send an enquiry for surgeon's gowns next. We can't afford to be too choosy these days,' she says.

'We don't do this kind of basic stuff,' I reply. 'You know that, Margaret. We're the high end of the low end.'

'The girls have too much time on their hands,' she insists. 'It'll keep everybody busy.'

'Shrouds are unlucky,' I say, picking up my wallet from the desk. 'My father always said that. And what kind of skill does it take? Tell me that. We might as well ship in some gunny sacks from Dacca and stuff the bodies in.'

* * *

A new sort of schedule starts to dictate the slow, quiet poison of these days, following a compass swinging between work, home and Esther. I casually stroll into the Didsbury Queen, place my cash on the counter and ask if room six is free. It always is. Soon Marvin, the receptionist, stops holding my fifty-pound note up to the light – I have become a regular. Sometimes I slip him a tenner, just to remind him not to ask questions. I even crack a joke or two. That's how invincible I feel.

Us. Esther. Me. We grow familiar with the afternoon slant of shadows across our hotel bed. Cedric travels a lot, building up his business empire in Eastern Europe, and I start leaning more on Margaret, sending her to meetings in my place and cancelling appointments so I can be with Esther. Geeta has started leaving my dinner on a plate by the microwave. But she still stays up for me, waiting until she hears my step in the front hall.

'The gods are smiling on us,' I tell Esther.

She touches her Magen David pendant. 'Don't tempt the gods. They can be cruel.' Esther, otherwise so different to Geeta, is so much like her when it comes to fearing God. She goes to synagogue every weekend and speaks of her rabbi in quiet, hushed tones.

'What do you think the rabbi would say about this?' I joke while we're lying in bed together, my hand on her thigh, my mouth nuzzling the nape of her neck.

She gives me a long, steady look.

'What we do inside this room has nothing to do with him. It is our birthright to be happy.'

I've not made another person happy in a long time. I'm grateful to Esther.

* * *

The Didsbury Queen is like my warehouse, an unfinished dream. The Pakistani owners who set it up have fled to Dubai, hounded by debt collectors and the taxman. The paint is peeling, the bannisters are broken and the pile of free circulars and newspapers on the reception desk grows higher each week. Even Marvin is biding his time. He studies accountancy in the evenings at a local adult-education centre and has dreams of starting again in Australia.

'Sydney's the place for me,' he says. 'This country's fucked, man. They're letting in too many immigrants. Who the hell can afford a hotel room these days, except hookers and married men having a fuck on the side?' He winks.

I lean on the counter and offer him a cigarette, making small talk, killing time until the clack of high heels and cloud of perfume announces Esther's arrival, the promise of good times in her eyes.

He accepts the cigarette grudgingly. He's trying to give up smoking – not because of his health, but because of the cost. 'It's nearly a fiver for a packet. Can you believe it? It's the government's way of screwing the poor.' There's rage in his voice. 'Kill every little joy they have. Beat them back into their hole. Do they put taxes on hunting, these posh boys, or shooting with the la-di-das?' He spits contemptuously into the wastepaper basket.

'Is business no good? How come I never see anyone else here?' I ask. I've never seen another guest loitering in the lobby or scuttling up to their room.

'It's mostly asylum types,' he says. 'Somalis and Bangladeshis. They spend a night or two before being shooed off to deportation centres. They hide in their rooms, eating their smelly food and praying. But why would you care? You're a rich guy with money to burn.'

I like being called rich. Although money is tight and my mortgage is sky high, we're still better off than those we've left behind.

I think of my house in south Manchester, my Merc with its personal number plate and my warehouse the size of two football fields. The world of refugees and the homeless isn't my world. If only Father had seen it. But he never got around to visiting England. I wanted him to see my house, take him to watch cricket at Lord's, go for a spin in my Mercedes. I wanted him to walk the length of the warehouse, sucking in his breath at the size and scale of it. I wanted him to see me as I saw myself – a success. It never happened. He never set foot in my house.

Going through his belongings after his death, I found the business-class tickets I'd sent him lying intact in their blue plastic sleeve. Next to them was a bundle of letters from Geeta, which she had dutifully written every month. They hadn't been opened. Father died still thinking I was a loser.

Esther and I are good together. These are afternoons of unhurried love and conversation. Sometimes she gives me suggestions, nuggets she's heard from Cedric in passing – 'I think animal prints are going to be big next summer,' or 'Why don't you branch out into home furnishings?' One day, when I show her my drawings, she says, 'You have a knack for design. Just look at the way you've nipped in the waist of this peasant blouse and teamed it with velvet trousers. Why don't you go into couture, PK? Leave the low-cost stuff to low-cost minds?'

'I don't think I can,' I say. 'I should have done it years ago, but at fifty-five I think I'm too late.' And there the conversation ends.

The slow unbuckling of a belt, the soft tearing of a zip being pulled down, the weight of her bare foot in the palm of my hand, the unhurried rub of our bodies against each other. These are heady days. I begin to love Esther for all this and more. Her shoes are usually suede with a four-inch heel. They're hopelessly unsuited to the rain, which is beating against the window of our hotel room, but I love her for the impracticality of these shoes, for the fragility of her silk dresses, for her increasing childish belief that us being together is the result of some divine destiny.

She never tires of telling me how good I'd looked that evening at Mowbray Hall. 'In your new-new suit with the cigarette held tight against your mouth and the sleepy way you spoke. I couldn't take my eyes off you.'

'All love stories are accidents,' I reply. 'A crazy lurch in the dark, and if we're lucky someone steps out to catch us, to break our fall.

I close my eyes and hold on to her, my fingers running through her hair, lingering and exploring the back of her neck, stroking the dark dusting of freckles on her naked shoulder.

'I wish I'd met you before,' I say, 'when I was free and young.'

'Don't think of before and after. Think of now,' she says.

* * *

The Didsbury Queen begins to feel like home. A different kind of home that doesn't carry the staleness or sadness of my Timperley house. Esther starts bringing things to the hotel – little titbits of her life for us to enjoy: candles, a crystal vase, even bottles of champagne swaddled in fragrant tissue, all carried inside a grey Gucci overnighter she pulls behind her with the primness of a BA air hostess.

I watch her light the candles. They smell rich and expensive, just like her. 'Where did you buy them?'

'From a little bijou shop in Paris, just behind the Avenue Montaigne.' She pronounces the name the way a French person would. 'A delightful place. It's been there for nearly a hundred years. You must know it?'

I know the road, all right. One afternoon I'd ditched the trade show at the Parc des Expositions and took the metro to the heart of the city. I spent hours lingering outside the dove-grey windows of the Dior showroom on Avenue Montaigne, finally plucking up the courage to go inside. The shop girls with their tailored suits and tight chignons followed me as I went from railing to railing, my greedy hands running over the furs and the silks. They stood at the front door and watched me leave, their faces expressionless.

To me Paris is a city of budget hotels on the Périphérique and cold crêpes and free airport shuttles to the prêt-à-porter shows on the fringes of the city, where tall apartment blocks raise their ugly heads to the sky. I've only ever managed to see the Eiffel Tower once, and even then in a rush between sample-shopping excursions. It looked like a giant misplaced electric pylon.

'My Paris is very different to yours,' I confess to Esther, my hand closing around her breast, my cheek resting against the soft mound of her stomach. There are parts to her I'm still discovering, like the ink-blue mermaid tattoo under her belly button, just above the thick flair of her woman's hair.

I want a picture of us in moments like these. My breath warm and urgent upon her skin, the afternoon sun sneaking in through the broken slats of the window blind, our taste, smell and touch mixing until I forget where my flesh ends and hers begins. I want to store the knowledge of such moments deep within me, so when darkness comes calling I can unfold this memory and relive it.

'Do you ever think of me when we are away from each other?' I ask her.

'Sometimes,' she says, and smiles. 'I'm also a wife and a mother. Life gets in the way, and I have to forget that a wonderful, caring mensch is waiting for me in a shabby hotel room.'

We straddle two separate worlds that could collide and disintegrate at any time.

There are days when Esther's mobile is silent or she fails to turn up at the hotel. I'm no different. I shut the hotel door, walk out on to the street and get so caught up in drumming up new business or fretting over Amar's grades that it takes me a while to remember the taste of Esther's mouth or the way her body opens up to mine.

We are married and middle-aged and tied for ever to other lives. The thought of Geeta and Cedric lingers inside our hotel room like a party balloon long after the party has ended. We try to chase the thoughts away – they have no meaning inside our bed, inside our love – but I don't think we ever succeed.

Dear Lopa didi,

Do you ever have to heat up Jijaji's dinner in the microwave? It is happening often to me now. PK comes home late, looking moody and angry. He suddenly has so many new customers that he has to entertain – but then he also says business is bad. I don't get it. He comes home, goes straight to the fridge and asks for food. He is always hungry. He eats the food standing by the sink, not bothering to even heat it up unless I microwave it for him. Afterwards it's straight to bed. I am worried about him. It was enough dealing with Amar's bed-wetting, but now it's like having two teenagers in the house. He doesn't want to be romantic any more. I wear new nighties and put on lipstick, but nothing doing. I know you will say it's because I am fat. But my snacks are the only thing keeping me happy nowadays. What exercise should I do? Easy for you to say it. You can go with your friends to the Hanging Gardens or walk on Marine Drive. There is no sea here in Manchester. It's always raining and cold. At least my garden is beautiful. That's one good thing about the rain – it makes the grass stay green all year around. If only the sun would shine, then PK's mango tree would grow. So many years and it's still an ugly little stump. You are right – I will try Weight Watchers. There will be a centre near me. Maybe I will ask Mrs Ahmed to join me. I won't ask the other Indian ladies. They will laugh at me. I will be a joke in the community.

Geeta

19

A HISTORY TOGETHER

One day Esther doesn't show up at the hotel. I stand by the window willing her red Mini to appear. Her mobile rings out and I don't have a landline number. This is how it is – huge chunks of our lives remain beyond each other's reach. Our relationship is built on mobile-phone numbers and a pre-booked dingy hotel room.

When I get home Haroon and Geeta are having tea in the kitchen.

'What a surprise – you're home early,' Geeta says, just as the cuckoo clock chimes four. I wait until the bird has finished its irritating jingle before trotting out my usual excuse of a cancelled meeting. I speak carefully, giving a detailed account of the meeting, but I make sure my face is averted from Geeta's questioning eyes.

Haroon stands up clumsily to greet me, spilling some tea on his shirt. Dressed in a white shirt and tie, he looks as though he's on his way to a Wall Street boardroom rather than giving maths tuition to a sulky teenager in Timperley.

'How is everything, Uncle? Have some tea with us,' Haroon says. He remains standing respectfully.

I tell him I would prefer something stronger. I go to the drinks cabinet in the lounge and find it locked.

'I've got the key,' Geeta says. She's followed me. 'Why don't you have tea instead? It's too early for alcohol.'

'I've had a stressful day. I need a drink.' I say, extending my hand.

She sighs and fishes out the key from inside her bra. Geeta's bra functions like a kangaroo's pouch: keys, the odd five-pound note, bills she's trying to forget all find their way into the talcum-powder-scented Marks and Spencer D cup.

I drink the whisky neat, straight from the bottle. A generous swig and I'm better. Esther is probably caught up in some domestic drama. I can call her later.

When I join them back in the kitchen, Haroon and Geeta are deep in conversation. With his head cocked to one side, a foot tapping under the table, Haroon is filling her in on gossip about Mrs Ahmed's mother-in-law, who is visiting from Pakistan and has overstayed her visitor's visa.

Geeta listens, rapt, stirring more and more sugar into her tea.

'How is Amar doing with maths? Any progress? He's terrified of algebra,' I interrupt them. I'm not paying Haroon ten pounds an hour for him to be sitting around chit-chatting with Geeta.

He glances at Geeta, who leans forward and squeezes his arm.

'Amar has forgotten about today's lesson, naughty little child. He's at Alice's house. Haroon will make sure he catches up next time,' she says, reassuring me.

Haroon nods energetically. 'Of course, Aunty. Amar just needs practice, that's all. He is a bright boy. He showed me his paintings the other day – good stuff.'

Bright? Nobody has ever called Amar that before. Maybe Haroon has spotted his potential. I'm beginning to like him, and am even thinking of offering him a part-time job in accounts. Sometimes the numbers make my head spin. A young brain would juggle them better.

'Uncle, you have a Mercedes, right? A silver one with a personalised number plate?' He suddenly pipes up.

Haroon has his mouth full. He's snacking on the Bombay mix and salted peanuts that Geeta has placed in little brown Pyrex bowls on the table.

'Yes, I do. Let me know if you want to go for a spin.'

'I think I saw you driving it last week. I was at the bus stop on the top of Elm Road and you drove past. I waved, but you didn't see me.'

Geeta corrects him and says he is wrong. My warehouse is in Grotton, which is miles away.

Like a dog after a bone, Haroon won't let go. 'I'm sure it was your number plate, Uncle, PK1.' He repeats the registration number, shaking his head like Peter Sellers.

The front door slams and Amar comes in, his school satchel slapping against his thigh. He goes straight to the fridge. He hasn't seen Haroon. 'Anything good to eat, Mum? I'm starving,' he calls over his shoulder.

'Haroon is here for your lesson. You forgot, didn't you?' Geeta laughs, treating it all like a joke.

The Bombay mix is almost finished. Haroon and she are starting on the salted peanuts.

'You've still got half an hour of your lesson left. Just go upstairs with Haroon and you can eat later,' I say, reaching once more for the Scotch.

So Haroon saw my car near the hotel. What else had he seen? I can't be sure. He is young and inquisitive, with time on his hands. I don't want him hanging around Geeta any longer.

'He's quite a lazy fellow, this Haroon,' I say to Geeta as soon as the door shuts behind them. 'I've got a gut feeling about him. Let's get rid of him and find someone more competent.'

'But he is such a polite boy,' she replies. 'Strange how he thought he recognised your car. Where is this Elm Road?' She's clearing up the table and getting ready to start on dinner.

'He was seeing things. I'll just go and check on the mango tree.'

'Don't water it again. It's drunk enough rain to last it a lifetime,' she calls after me.

* * *

Out of earshot, I ring Esther. She picks up this time, but her voice is low and guarded.

'So sorry, my mensch, I couldn't make it today.' I hear the sound of running water and the toilet flushing.

I walk deeper into the garden, into the shadow of the hedge dividing our garden from Mr Peters. 'Where are you, Esther? I waited for you.'

I can see Geeta's silhouette through the patio door. She's hunched over the hob, stirring a pot.

'It's Cedric.' Esther's voice is tearful. 'He came home early complaining of a sore head. It was impossible to get away.'

'Couldn't you have made an excuse?' I feel bitter.

'You should see him, swaddled in bed like a baby, holding on to his blackberry and begging me to make him chicken soup,' she says, and laughs.

'And you were so busy nursing him you couldn't spare a minute to text me? I felt like a right idiot waiting alone in that room.'

'I'm his wife,' she says, and her voice hardens.

I imagine her sitting at her husband's side, an arm around his shoulder, feeding him his favourite soup. She would have made it just the way he liked it – not too much pepper, the chicken shredded to a soft consistency. He would belch his satisfaction and they'd lie down together, maybe discuss their children or holiday plans. They have history together. They will always have it. Just as I share a history with Geeta. However broken or flawed it might be. How long can I go on ignoring this? Our time together is borrowed. We have no right to own it.

'Perhaps it's best we don't meet, Esther,' I tell her. 'You'll always be a wife, and I'm still a husband.'

The patio doors open. 'Dinner's ready, come inside,' Geeta calls.

* * *

The next day I find Geeta sitting on the settee, the remote sleeping in her lap, the television on mute. Two bottles of Slim Fast chocolate milkshake sit on the table, untouched. The room feels sad without the friendly babble of the television, as though a family member had died or suddenly left the house.

She's staring into the garden.

'What's wrong?' I ask. 'How come the TV's not on?' I sit down beside her. Our legs touch, her plump thighs warm against mine.

She says she isn't in the mood to watch anything.

Rain begins to fall.

'This rain isn't good for the mango tree,' I say, looking out at the garden.

My tree stands forlorn, a skeleton of brown twigs. It looks like a refugee next to the thick, lush green of the other trees and shrubbery – an intruder with sad memories of sunshine days woven into its bark. It's no different to Geeta, who continues to live in the shadow of her sunlit Bombay youth.

'It was a mistake,' I say. 'I should never have brought it here. I don't think it'll survive another winter.'

Geeta says she's bought some mulch from the garden centre – she knows the mango tree is my pride and joy. 'Don't worry. Maybe this year it'll finally show some leaves.'

'I'll put the mulch down this weekend,' I reply. 'It should help with the rot.'

We sit there looking out. The tree is still only a foot high, standing just to the right of Geeta's washing line. It looks insignificant beneath the grey Manchester sky.

'If only the sun would shine,' Geeta says.

I light a cigarette and remind her she lives in the north-west of England. 'The sun is always on strike here.'

She doesn't find it funny.

'I thought you were going to quit smoking?' she says. 'You promised.'

'I've said before, it is not easy giving up things. How would you feel if I told you I was cancelling the Zee TV subscription?' The silence grows uncomfortable. There'll be more questions soon.

'I am thinking of starting a computer course – a beginner's course at Trafford College. Things like Excel and emails,' Geeta says suddenly, brushing unseen fluff from her blue tracksuit. Her hands fold into little fists in her lap.

'What's this new interest in computing?' I ask. 'Remember I paid up for your yoga classes at the Valley Lodge. How many did you attend? Two? Three, max?'

'It's different this time. I have more time,' she says, the frown lines slicing across her forehead deepening – a forehead that was once smooth and shiny like a baby's bottom. 'You are always busy with your work. I hardly see you any more. If I learn computing then I can start coming to the office with you, help look over the accounts. It's always good to have an extra pair of eyes – a family member you can trust.' She speaks cautiously, as though reciting a rehearsed speech.

'How do you think the staff will feel about the boss's wife coming in? Margaret will think she's not needed any more, and I can't afford to lose her. Anyway, you'll only come in to work for a week, and then you'll get bored – you'll want to meet Gupta's wife or go to the temple or a kitty lunch, and then what?'

'But I want to do something useful. Amar's growing up fast. He doesn't need me that much any more.'

'Why don't you just relax? Be like the other women in the community – join an aerobics class or something, do Meals on Wheels, go to Gandhi Hall.' I was trying to be helpful.

Her face turns away, she opens her fists, spreads open her palms and places them on her lap. She's examining the lines that criss-cross the plump pale flesh. Her face is like a room where the lights have been switched off.

Dear Lopa didi,

This is the second letter I'm writing you this week. I hate our phone calls. There is never enough time to say everything. It's 'How are you? How are the kids?' and before you know it, time's up. Anyway, I hate dieting. I went to one Weight Watchers class and that was enough. It was in a cold church hall and there were lots of English ladies sitting around, chatting with each other. When it was my turn to go on the scales, the organiser kept saying, Hurry up, hurry up – I had that many layers of clothing to take off. The others were in leggings and T-shirts. I'm not telling you my weight. It's double what you think I am. You can't eat this, you can't eat that – that's what the organiser said afterwards. She looked like a fat pig herself. The worst thing we can eat is our Indian curries. The whole class giggled when she said this. I felt so ashamed. I'm not going to make bean casserole or rhubarb pie – there's nothing wrong with our dal chawal. Anyway, I'm going to start computer lessons. This way I can reactivate my brain and help PK, and also keep an eye on him. He is drinking too much whisky, and whenever I ring the office Margaret always says he's busy or out at a meeting. I think George Bush and Tony Blair have more time on their hands.

Geeta

20

POLLUTING THE GODS

The empty look in Geeta's eyes troubles me. I think of ways of making her feel better. I put up the shelves in the garage she's been asking for and I order her a new washing machine from John Lewis – a top-of-the-range Miele with a five-year guarantee. One day, when she's at the temple, I arrange for a cleaning agency to come and scrub the house until it shines like new.

'How much did the cleaner cost?' Geeta asks, moving the sofas to check for dust on the skirting boards, drawing the curtains and running her finger down the windowpane, her fingerprints leaving a smudge behind.

'I had to get a loan from the bank,' I say. It's a joke, but she doesn't get it.

'You didn't…!' The handbag falls from her hand.

'It's a joke, Geeta, just a joke,' I say, patting her cheek. 'Lighten up, please, will you? I was just trying to make you happy.'

She's confused. 'Why are you trying to make me happy?' she says.

The next day, her eyes question me over her mug of tea. 'What's got into you?' she says. Instead of her usual bowl of crisps, a plate of chopped carrots and celery sit next to the teapot. She picks up a carrot stick and starts munching it slowly, laboriously. 'It feels like when we first came to this country. You were always so busy around the house, fixing things. And Friday was flower day – fresh flowers on your way back from work. Always roses, and when I complained about the cost you said beauty didn't have a price tag.' She has remembered my words, has carried them inside her all these years.

'Why are you bombarding me with questions?' I snap. 'Just be happy I'm doing stuff.'

Then Amar comes lumbering into the kitchen, making his way directly to the fridge. 'Mum, didn't you buy any Krispy Kreme doughnuts?'

'No doughnuts for you, mister. You're coming to the gym with me,' I say, pinching the roll of fat hanging over his school trousers, making him yelp. 'Time to get rid of this muffin top.'

I'm talking and behaving like a father, but deep down inside a small voice whispers, 'How long will this last?'

* * *

'Your head's in the clouds these days,' Gupta says when we meet at the Victoria. 'I've not seen you in ages.'

'Work is tough. Takes up all my time.' I raise my beer glass so it hides my eyes. My time is taken up by Esther – meeting her, thinking of her, dreaming of her. At fifty-five, I have become a giddy-eyed teenager, no longer in control.

'Work!' He spits out the word. 'Bullshit! You're not that much of a big shot. You need a schedule, little goalposts to navigate your days.' He smirks and sits back, arms folded, pleased with his homily. He's a great believer in rituals. Thursdays were the days he met me for a drink and fucked his wife; on Saturdays he did the weekly shop at Tesco, and on Tuesdays he checked his bank statements. His life ran in columns and figures, while mine felt like graffiti on a public-toilet wall.

A young woman comes in and walks up to the bar, a tight black skirt hugging her backside. In the old days Gupta would've nudged me – maybe even gone up to the counter to get a better look – but not today.

'What's wrong?' I raise my eyebrows. 'Aren't you going to pay her a compliment? Pass comment?'

'She's hot,' he admits. His eyes slide off my face and wander over to her. She has big breasts. Gupta had a weakness for those. As a student he'd bring home a shelf-load of Swedish magazines and lock himself in the bathroom for hours.

'Forget her. Tell me about the kids – how are they doing?' I didn't really want to talk about women when I knew it would just make me think about Esther.

'Anju's finishing the secretarial course next year,' he says, his face beaming with pride.

'And Ankit?'

The son is the black sheep of the Gupta family. He is studying literature at Hull. He's not interested in becoming a banker or a lawyer – he wants to be a poet. His choice sent shock waves through Manchester's Indian community, Geeta had told me gleefully. 'Mrs Kapoor and Mrs Sharma were horrified. Do I know their sons were studying finance at LSE? Yes, at least they'll get jobs with banks like J.P. Morgan. But there's no such hope for Gupta's son. He'll become a teaching assistant in a red-brick uni, begging for grants.' Ankit is the Amar of their family, muddling his way through life. At least their daughter has a future.

'What are Ankit's plans?' I go on. 'He can't bury his head inside books for ever.'

'Oh, him…' He snorts. 'He wants to go to Paris and write poems. He expects me to pay his bills.'

'Hey, steady on. He might be the next Shakespeare one day!'

'He might be more like skint one day. By the way,' he starts, apparently suddenly remembering something, 'were you in west Didsbury last week? It was a Tuesday. I'm sure it was you.' He's examining my face like a traveller poring over a map.

The pub goes quiet. A loud ticking starts up inside my head.

'Didsbury? It can't have been me, can't have been… I was at work at the warehouse. I had customers that day,' I gush, staring into my pint of beer.

Gupta shakes his head. 'It was you, all right. You were coming out of this hotel on Elm Road. You must have been checking in your Bangladeshi supplier. What's his name now? Ali? Aziz?'

A way out. 'Oh yes, I remember now. It was Ali. He wanted to stay somewhere central and cheap,' I say, frowning at the trivial detail as though I disapprove.

'Some shithole you put him in! Try the Holiday Inn near your office next time,' Gupta says. 'They give you loyalty points, too.'

'How come you were hanging around in Didsbury? Have you moved office?' It's my turn to probe.

'They've dumped me with a new account – Hades and Sons. A funeral parlour. Can you imagine what I've been reduced to? Settling the accounts of the dead.' He scowls.

'Cheer up, it could be worse.' I slap him on the shoulders and take out my car keys. The pub is filling up, and the girl with the nice boobs has disappeared. 'Let's go. You have a busy night ahead.' I wink to show him I've not forgotten about his Thursday nights.

Gupta lowers his voice. 'Sex is not always so easy these days. I get sleepy. To be honest, I'd rather watch cricket on the telly instead.' He shrugs.

His wife would be waiting in bed, her petticoat rolled up high around her dimpled thighs, a romantic Lata Mangheshkar song playing in the cassette player on the windowsill. Once, long ago, that was my love story too.

We get up to leave and Gupta hands me an invite. It is for an evening satsang, a prayer meeting at the Jai Govind temple in Chorlton. 'It's next Friday. Bring the family. The prayers will start at five sharp – BST, not IST. Preeti Bhojan will be served promptly afterwards.'

'Why are you doing this nonsense?' I toss the invite with its picture of a grinning blue flute-playing Krishna on the table.

'It's a simple thank-you to God, that's all,' Gupta says. 'The wife's wanted to do something for a long time, and now that the children are grown up—'

'What's there to be thankful about?' I interrupt. 'You just told me you're doing a dead man's accounts and your son's turned out to be a poet.'

'England's been good to us, PK,' he says, clicking his briefcase shut. 'I've got my house, my car, a lifelong pension. I don't know about you, but I have a lot to be thankful for.'

This is Gupta's problem. Always ready to settle for bite-sized pieces of happiness.

'Bullshit!' I spit out. 'Who knows what we might have become had we stayed on in India or gone to America.'

Gupta folds his right hand into a fist and slams it on the table. The invite slips off the table and lands near my feet. Gupta picks it up, presses it to his forehead and his chest, does the sign of a cross and finally slips it inside his jacket pocket.

'That's the trouble with you, PK,' he finishes. 'Always wanting more out of life. Look at me, I'm just grateful to have a life.'

I promise to attend the prayers. Geeta loves going to the temple. It would mean chatting about the latest Hindi films and free vegetarian food that flows like the Ganges.

* * *

The following Friday Geeta's ready for the temple, in her going-out silk sari, a beige pashmina shawl folded neatly over her arm. Amar stands next to her in an ironed checked shirt and his smart grey school trousers. He's fiddling with the Nintendo DS in his hand.

I pretend to read the papers, a mug of tea in my hand.

'Still not ready? We will be late,' Geeta says.

'I thought I'd work on the garden for a bit and join you later. The mango tree needs some more pesticide,' I say, and pick up my gardening gloves and go to pull out a gardening manual from the shelf that holds Geeta's cookery books. I'd bought a book on Capability Brown after the trip to Mowbray Hall.

'We'll be late for the temple,' she repeats.

'Indian things never start on time,' I answer.

Geeta's mouth turns down, the slow, tilting sag of disappointment spreading out. One day her face will collapse, like the walls of a house bulldozed in slow motion. She has looked forward to the temple and the social catch-up with the other women, and here I am, intent on spoiling it for her.

'I know what we'll do,' I say, smiling brightly at both mother and son. 'I can drop you at the temple, pop into B&Q, pick up some stuff, catch up on the gardening and join you later.'

I'm proud at how simple and effortless I've made it all sound. But there is nothing to be proud of in what I am going to be doing.

* * *

Our lover's tiff is forgotten.

'I am full of sadness, PK. And this sadness has everything to do with you,' Esther says, folding herself inside my arms. 'We've not seen each other for a month.'

'Twenty-two days,' I correct her. I stroke the pale silk of the blond hairs on her arms. So many months together, but here she is, still new, still exciting. Still so different to Geeta.

'Didn't you miss me…?' She pauses and her fingers slip down, holding me long enough to make me forget Gupta and Geeta and the bright blue flute-playing statue of Lord Krishna waiting for me in the temple.

Esther has just returned from a trip to New York. 'It was exhausting. All those charity dinners and self-centred speeches. The hypocrisy of it all! The donor set – all they're after is an invite to the White House,' she says.

'I wouldn't know,' I reply. 'Signing charity cheques is a luxury I've not had. Too busy keeping up with my mortgage payments.' I say this quietly and she doesn't seem to hear me.

* * *

Being away from each other for so long has made us greedy for love. Afterwards Esther is happy to stay in bed, her bare legs entwined in mine, her hair tickling my nostrils.

One long arm reaches out lazily for her bag, which lies on the floor besides the bed. She pulls out a brightly wrapped packet and gives it to me. The orange gauze wrapping paper is embossed with an intricate navy-blue paisley print.

'Go on, open it, open it!' she says, clapping her hands together, her eyes shining.

I unwrap the parcel. It's a tie – an expensive Hermès with a parade of tiny elephants embroidered across the centre. Nestling beneath the tie is a two-CD set, *The Best of Neil Diamond*.

'You can listen to it when you're on the road visiting customers. And you can wear the tie when you win business contracts. It's going to be your lucky tie.' She sounds like a child.

'I'll keep the music, but you'd better keep the tie – Geeta will ask questions.'

'Why would she know? Is she in charge of your wardrobe?' She gives me a searching look.

'I'll wear it when we go somewhere special,' I say.

'Well, why don't we go somewhere special, then, instead of always meeting in this dump?' She pulls away from me, her face averted, her arms folded and unyielding.

'I agree it's a dump, but it's the safest place to meet,' I say. 'No one will think of finding us here,' I add, forgetting for a moment that both Haroon and Gupta have spotted me on the street.

'I spend hours thinking of all the things we'll do,' Esther says. 'We'll go to restaurants, do ordinary, happy things that people in love do. And then I realise that we'll never get to do even half those things – there's a taxi meter ticking all the time between us. Everything's so rushed. It's like playing hide and seek with life.'

'Where can we go?' I say, looking over at the window, criss-crossed with metal bars, and the slow, sickly spread of damp across the ceiling above it. The world is small when you're betraying a family.

But Esther has plans. Her body relaxes and she nuzzles her face against my cheek. 'Let's go to Europe, darling. What about Spain? We won't meet a soul.' She makes it sound simple and effortless.

Swept away in her excitement, I agree. It would be easy to slip away for a night or two. I could invent a trade fair or a business meeting. 'Let's go for it,' I say, feeling as reckless and brave as a twenty-year-old on the verge of a new life.

* * *

The sky is tinted with darkness and the prayers are over by the time I reach the temple. I hesitate at the door. Gupta, his head bowed and hands folded, is sitting with his family at the front, near the statues. Elaborate silver platters of fruit and flowers are arranged like a boundary wall in front of the deities.

His wife bends forward and rearranges the fruits, shifting the apples and the oranges, forming them into little pyramids. Geeta and Amar sit behind the Guptas. Geeta keeps turning around, fidgeting with the shawl around her shoulders. Sitting on the floor can't have been easy on her knees. She spots me, and her trusting face breaks into a smile.

She pats the empty space next to her, but I shake my head. I have no business polluting the gods. She whispers something to Gupta, who's swaying his head to the beat of the cymbals.

He gets up and makes his way towards me, stopping to greet his English colleagues, who sit on chairs at the back of the room, fanning themselves with the invite.

'You're running on Indian Shit Time,' Gupta hisses, and holds out his wrist for me to check his watch. 'You've missed the best bits. Guruji was talking about the family and how to bring up your kids with the right Indian values.' The Guru had been specially flown in from India for the occasion.

'He looks costly,' I whisper to Gupta.

'Actually, I got a real deal,' he whispers back. He was in Manchester for a wedding – some big-shot from Hale flew him over – and this appearance is a bit of extra pocket money on the side. He's going on to Birmingham and Derby before flying back to his ashram in Kanpur.

Perched on a round orange cushion, his backside spilling over the corners, the Guru surveys the room, bird-like eyes darting around. The white sandal-paste tilak on his forehead is smudged, and tiny white droplets travel slowly down his nose like a row of ants. His small feminine hands hold the mic cautiously, as though it's an egg he's afraid to crack. I recognise the tune he's humming. It's the Gayatri Mantra. My mother often used to sing it in the mornings as she watered the Tulsi plant on the balcony.

The prayers end and the action moves to the temple's dining hall, where the food is being distributed. Large brass pans filled with steaming dal, dhokla, pulao and halwa rest on long trestle tables. The air smells of sandalwood incense, old socks and fried poppadoms.

There's a frenzied scramble as people rush to the shoe racks, trying to retrieve their shoes and sandals before grabbing their chairs at the table. I wait for my family to join me.

'You should have come inside and sat with us,' Geeta says. She's limping slightly, and holds on to Amar's elbow for support.

'Why didn't you sit on a chair?' I ask. 'Your knees aren't up to it.'

'It's disrespectful to the gods,' she says, and asks me again why I've been delayed.

'I was so busy in the garden I forgot the time. Sorry,' I say.

She nods understandingly. 'I know. That mango tree is like your second son.'

The Guru shuffles past us on his way out to a waiting cab.

'Guruji, Guruji…' Geeta catches hold of his arm. 'Please give an extra-special blessing for our family.' She pushes Amar forward and he bends his head obediently. The Guru shuts his eyes and blesses the bowed head, muttering something under his breath.

It's my turn next.

'Now, please, my husband, please. Blessings for his long life, for his business.' Geeta's voice rises in excitement.

The Guru looks at me, stares hard for a time, then shakes his head, wagging his finger like a disappointed teacher.

'No, not him. Not him,' he says, and then a lackey comes rushing over to tell him that the taxi is waiting.

21

WHEN DARKNESS CALLS

'I don't know why Guruji didn't bless you. Never mind, next time,' Geeta says when we get home. Her face is contented. She loves her temple outings.

'The food was yummy, but there wasn't enough for seconds, Mum,' Amar whines.

'I loved the carrot halwa. Kamala behan did a good job. It wasn't too oily this time,' Geeta adds, on her way to the television. She sees my gardening gloves on the kitchen table and picks them up. They're pristine – not a dab of mud on them. 'But you didn't do any gardening! Why did you come so late to the temple?' She holds the gloves delicately like a murder weapon.

'Accounts… I had to finish some accounts,' I mumble.

'But Margaret does the accounts.' Her forehead knits in worry.

I turn to Amar. He's by the fridge devouring a vanilla slice. I pinch the soft jelly flesh on his arm. 'Looks like you've stopped going to the gym. You should've seen me at your age – thin and strong like bamboo.'

'Leave him alone. He's a growing boy.' Geeta's voice rises. She asks Amar if he wants an omelette. She's already slicing the cheddar and cracking the egg.

The walls of the house and the family are closing in, crushing me with their small disappointments and small dreams.

'Stay longer with me, won't you,' Esther had said when I was ready to leave for the temple. She lay naked, the blanket carelessly thrown to the floor, the deep-blue vein in her collarbone pulsing quietly, her arms reaching out to stop me going.

'We'll go somewhere nice for the weekend. Something to look forward to,' I promised her as I left for the temple.

* * *

I sit at the kitchen table, thinking of my promise to Esther. But Amar is saying something. He's a blur, tugging my sleeve.

I hear him say he wants us to paint together. Would I please, please help him paint?

'What's the matter with you?' Geeta says. 'You're not even listening to your son. Is everything all right with accounts?' She stands at the sink, Marigolds on her hands, her dark eyes boring into mine, her hands frozen on their way to turn on the tap.

She must know. Surely, she must know. The thought sticks in my throat like a stone. I go to the sink, fill a glass with water and drink it quickly.

A feeling of unease enters the room, a foul smell only Geeta and I can detect. But Amar picks up on it too, and bursts into tears.

'You both look angry. Dad, are you angry with me? Mum, are you angry with me?' On and on he goes, his face blotchy with tears.

'Your mum is tired, that's all.' I say. 'Let's leave her in peace and go and do some painting.'

'You won't get bored watching me paint?' He's stopped crying, but his eyes are still worried.

'Course not. I'm your dad. I want to spend time with you.'

A smile splits his face. 'Mum, you have the omelette. I'm painting with Dad.'

We leave Geeta standing by the sink, a distracted look on her face.

'What's wrong with Mum? She looks awful,' Amar says.

'She is just tired. All that sitting on the floor at the temple and chit-chatting, it can drain anyone.'

Amar giggles. 'She's too fat,' he says. 'She needs to go on a diet. She'll be happy then.'

* * *

Amar's room is like a science lab, orderly and clean. His cleanliness is a constant surprise. He spends Sundays dusting every nook and cranny and then comes down wearing mismatching socks and a shirt smeared with food stains.

'I don't get it,' I used to say to Geeta. 'He forgets to shower, but he won't forget to plump the pillows on his bed.'

Neat rows of Encyclopaedia Britannica, still sealed in their plastic covers, stand like soldiers on the shelves. A travelling salesman had palmed them off to Geeta, spending hours talking to her about Scientology. The stack of red plastic IKEA boxes near the desk hold Amar's collection of Matchbox cars and dinosaur models.

While Amar hunts around for his paints I open his drawers, more out of boredom than curiosity. His pens are tied together with a rubber band and his notebooks are covered in the same brown paper. Geeta has printed his name and the subject on white labels in the centre of each cover. I check his wardrobe. T-shirts are stacked neatly, and there is a wire basket full of socks arranged by colour.

The walls aren't covered in the signs of boyhood you might expect – there are no Man U posters or cricketing heroes blu-tacked to the walls, only a large map of the world and a brass statue of Ganesh on the bedside table, placed there by Geeta for his night-time protection. I go over to the map and look at Europe, at places where I could escape with Esther for a weekend break.

Amar spreads a newspaper on the carpet and opens up his sketch pad. I yawn and walk over to his desk and open another drawer. A quick snoop into my son's life, that's all. There's a small Tupperware filled with sharpeners and staples and a set of postcards of Egyptian mummies from a school trip. It's all innocent stuff. I'm about to shut the drawer when I catch a glint of gold.

The corner of a magazine cover peeps out from under an atlas. The glossy finish reminds me of the magazines Gupta hoarded in our early days living together.

'Hey! What's this, Amar?' I show him the magazine. A naked blonde woman is on the front cover, sprawled on a bed, eyes shut, legs open, squeezing her own tits.

Amar goes quiet. His eyes turn shifty. He has the same look he used to have when he was a child and broke something precious.

'Where did you get this shit from?' I wave the magazine in his face. 'You're only fourteen, for God's sake. Who got it for you?' I imagine an older boy – a sixth former, perhaps – getting it for him.

'Alice gave it to me,' he admits, and slumps on to the bed, holding his head in his hands like an old man. Tears hang from the tip of his nose, and his eyes get puffy as he sobs.

'Why would she give you this rubbish?' I sit next to him, my arm around his sobbing shoulders. The world is a dark, dirty place, but I don't want its shadows falling on my son. Not just yet.

'Now you will hate me even more,' Amar snivels.

'I'm angry, but I don't hate you. How can a father hate his son?'

Easily, I think, my Father's face coming into view in my mind's eye. 'You are selling ladies' clothes?' he wrote back when I told him I'd jacked in the idea of going to America. 'You could've joined the civil service, become an ambassador, a brain surgeon, and you ended up fixing hemlines in Manchester. What a loser.'

I flick through the pages of Amar's magazine. Pornography doesn't move with the times. Things haven't changed much since my youth – the same bodies flaunting the same bits. I see Amar has scribbled and then crossed out what he's written on some of the pictures.

'This Alice…' I begin carefully. I want him to tell me more. 'Don't you think it's strange for a girl to give you this sort of thing?'

'She thinks I'm too much of a baby. I need to know about things. She takes them back after I've had a look. She says it's sex education.' There's no embarrassment in his voice.

'I don't think you should be her friend. This is dirty. You shouldn't be reading this.' I keep my voice low so Geeta can't hear us and come rushing up to defend him. I take some scissors from the desk and methodically go through each page of the magazine, slicing through each breast and buttock, until all that remains is a little mound of paper sitting forlornly in his rubbish bin.

'Good riddance,' I say. 'We've got rid of the filth. I have a good mind to ring Alice's mum and tell her about what's been going on.'

'No, Dad, she really is a nice person,' Amar insists. 'The other kids in the class laugh at me. They don't want to sit near me, but she eats her lunch with me and says it's not cool to play games. It's much better to paint.' He breathes out heavily; the long explanation has tired him out. I keep a firm grip on him, holding on until his shoulders sag and his head falls on my shoulder. His toes curl up in surrender.

He is wearing his favourite lime-green socks, the ones with Bugs Bunny embroidered on them. I just can't connect the smuttiness of the magazines he'd been reading with the childishness of those socks.

What can I do? I could ask Gupta, but his kids are college kids. He wouldn't remember the dark tunnel of temptation through which he has led them to light and safety.

'You hate me, Dad,' Amar repeats. 'It's there on your face. You have the same look you had when you hit me with the cricket ball.'

'That was an accident, Amar. Believe me, I didn't hit you on purpose. You know that, don't you?'

But he shakes his head and pulls away from me and falls back on his bed, dragging the duvet with the blue dinosaur print right over his face.

I sit beside him, my hands by my side like a dead weight, the skin hanging slack, the hair on the wrists grey. I came to fatherhood too late. I was in my forties by the time Amar was born. At fifty-five I lack the quickness and the alert nose to catch the scent of changing times. I look at Amar again. I see him as though I am seeing him for the first time. Memory works like that. There are gaping holes where once entire continents of emotion stood.

But there are some things I can never forget. I remember Amar as a newborn, checking him for all ten fingers and toes, studying his rosebud mouth, the soft fragility of his head.

'He is perfect,' I whispered to Geeta, grateful that he hadn't been born deformed or disabled or dead.

'He will make you proud,' she said. 'He'll be a great man when he grows up.' Geeta has always dreamt big when it comes to Amar.

'Maybe we should try for another child,' I said to Geeta on Amar's second birthday. 'It will be good for him to have someone to play with.' She agreed, even though her body was already battered with three miscarriages.

'Please don't make a scene, Dad. Please don't tell Mum,' Amar whispers in a tired voice. His voice floats up muffled and small through the duvet. 'Alice says she's got a roomful of them. She reads them every night. She's going to be mad at me.'

He says it isn't Alice's fault – he's to blame; he was curious; he'd seen a film and wanted to know more. 'I'll be fifteen soon,' he says.

'Look, I'm your dad. I can tell you about these things,' I reply hesitantly.

'But I don't want to listen to your lectures. You're always telling me off.' Amar throws away the duvet and hunches up, his belly pressing against his thighs. His hands fly up and press hard against his ears, as though he's blocking out my voice. He screws up his face and shouts, 'Headache! I have a headache. It's hurting me, where you hit me with the ball.'

I run to the landing and call out to Geeta. 'Get some water for Amar, Geeta, and his painkillers.'

He's done this before, collapsing with a headache or stomach cramps when pushed into a corner. There are things I want to tell Amar, but then I think of what I get up to in a hotel room with a woman who is not his mother. There are life lessons he needs to learn, but I'm not the right teacher. By sleeping with Esther I've abdicated all the duties of a good father.

Geeta soon arrives, bundling Amar into her arms, massaging his temple with Tiger balm, cooing to him until his breath steadies and he falls into a fitful sleep. I leave them, but as I leave my foot knocks against the paint pots Amar has arranged so neatly on a newspaper. The red paint slowly seeps out and bleeds into the carpet.

* * *

'Why was Amar so upset? Did you tick him off for something?' Geeta asks when we're getting ready for bed. She's brushing her teeth, but her eyes are on me in the mirror.

'His teachers say he has real talent. You should be encouraging him with his painting,' she continues.

'I'm sure he's got talent, but let's not fool ourselves that he's something great. I've seen his stuff. He uses unmixed colours, and it's all a bit basic. He's hardly going to be an M.F. Hussein or Picasso.' I remember the paintings I saw at the Manchester gallery with Esther on that long-ago afternoon when my life as I knew it started unravelling. I remember their grace and beauty.

She stops brushing her teeth. 'That's just so typical of you. You've never encouraged him.' The toothpaste daubs her lips white.

'He had a dirty magazine in his room. Did you expect me to encourage him in reading those? Maybe buy him an annual subscription?' My voice trembles with rage.

Geeta forgets to rinse the toothpaste out of her mouth. She sits on the bed, the toothbrush clutched tight in her hand like a magic wand. 'This wouldn't have happened if we had stayed back home. This place is corrupt. I see it on TV: girls as young as thirteen becoming pregnant.' Her face twists in disgust as she leans against the headboard, her eyes dark, hooded with unhappiness. Thirty years in Manchester and 'home' is still elsewhere. Home is still India.

'Don't be so melodramatic. He's a boy, he's growing up. I was surprised, that's all. I still see him as an overgrown baby.' I make light of things. 'But keep an eye on his friends. Keep an eye on that Alice.'

* * *

'Remember the computing course at the Trafford College I talked about?' Geeta says the next day. There are dark circles under her eyes. I'd heard her all night, shifting about the room, moving the knick-knacks on her dressing table, opening drawers and dragging out the suitcase she kept under our bed. She was looking at our wedding album.

'I told you I don't need you at the office. There is no need to go on any computing course. You won't like it.'

There's a pattern to Geeta's life that I'm just recognising. Every two years she enrols in a self-improvement course – yoga one year, Chinese cookery the next. A wave of enthusiasm lifts her and she rushes out to buy the stationery, the notebooks, the yoga mat, and then the wave subsides, she starts skipping classes, making excuses, and goes back to her television.

'I've already enrolled,' she says, and adds that the fee wasn't much.

'Don't you have enough things on your plate?' I ask.

Her voice is quiet and firm. 'You're never around these days. Nine days out of ten you ring me to say you won't be home for dinner. I don't want to just kill time, I want to be useful.' Her words rush out like beads rolling off a snapped necklace thread. 'I spoke to my sister in Bombay, and she said the same thing. "Geeta, get a job. Start a business. Start a life." Lopa didi has opened a boutique in her garage. She has hired a tailor, and she makes good money. In the evenings she is running laughter yoga classes on her terrace.' Geeta's already-small voice fades into a whisper.

I see her imagining her sister's life in Bombay, the cheerful hustle and bustle of it, while she sits here alone, flicking through the Asian channels on her TV, marooned on a distant rainy island.

I reach out and squeeze her shoulder. 'You're right. I think it's a good idea, Geeta. You'll make new friends.' She has every right to grab any happiness she can find. Aren't I doing the same?

Dear Lopa didi,
I did it. I rang up the college and asked if they had any computer courses for beginners.

I am so excited. It isn't cheap – two hundred pounds, or almost twenty thousand rupees. But it will keep me busy. The last few weeks have been very mixed. PK is being helpful around the house. He even organised a professional cleaner to come home. I think I can do a better job, to be honest, but it shows he cares. I wish he would be as caring towards Amar and the Guptas. He missed their important Puja at the temple, came right at the end. I know PK is very modern – he doesn't believe in God – but he could at least respect other people's feelings.

Amar had another meltdown. PK found a dirty magazine in his bedroom. It's this sneaky school friend of his – her name is Alice. She's no good. She wants Amar to get into trouble. Amar would never read such horrible stuff. He's still a child. But PK thinks he is corrupt. My head just starts spinning when I think of all this. I wish I could be there on your terrace, the sea wind blowing through my hair, practising laughter yoga and watching the sun set. But that's not my destiny.

Geeta

P.S. Congratulations on Chintu's results. To come first in final-year exams is no joke. All credit to the parents.

22

IS THIS HOW LIFE IS MEANT TO BE

Towards the end of summer, when the trees lining the roads sway under the weight of blossom and the sunlight hits the rooftops early in the morning, Esther and I catch a flight to Marbella. Just as she promised, she's organised everything: the dates, the tickets, the excuses we need to give. All I had to do was book a hotel and turn up at the airport, an overnight case in hand.

Getting away is easier than I had imagined. I leave for the office early while Geeta's still asleep. Later that morning, I ring home and explain that one of my shipments is stuck at customs. 'I've got to go to Dover to get it released. The shipping agent will meet me there. I might even have to stay a couple of days.'

'You didn't mention it before,' Geeta says. 'Aren't you coming home to pack?'

'There's no time,' I say. 'I'll pick up some stuff on the way. I'll be back by Sunday. It's a short trip.'

'It's Amar's birthday on Sunday. He's so excited about Alton Towers.'

'Geeta,' I assure her, 'of course I'll be back for Amar's birthday.' I'll fly back Sunday morning, be home by lunchtime – ready to be a dutiful father and husband again. 'We'll have a great time at Alton Towers,' I say. 'The Guptas are coming along too.' I know that will make her happy. Our family outings always work better with outsiders around.

* * *

Esther and I check in separately. Even an airport has eyes, I tell her. The Monarch flight isn't busy and I move to the empty seat next to her. We hold hands, dizzy with the excitement of finally being together outside Manchester, outside the four walls of the Didsbury Queen. I wait until we have had our fill of the champagne from the trolley before telling her about the hotel I've booked. It's the Hilton near the airport. I managed to get a last-minute deal, a suite with breakfast thrown in. 'It's a large hotel,' I say, stroking her cheek. 'I know you will like it. There's a rooftop pool where you can sunbathe.'

I can see us there, lying on deck chairs, her face turned up to the sun and our hands linked. There will be cocktails and dinner and slow, unhurried hours of making love in a bed that doesn't smell of deceit. It is going to be perfect.

'It sounds dreadful,' Esther says, biting her bottom lip and turning her face to the window. 'I know that hotel. It's just off the roundabout, right on the motorway. Whatever made you choose it? You always go for such faceless places.' She pulls out the airline magazine from the front pocket of the seat and starts flicking through the duty free pages.

'I didn't realise you were such an expert on hotels on the Costa del Sol?' I say.

I unfold my *Daily Mail* slowly and deliberately and go straight to the sports section. 'BECKHAM SCORES HAT TRICK FOR UNITED', the headline says, but even that fails to lift my mood. I don't like the way Esther is taking ownership of the weekend. I'd chosen the Hilton to make sure we caught the return flight in time. It's Amar's birthday, and I don't want to miss the flight home because of a traffic jam on the motorway. Everybody knows the Spanish are the worst drivers in Europe.

The rest of the flight passes in silence, but as the plane taxies into Malaga airport, Esther slips her hand in mine and says that we'll have the most memorable time ever. It's her way of saying sorry.

Esther tells the cab to take us to a hotel in Puerto Banús. 'It's a jewel of a port,' she says. 'Only an hour away, and you'll love the boats. Even the Aga Khan has his yacht docked there.'

I smile at her excitement and ask her about the hotel.

'It's called Don Leone. It's featured in this month's *Vogue*. It's very exclusive, only twenty rooms, but I'll make sure we get in,' she says, her chin tilted in defiance.

Small and exclusive can only mean one thing: money running through my fingers like water. I've already lost the deposit on the Hilton by not turning up. I move closer and put an arm around her. Esther's right – what do I know about the glitz and glamour of a beach holiday? The only beach holiday I've had was at Blackpool.

* * *

I imagine golden beaches, palm trees and a sea so blue it hurts the eye, but it's a different kind of Spain that we drive through. The taxi drives past cement-plastered office blocks and shopping arcades styled like faux Arab palaces, with arches and domes and restaurants advertising a full English breakfast. Billboards for sea-view villas and golf courses block out the distant mountains. The hot, dry landscape makes me thirsty.

'Has it always been this ugly?' I ask Esther.

'Malaga's changed a lot,' Esther admits. 'They went mad with construction in the sixties, and the Brits didn't help, coming here in hoards on cheap budget airlines. They should be banned.'

I grin and pat her hand. 'We'll have a good time, and that's all that matters.' I don't want her to feel responsible for the plainness or the heat.

We spend the rest of the journey chatting about places we'll visit one day. Esther has a ready-made list: Venice, Paris, Budapest, followed by a trip to New York in the autumn. New York is her favourite city. The energy of the place makes her feel twenty years old. 'You would suit New York,' she says, nuzzling my ear. 'I can imagine you in a black polo neck, visiting art galleries with me and attending the Met Ball. We'd have a loft in Soho with Warhol on the walls.'

Listening to her is like listening to a fairy tale. I know none of it is real, but I like hearing it.

The taxi is fast and the sea streaks past us, a ribbon of blue light and shade. Elvis Presley songs blast from the radio. I ask the driver to tune into a local station, but he doesn't understand me.

When we reach the hotel, the taxi fare's almost as much as a train ticket from Manchester to London. 'We should have taken the bus,' I joke, paying the driver. 'It would've been a lot cheaper.'

Don Leone stands on the edge of a private beach. A few short steps and the Mediterranean would be biting our feet. I follow Esther into the hotel. The manager greets her like an old friend. He's short and bald with a wide forehead and a bright blue tie that mimics the colour of the sea outside. I wonder if he fancies her or if she's just a regular. Whatever it is, we're in luck. There is a superior room available. Esther stands at the reception desk, fanning herself with my folded newspaper. It's late morning, and the air in the hotel lobby is stale and heavy.

The place resembles a monastery, with its stripped wooden floor and the whitewashed walls. Huge clay pots with lemon trees cluster in the centre. I sit on the cream-coloured sofa by the pots and let Esther do the form-filling, staying in the shadows until we're shown to our room.

'Now, isn't this lovely?' Esther turns to me, beaming with pride.

The sun pours through the windows, lighting up the large bed and revealing the outline of Esther's legs through her thin linen dress. She looks girlish and young, the sunglasses poised on the top of her head, the deep, dark shadow of her cleavage damp with sweat.

'Let's try out the goose-feather pillows,' I whisper into her hair. The bickering on the plane and the long taxi ride don't matter any more.

When we finally come out of the room, the sun dips low in the evening sky and the port is busy with the clink of wine glasses in restaurants and the buzz of holiday voices. Esther takes my arm, leaning against me, our shoes sinking in the sand. We walk to the bar the concierge had recommended. A local, authentic place, he'd said. It's at the far end of the beach near the lighthouse – a little shack with fairy lights wrapped around wooden poles and a stone Buddha perched on a rock. A blue-and-white-striped boat, crammed full of beer bottles, lies beached on one side of the bar. The stools and the coconut ashtrays make me feel like a student again.

'Isn't this how life was meant to be?' I say to Esther as we sit drinking our mojitos.

She nods, her eyes sparkling dreamily. 'Manchester seems so far away,' she says.

'It doesn't even exist,' I reply, pushing a little plate of black olives towards her. The trip to Alton Towers, Geeta's chutney sandwiches, the slap of rain against the car window and the slow-moving, sullen ticket queues – they belong to someone else's life. I lean forward and kiss Esther.

'I came to Puerto Banús with Cedric once. A long time back. It was so different,' she says. 'He was either ringing his office or wanting to go to the casino. He'd hate coming to a bohemian place like this. It would be all…' She makes her voice deep, imitating him, 'Esther, book us the best restaurant in town, and make sure the food's kosher and the wine's expensive.' She giggles and hiccups quietly.

'Let's not talk about him,' I say, lighting a cigarette.

The waitress, a young girl wearing a shiny stud in one nostril, comes over to our table. We watch as she takes out her lighter and tries to light the candle that's stuck inside an empty wine bottle. Her hands shake as she finally lights it.

'More romantic this way,' she says. She has a strong Irish accent. I wonder if anything was Spanish in Spain.

Esther orders a third Bloody Mary. She slurs her words and her eyes are distracted.

'Let's switch to water,' I suggest, but she won't have it, clapping her hands and telling the Irish girl to be quick with our drinks.

'Are you OK, Esther?' The excitement of being away on this clandestine trip has gone to her head, that's what I think.

She clears her throat a few times before speaking. 'I've been doing some serious thinking lately, my mensch. We need to talk. I think the moment has come,' she says.

A group of small kids run squealing into the waves, their arms outstretched, their mothers shouting at them to come back. I think of the sea in Bombay, of the sewage pipes that empty their filth into it. No one would swim in it.

'I want to end my marriage,' Esther announces. 'It's run its course. Being with you has brought it home to me. I'm going to ask Cedric for a divorce.' She says this quietly, her chin resting on her hand, the sea breeze pulling at her hair.

The postcard moment disappears. This is real life.

'You're not thinking straight,' I say, taking hold of her hand. 'It's the drink and the heat. It's made us giddy. We need to be serious about this. You can't just end a marriage. Imagine the damage.' I feel the dull start of a headache.

'But don't you love me? Don't you want to leave Greta? Or… is it some sick sense of Indian duty that's tying you down?' She pushes away my hand and gulps down her drink.

I can't imagine a life with Esther coming true. There are too many people standing in the way. This woman sitting across me with her dreams of New York living and Parisian candles feels as much a stranger as Geeta with her pining for Chowpatty and Bombay bhel.

'We need time to get to know each other,' I say.

'We need love,' she replies. 'You want to open a window to love and have a peep, whereas I want to kick open the door and walk right in.'

Esther stares past me at the sea slapping noisily against the beach. The water is as dark as the starless sky above.

I slip my fingers through hers. They are cold.

'These things can't be rushed,' I say. 'We have to think carefully about the hurt we'll cause. We're not teenagers. We're responsible adults.' I'm like a doctor diagnosing a condition.

She lets out an impatient sigh.

'Forget it, then. Let's eat somewhere nice, get drunk and fuck.' Her voice falters and she slides back on her Jacki O sunglasses, which are large and black and hide most of her face.

The air thrums with things left unsaid.

When I come back after paying the bill, Esther has gone to the toilet. I wait, watching the kids, who are now settled on bar stools eating ice cream. Kids are the same everywhere. Even Amar loves his ice cream. He could go through an entire tub of Ben and Jerry's in one sitting.

'I know this restaurant at the port that does the best paella in town,' Esther says. She's retouched her make-up, but her voice lacks its cheerful chirpiness.

Los Bandidos is full, but the waiter manages to find us a table at the back, near the toilets.

'We should have got the concierge to book,' Esther says with a frown. She asks to see the manager, but I don't want her to make a fuss. 'OK, let's go to another place,' she says. 'There's an Argentinean that does good steaks. It's only a ten-minute walk.'

'It's only a meal. We'll soon be out of here,' I reply. I want us to go for a long walk on the beach, stroll towards the distant lights of Marbella. We have the luxury of an entire night together before us and I don't want to squander away the hours bickering over a restaurant table.

'It's going to be smelly and noisy,' she says, sitting down reluctantly.

I check the wine list, making the switch from euros to sterling, calculating the price of the wine Esther wanted. It's the most expensive one on the list. 'What about Sangria?' I suggest. 'We're in Spain – what's the point in drinking French wine?'

She makes a face, looking at her hands, holding them up to check her nails. The light bounces off their crimson sheen. 'The problem with Sangria is they dilute it with water and the cheapest plonk. The best place for Sangria is at the Marbella Beach Club. We could've stayed there, but I'm not sure if you would have liked the rates.'

I put down the menu. When did she become so obsessed with the price tag? Or has she always been like this, and I'm only noticing it now? The couple at the next table are smiling, and their glasses clink in a toast. The man says something and the woman blushes and brings his hand to her lips, kissing each finger slowly. I'm jealous of their intimacy and am suddenly nostalgic for our shabby hotel room back home.

'Fine,' I say, pointing to the wine list. 'Have it your way. Let's blow the money on the costliest shit they have.'

'I've noticed this about you,' Esther says, moving her face closer to mine. 'You always get touchy when it comes to money. You were moaning about the taxi fare and I saw the way you checked the hotel rates twice, and now this. Why can't we ever talk about sailing or horseback riding or music?' Her shoulders sag as she reaches into her bag for a cigarette. 'Beautiful stuff,' she continues. 'We don't talk enough about beautiful stuff.'

My hands tremble, but my voice is steady as I answer her. 'I would love to talk about beauty, but I'm sorry, right now all I can think of is money. My business is failing and I have a son who's…' I stop. I can't believe this is the first time I've felt like sharing the inadequacies of my life with Esther. Maybe it's the start of a new kind of honesty between us. If she probes me more I might tell her about having to sack the girls on the hemming floor. I might even tell her about the time I suggested Geeta bought Amar's school uniform from the second-hand uniform shop, but the shame of it makes me stop. I try again. 'Esther, try and see life from my side of the road sometimes. I'm not Cedric Solomon.'

She doesn't want to know more. She winces when I say Cedric's name.

'You've misunderstood me. Money isn't everything,' she says. Rich or poor, it doesn't mean a damn thing if there's no love.'

LOVE. I repeat her word. The immensity of the word feels lost inside my mouth, and I can't picture the bricks and cement or the warmth that accompany it.

The waiter comes over. It's been a busy night, he tells us, and they've run out of paella. Would we be happy with risotto made Spanish style with chorizo and olives?' He's an Arab, trying to pass himself off as Spanish, but I can see from his expression and the way he smiles and nods too eagerly at my choice that he belongs to the same homeless tribe as me. He has come to Spain to make money, not to stare at the sea. His kids would one day enjoy the luxury of beautiful things, but not him.

'We'll have champagne and the sea bass baked in salt,' I tell him. 'Dom Perignon.' I'm determined to show Esther I can afford beauty like her if I want.

* * *

The weekend is a blur of hours spent walking on the beach, toes sinking into the sand and Esther's excitable voice pointing out the sleek yachts that bob in quiet contentment in the marina. She reads out the names – *Laila*, *Nightingale*, *Chelsea Bird.* She's even partied on one that belongs to a business acquaintance of her husband's. It was caviar on tap and non-stop dancing.

'Money is wasted on the rich,' I tell her. We stroll past designer shops and overdressed holidaymakers. I buy Esther a Spanish shawl in black crochet and we take the little toy tourist train around the backstreets. I feel like an imposter gatecrashing someone else's life.

On Sunday morning I make sure we're at the airport hours before check-in.

'What's the rush?' Esther grumbles, running an agitated hand through her hair.

'I'm taking Amar to Alton Towers, and I don't want to miss the flight. He's waited for this all year. It's his birthday. He's fifteen.'

'You're just getting paranoid for no reason. Of course we won't miss the flight,' Esther says, walking towards the duty-free shop. I say we should wait at the gate. She won't listen.

I follow her. She moves swiftly from one aisle to another, picking up bottles and jars, spraying scent on to her neck, her hair, her wrists. The artificially lit shop mirrors throw back our image. There we are – me with my puffy eyes and Esther in a too-tight dress that strains against her belly. I see us as the world saw us: an ordinary, middle-aged couple.

Once the shopping is over, Esther suggests breakfast. 'Churros with hot chocolate?' She smacks her lips like a child, her voice petulant. 'We didn't get to try them at the Orange Square last night.'

'We'll miss the flight,' I say. 'Let's grab a coffee at the gate.'

Esther points to the flight board. The Monarch flight is delayed by two hours.

'It's a technical fault,' the girl at the check-in counter explains, handing us a voucher for refreshments.

'How long before take-off?' I ask.

The girl shrugs her shoulders.

A queue forms behind me, but I don't care. I keep thinking of Amar's disappointed eyes. The girl taps a little more on her keyboard and mutters something in Spanish to her colleague.

'You're making a scene,' Esther says angrily, pulling at my sleeve.

There is nothing to do but wait. It will be evening by the time I get home. Amar will understand. I just have to explain and give the right reasons for the delay.

'At least,' Esther says, 'we'll get to eat those churros.'

* * *

I get home late. The front hall is lit. Music is coming from the lounge – a room we hardly ever use. I open the door, ready with a flurry of excuses and apologies. Geeta, Amar and the Guptas are sitting around the coffee table, where a big chocolate cake sits, with fifteen extinguished candles. Red and yellow balloons dangle from the curtain poles. Amar sees me and runs out of the room.

Gupta taps his watch. 'Indian Shit Time, not BST. You're back, my friend – we were about to call the police!' He slaps my back and addresses the women. 'The Prodigal Father returns… Just kidding! Here, have a slice of the delicious cake,' he says, cutting me one.

'The flight was delayed. Some technical problem,' I say. 'I'm sorry.' I sit down next to Geeta. She won't look at me.

'Well, you managed to miss your son's birthday party. Great timing, as always, PK,' Gupta says, taking off his glasses and wiping them with a handkerchief.

Gupta's wife, who always has a way with descriptions, tells me about their outing. They'd made a day of it, and packed a picnic of cheese sandwiches, samosas and sausage rolls. Even the rain stayed away.

'Wasn't it great that Amar went on the Big Dipper twice?' Geeta says to Gupta, but she still doesn't look at me.

I smile and nod, sitting on the edge of the sofa, the plate balancing on my lap, an outsider in my own home. 'I thought he hated those kinds of rides?' I say.

'Not any more,' Gupta pipes up. 'Actually, the credit goes to his friend. She told him he has to man up now that he's a proper teenager.' Gupta's wife giggles.

'Where's Amar?' I ask Geeta. She's collecting the used plates, piling them on top of one another.

'He must be in the kitchen, helping Alice make the tea,' Usha says helpfully.

* * *

They're in the kitchen, hunched over the kettle, shoulders touching. A tray with cups and saucers stands ready on the kitchen table.

'Hello, Alice,' I say, tapping her lightly on the shoulder. She whirls around, nearly knocking over the kettle.

'Hi there.' She looks me right in the eye. She's a big girl, with a woman's body and yellow hair straight out of a bottle. I'd imagined her prettier – more petite and delicate.

'You can't have my cake, Dad,' Amar says, snatching away my plate. 'You didn't come to my party.'

Alice laughs and tells my son to behave. She says they'd baked it together, with real Belgian chocolate they'd bought from Tesco and melted in a saucepan.

'It was such fun,' Amar says. He is happy.

'We had fun in Blackpool, didn't we, Amar?' Alice says in a low smoker's voice, edging closer to him. Her fingers brush against him as he pours tea into the mugs.

'Careful! You're so clumsy,' I shout, as he spills some on to the table.

'You missed a great day out.' Alice is still speaking. She has a slow, lazy way of speaking.

'I had a business trip.' I'm justifying myself to a teenager.

'You were naughty, missing your son's birthday,' she persists, leaning against the fridge door, a hand on her hip. Her cheap imitation-leather boots are scuffed around the front, like she's been kicking something hard.

'I'm taking him to Euro Disney next year,' I reply. I'd thought of it on the way home: a perfect peace offering.

Amar hands me back my plate. 'You can have some cake now,' he says. He's clapping his hands and whirling around the kitchen like a dervish. 'I'm going to Disneyland! I'm going to Disneyland! I'm going to meet Micky Mouse,' he chants.

'He's had too much sugar. It's done things to his head,' Alice says, grinning.

* * *

The Guptas are leaving. Gupta's wife is squeezing herself into her coat. 'Stay a bit longer,' I say. I don't want to be alone with Geeta's anger.

But Gupta says I must be tired from my trip. 'Where was it again?' he asks.

I tell him I'd gone to Dover to release a shipment. Some papers were missing – only a formality, but it took up the whole weekend, I say.

'Oh yes, yes… Dover. I thought it was Felixstowe for some reason,' Gupta says, as though he didn't really care where I'd been. 'Geeta was saying something about that. I didn't know you worked weekends.' He pauses and pulls out a toothpick from his trouser pocket, sinking back on to the sofa, the toothpick busy in his mouth, the golf T-shirt tight against his belly.

He's forgotten to dye his sideburns, and the grey hair looks false against his nut-brown skin.

'I'm busy with our new account,' he says. 'Hades and Sons. The funeral people. Remember? I told you about it.'

'I thought that was a small job?' I reply.

'Nothing's small these days. Especially with the dead – their mess goes on for ever.' He gives an exaggerated sigh and looks at me. 'Something's not quite right, PK. You're not yourself. You're not ill or anything, are you? Have you had your prostate checked? Your blood pressure?'

And Gupta bends over me like a nurse, kneading my shoulders. His hands are like a woman's: smooth and hairless. What else hadn't I noticed about him before? I notice as if for the first time the way his eyes glint behind his glasses while he's making a point, the way he jabs his ivory toothpick to get at his fillings.

'I'm fit as a horse,' I say, and flex my arm so he can feel my muscle.

'How is the Didsbury Queen? Your suppliers still happy with it?' Gupta changes the topic, the toothpick dangling from his mouth, his hands clasped together on the table as though in prayer.

* * *

'How could you forget Amar's birthday?' Geeta asks. She's sitting on the bed, still wearing the blue silk tunic and trousers she saves for special days. The bedroom lights are on, the door shut. There's nowhere to hide.

'I told you, the flight got delayed. I'm sorry. There was no way of catching another one.' I refuse to meet her eyes.

'I don't understand you,' she says. 'On one hand you're saying business is drying up and no new orders are coming in, and the next thing I know you're too busy to spend your only son's birthday with him. Have you forgotten the difficulty we had in having him? After those three miscarriages… he's a gift!'

'We'll have another celebration,' I promise her. 'We'll go away over the summer. Maybe go to Paris – we'll stay in the best hotel. We can take him to the Eiffel Tower and Euro Disney.'

'You should've seen him. He ran to the door every time he heard a car. Thank God the Guptas were there. And Alice saved the day – she was so nice. She kept saying dads don't matter.'

I reach out and hold her hand. 'It won't happen again, I promise.' I mean it.

'I know you've got worries at work,' she says. 'Gupta told me there's a lot of competition and you're under pressure.' She clasps my face in her hands, her eyes welling up with tears. 'Talk to me, PK. Tell me what's going on inside this head of yours.'

She's so close I can smell the cumin from the samosas in her hair.

Lopa didi,

I can't forgive him. He missed our Amar's birthday. Thank God for the Guptas and for Alice. They saved the day. They took us to Blackpool. God was kind to my little boy – he kept the rains away. Blackpool looked beautiful in the sun. The sea was sparkling away. We sat on benches near the beach and Usha brought the most delicious gobi parathas. These seagulls flew down and surrounded us. So much cackle and noise, but they're just like glamorous crows, to be honest. We fed them samosas. Such a pity all Amar wanted was a Happy Meal from McDonald's. I've started liking his friend, Alice, again. She ate three parathas and took Amar on the Big Dipper and held his hand. Even your Chintu would find this ride scary. PK came back very late from his business trip, like a thief in the night. He looked a mess. His shirt was crumpled and his mouth stank of alcohol. Gupta thinks he may be keeping bad company. He has told me to be alert. To look through his pockets and check his statements. I had to laugh when he said this. We have been married nearly thirty years – how can I go snooping through PK's things? You tell me. Would you do that to Jijaji?

Anyway, I must go now. I can hear Amar crying in the next room.

Bye,

Geeta

23

YOU CAN'T GO WRONG WITH PEARLS

Gupta wants to meet. There are things on his mind that need sorting out over a pint of orange juice and a packet of crisps. He's having trouble over the accounts at the funeral parlour next to the Didsbury Queen – apparently there are dead people claiming child allowance and benefits. He groans about it every time we meet.

I wait for him at the Victoria. An elderly couple arrives at the next table. The woman's silver bob and neat beige cardigan remind me of Margaret Thatcher. She even has a string of cream pearls around her neck. The husband waves to a waiter as he settles down to read the menu.

They reach for their glasses and their cutlery like a pair of synchronised swimmers. That's how they'll be now to the end of their days, ordering their fish and chips and a glass of chardonnay, booking a week's holiday in Cornwall with their grandkids. They will be moored and anchored to this world, while Geeta, Amar and I remain floundering and flailing, neither English nor Indian, no roots, no branches, for ever in limbo, like my mango tree, fighting to bear fruit beneath a cold foreign sky.

There's still no sign of Gupta.

I think of ringing Esther, but then I remember her behaviour in Marbella. We've not met since, and I'm in no hurry to be with her again. I let Amar down big time, and I blame her. All of a sudden there's a ping and a text message appears. 'My darling Mensch, wasn't I a bitch in Marbella. Sorry, blame it on my menopausal hormones,' followed by at least ten kisses.

I call her.

'Have you forgiven me, my handsome mensch?' Her voice is warm and comforting like chicken soup.

'I blame myself too. Guess we just weren't used to spending so much time together. It felt illegal. So what are you up to?' I want the couple at the next table to think I'm talking to someone close.

'I've been cooking today,' Esther replies. 'It's Purim, and Cedric's family is coming over for dinner.'

I feel a stab of jealousy. She'll never cook for me. I'll never be a part of her daily habits, doing things that people do when no one's watching, like brushing her teeth or reading a magazine while picking at her feet. She'll always come to me sleek and smooth, her body perfumed, her best lingerie on.

'Lara's coming too,' she says. 'I'm making her a cake – an apple and honey one. It's her favourite.' Esther's daughter Lara lives in Tel Aviv, working at a specialist school for children with learning disabilities. I know this much about her, but nothing more. Like so many things about us, our children's lives are faceless and out of bounds.

'Let me see a picture of her,' I'd said to Esther once. 'Let's see if she's got your looks.' She shook her head and turned away, but not before I'd seen the glitter of tears in her eyes.

'Save me a slice of your cake,' I say. I'm still smiling when our phone call ends and I'm back on my own in the pub with my pint of beer.

'I was speaking to my wife,' I lie to the woman at the next table. Her husband has gone to the gents' and she's on her own.

'She's baking for you?' she asks. 'I'm sorry, I couldn't help overhearing.'

Something foolish makes me say yes. 'It's our anniversary, and she's baking me a cake.'

The husband is back. He sits, arms folded across his chest, waiting for our chit-chat to end. But the woman's interested. 'How many years have you been married?'

I laugh. 'Oh, too long to remember.'

It is indeed an anniversary the next evening, and I'm going to meet Esther in the evening.

'Nearly a year since we first saw each other,' Esther said on the phone, making it sound as though it's a milestone as grand as a twenty-fifth.

'A year!' I'd let out a long, low whistle, not quite believing the ticking of time. 'Is that all? It feels like a lifetime.'

'What should I get her for an anniversary present?' I ask the interested woman.

She looks confused, and the colour runs to her cheeks. Glancing at her husband, she shyly fingers her necklace. 'Pearls would be good,' she says.

'You can't go wrong with pearls,' her husband agrees, pointing to her neck.

'For our twenty-fifth,' she reminds him.

What did I get Geeta for our twenty-fifth? I'd surprised her with a trip to London and an afternoon tea at the Hilton, where I studied her long face as she studied the menu. The finger sandwiches were too small and the scones weren't sweet enough. She insisted on tap water, not the bottled stuff on offer. Back in the suite I had quietly got drunk on the whisky from the mini bar before we went to see a show at the West End. I can't even remember the name of the musical. She would have preferred a big, flashy party in a restaurant.

But Esther was different. She appreciated beautiful things. The pearls would light up her face.

* * *

There's still time for a quick detour to the Trafford Centre to buy a present. At that time of evening, Cartwright's is empty, except for a young man cleaning the glass display cabinets. He frowns when he sees me enter. It's almost closing time.

'I'm looking for a gift,' I say to him. 'A pearl necklace. The best you have.'

Wiping his hands on his trousers, he enquires what kind of pearls I want. 'Freshwater or cultured? We've just got some South Sea ones in. Absolute beauties.'

I don't have a clue. I just want to get a feel of the price.

He brings out a dark velvet tray that is crowded with pearls – long ones, short ones, round ones, tear-shaped ones; night-dark, delicate pink, soft creams and peaches.

I know the one I want right away. It sits slightly apart from the others: a medium-sized necklace with plump, round, creamy pearls.

The salesman compliments me on my good taste. He swings the strand against the light.

I can already see them on Esther's neck. I ask him the price.

He punches a few numbers into his calculator. 'Twelve hundred pounds.'

I like the way he's arrived at a neat, round figure. 'Eight hundred and fifty and I'll take it right away. I'll pay cash,' I offer.

'It's a fixed price, sir. We don't bargain. This is the best quality you'll find. It's not made in China.' He starts putting the tray away.

I imagine Esther's face as she opens the pouch. I think of my hands fastening the clasp, my fingers against the warm skin of her neck, her long hair brushing against my chin as I bend down to slip it around her neck.

'I'll take it.' I pull out my wallet. It is an anniversary gift, after all – it needs to be special.

I stuff the receipt in my wallet and head home.

24

AN ATOM BOMB

Geeta's still at college when I get home. The house feels empty without her bustling presence. I'm filling the kettle in the kitchen when I hear a noise upstairs. It must be Amar, I think, so I go up to find him. It's time to reconnect with him – I'll tell him how sorry I was to miss his birthday and how the trip to Disneyland is just around the corner.

His room is dark and the windows are wide open. The street lamp throws crooked shadows on to the carpet and the walls. My eyes slowly adjust to the darkness, and I make out a figure sprawled on the bed. It's Amar. He's in bed, a sheet pulled halfway across his body, a magazine lying face down on his bare chest. His eyes are shut, his mouth open. I see his hand move rhythmically up and down beneath the sheet. I don't recognise this boy.

I stand watching, my hand frozen on the door handle, as he lets out a moan. A deep shudder goes through his body and a sour, acidic smell fills the room. I leave before he opens his eyes.

Outside in the garden, the night sky is clear, shot through with a thousand stars. I go up to my mango tree and stare at its polythene-wrapped limbs, naked and thin. They look like Amar's limbs when he was just born.

A hand touches my shoulder. 'You'll catch a cold, standing outside like this. Come inside.' It's Geeta. I follow her in. She starts peeling the potatoes and then stops, letting out a big yawn. Her eyes narrow into slits of fatigue.

'Don't bother cooking,' I say. 'I'll order a takeaway.'

'That would be nice,' she says, and, leaving the potatoes, goes to the table where her plastic college folder lies. She starts flicking through the pages in an aimless, listless sort of way. 'I've got work to catch up on. I'm too tired to cook tonight.'

'I told you it was a bad idea, becoming a student at your age.'

Geeta hesitates. 'I'm not really enjoying the course,' she admits. 'The day is too long and the other students are so young. The teacher speaks too quickly. I can't understand a thing. He has such a strong Scottish accent.'

'How about your Indian accent? Does he find that a problem?' I joke. Geeta has stubbornly clung to her Indian intonations and expressions all these years, unwilling to adapt. I'm different. The first thing I did on moving here was to mould my voice to the Mancunian way, shaping my mouth to the broad vowels. It helped me win business in the early days. Customers were surprised when they met me face to face, unable to connect the white voice on the phone to the brown face smiling back at them.

Geeta ignores my jibe and switches on the kettle. 'My brain is old. It's not used to being clever any more.'

'You fret too much. Just enjoy being a housewife,' I say. 'If you're that interested in computers, just come to the office and maybe Margaret can explain the basics. You know – how to send emails and that kind of stuff.' Listen to me pretending to be an understanding husband.

'Maybe I'll come to the office one day – I don't know when,' Geeta says, but she doesn't sound convinced.

I know how much she hates coming to the warehouse. The awkwardness of being the boss's wife, of making small talk with the girls and pretending to know the stock flow and the seasonal trends. The last time she came, she stayed outside, waiting in the car, the engine idling, while I brought down some documents for her to sign.

The kitchen door opens and Amar is there, wearing mismatched Disney socks, one red, one green, and some white tennis shorts. His T-shirt strains against his tummy. I can't meet his eye. I see him again in his darkened bedroom, the smutty magazine open, and his feverish hand moving up and down.

'Why don't you go for a run, Amar? It'll clear your head.' I look pointedly at his tummy. 'It'll do you good.'

'It's late, Dad. I'll get mugged if I go out, and I've got school tomorrow and…' He opens the fridge and then the microwave and turns to Geeta. 'Where's dinner, Mum? I'm hungry.'

'Go upstairs and finish your homework,' Geeta says. 'We're getting a takeaway. It will take time.' There's a new edge to her voice and Amar notices it.

'But you always have my food ready, Mum,' he says, his bottom lip quivering. 'I don't want you to go to your stupid college any more! You only want me out of the way so you can complain to Dad about me.' He leaves, slamming the door behind him.

Geeta stands by the fridge, the door held open, her head almost buried inside the icy blue-lit interior, her cheeks shiny with sweat.

'What kind of an awful mother am I? I didn't even have dinner ready for my son,' she says, her eyes filling up.

'Ignore him. He's a teenager. They're selfish. This computer course of yours, it's causing you too much stress,' I say. 'Just leave it.'

'But I like getting out of the house, meeting new people. There are two nice Polish girls, and they want to learn how to make chicken curry…' Geeta stands there, holding open the fridge door, talking more to herself than me.

'You're tired, Geeta.' My voice softens. 'You can't manage the house and be a student and look after Amar.' I lower my eyes and almost whisper. 'We all know he's a difficult child.'

We only talk about Amar's behaviour when there's a crisis.

'He's changing. He doesn't want to talk about school any more. Tells me to shut up when I ask about his friends,' Geeta continues, a tremor in her voice.

'He's told me not to go up to his room any more,' she adds.

'You're worrying too much,' I say. 'Just order some pizza from Goodfellas'. Get the thin crust ones – they're healthier.'

'I'll order some chocolate-chip cookies too for Amar. He loves dunking them in his milk.' She reaches for my jacket that I'd flung on the chair, her hands fishing inside the pockets to get my wallet for the credit card.

I suddenly remember the receipt for the pearls. I grab the jacket before she can get to my wallet. 'Here, give it to me. I'll place the order.'

'All right, all right.' She flings up her arms in exasperation. 'What do you have inside, an atom bomb?'

Dear Lopa didi,

You were right. The computer course has done me a world of good. It's only twice a week, but it's so nice to dress up, pack my sandwiches for lunch and catch the bus and just get out. I almost feel like a college girl again. The course is tough. There is word processing, spreadsheets and slide-show presentations to learn about. The teacher, Mr MacDougall, is kind – he repeats everything twice for my benefit. The best part is the break. There is a lovely glass-roofed cafeteria with potted aspidistra plants. I usually sit with two Polish girls who are here as au pairs. Au pairs help around the house, but they are not like servants. These girls have lovely smiles and keep asking me about Indian recipes. They tell me Polish food is mainly potatoes and meat. I wish one of them could help me with Amar. He is becoming very moody, and also he is piling on the weight. I want PK to go with him to a gym instead of just ordering him to go. Children learn so much better when parents set an example. I'm not sure whether I will continue with this course. I don't know how you juggle your boutique, yoga, Jijaji and the kids all at the same time. I am always so tired. No time for romance or going out alone with PK. Where would we go? What would we talk about? He is always checking his mobile, doesn't pay attention. Anyway, Diwali will soon be here. Please send me your recipe for besan burfi.

Love to the kids,

Geeta

P.S. Have you started looking for boys for Bubbly? She will soon be nineteen. Find a nice boy with a good salary and family values.

25

DAYS FILLED WITH WATER

When I try to remember my life before Esther, all I see are blurred outlines of a man stumbling through his days.

'Soon it'll be one year, than two… and then one day you'll finally say, "Yes, Esther, I'm ready. I'm ready to begin again,"' Esther says, closing her eyes, her long lashes soft against her cheek.

'Aren't we lucky we've not been caught?' I say.

'Don't tempt fate. The gods are watching.' Her finger presses against my lips as she mumbles a prayer. I bow my head, shut my eyes and listen to the questioning beat of my heart. It's the nearest I'll ever come to God.

We are in the Didsbury Queen, getting ready to go out to celebrate our anniversary. Esther pouts into the bathroom mirror and applies her lipstick. The pearls I gave her glow around her bare throat.

Our eyes meet in the mirror. I pull her closer, my mouth brushing the nape of her neck, where a tiny pulse beats in excitement.

'I forgive you,' I say.

She frowns. 'Forgive me for what?'

'For ruining my life.'

'I've improved your life, not ruined it. We don't *have* to be together, you know…' She says the words lightly, but it feels like a threat. She reaches for her dress, weaving her arms through the blue silk sleeves like a dancer. It has wide bell-shaped sleeves and a fluid shape, and its cut makes it look like a kimono. I twirl her around like a ballerina.

'This dress is Issey Miyake, isn't it?'

She nods. 'You should design something like this for next season. I heard Cedric say that Japan is going to be big next year.'

'I'm sticking to twenty-pound jeans and polyester lace skirts, thank you very much,' I say. 'You can't go wrong with them. All this talk of recession is making everyone nervous.'

She shakes her head, and says now isn't the time to talk about problems. Opening her handbag, she sprays her Chanel fragrance into the room and walks through the cloud. There's no room for drabness in Esther's world.

* * *

We leave the hotel together. There's no one at the reception counter, but I can hear Marvin whistling in the back room, which also doubles as his kitchen. The lobby smells of Maggi noodles and garlic.

'Let's hurry. Our reservation is for eight p.m.,' I say, holding Esther's hand and helping her to cross the road like a child. I've booked the French restaurant in Chester for our anniversary dinner.

'Remember how nervous we were the first time? Little did we know how things would turn out,' Esther says.

We walk to my car. This is the first time we've been outside in public, flaunting our affair, hand in hand. I put my arm around her. There are goosebumps on her skin. So many months have gone by, and I still can't get over the surprising, joyous touch of her. I'm a lucky man.

I check again if Cedric is in town.

'He's in Moscow till Monday. He's signing up with some new stores…' Esther's voice trails off. She knows how much I hate hearing about her husband's business success.

Light rain is falling. Faint, wispy drops that warn of days filled with water. Another year is dragging to a close. I wonder if we will still be together in a year's time. I can't see beyond the murky, messy, exhilarating present.

'I had a strange dream last night,' Esther says. 'I dreamt that I lost you in a crowd, and when I finally found you, you refused to recognise me. You nodded politely, gave a little wave and walked away.'

I shake my head, my hands going through my pockets, searching for my car keys. 'You're talking crazy tonight. Would I ever do that to you? Would I ever?'

'Where the hell are your keys?' she says, brushing an impatient hand over her hair, smoothing it down. 'This damn rain – I hate that about Manchester. It ruins my hair. I'll look a right state in the restaurant.'

A car slows down as it passes us. I don't recognise the black Ford Fiesta right away. The windows roll down and Gupta's sallow, pointed face floats into view. The steel frame of his cheap glasses glimmer in the light of the street lamps.

'Hi PK! Is that really you?' he says, his head sticking out of his car window. 'What awful weather.'

'What are you doing here?' I say. The car keys fall from my hand, hitting the pavement with a steely tinkle. Esther quickly bends down to pick them up.

Gupta stares at Esther. 'I left some files behind at Hades. I thought I'd catch up on some work. Just imagine – they've not filed their returns for nearly five years… enough to make a man turn in his grave.' He gives a dry chuckle and waits for me to speak again.

I want Esther to get into the car and fade away into the background, but she stays by my side, her body pressed against my arm, the rain gluing her hair to her cheeks, an anxious half-smile on her lips.

'Won't you introduce me to your friend?' Gupta says finally. His hands grip the steering wheel. One finger lightly taps it, as if to the beat of some unheard drum.

'Her name is Esther,' I say. I don't have time to invent another name.

'Esther... what a beautiful name. Jewish origin, isn't it? But Esther... who?' His face is expectant.

'Esther Solomon,' Esther says, loudly and clearly.

She tells me later that it was just plain nerves that made her blurt out her correct name – the fright of being caught out at last catching her off-guard. 'Your friend – his eyes were like skewers.'

Gupta gets out of his car, slowly, gracefully, like a dancer in slow motion. He opens his car boot, pulls out a large golfing umbrella and unfurls it over Esther's head, and then, taking Esther's hand in his, he brings it to his lips.

'Miss Esther Solomon, it's an honour to meet you. Any friend of PK's is a friend of mine. The name is Gupta. I'm his oldest friend. We used to chat up girls together in Bombay. But you know that already, I suppose?' he says.

Esther nods and pushes strands of hair behind her ears. Her features are blurry and raw in the rain.

I check my watch and tell Esther to get into the car. I slide in, ready to slam the door on Gupta, but he's quicker than me. He grabs the car door, jamming it open with his bony hip, and brings his face close to mine.

'Not so quick, my friend. Tell me, are you going anywhere nice? You know I'm always on the hunt for a good restaurant.' He clears his throat and tightens his grip on the umbrella handle. He is a small man and the umbrella shakes in his hand.

'Miss Solomon is a business contact. We had a late meeting, and we're just going to grab a quick bite.' I sound pathetic.

He examines my face closely. 'A business meeting,' he repeats slowly.

I manage to close the car door and start the engine.

'Goodbye, Miss Solomon. It was a pleasure to meet you. Please don't let him work you too hard,' he shouts after us. I see him through the rear-view mirror, his eyes burning holes in my back.

Esther is shivering and weeping, her head pressed against the dashboard.

'It's over. It's over. He'll never believe we're only work contacts,' she sobs.

'The bastard! The bastard! He was stalking us. He's seen me come out of that hotel, and it didn't take him long to put two and two together,' I fume. There's blood on my brain. If I had a gun, I would put a bullet through his heart.

'Take me home. Please just take me home. I don't feel like going out for dinner,' Esther says.

The restaurant is forgotten. The pearls are forgotten. The anniversary feels like a funeral.

* * *

Esther lives in a large, old-fashioned Victorian house on a quiet road close to the university, not far from the bakery where we had stumbled upon each other. The area was sought after once, because of its proximity to the centre, but is now occupied mainly by academics or middle-management types. The more affluent have moved to suburbs like Wilmslow and Hale, where they live in big gated houses, rub shoulders with United football players and their glossy wives and pretend they are in Beverley Hills. Large rhododendron bushes screen Esther's house from the road. I have imagined her house a thousand times, imagined Esther's life swimming effortlessly within its four walls, and now I am here.

'Are you sure you want me to come in?' I ask her.

'Of course. I've already told you Cedric's away. I'm by myself.' Her voice is petulant and harsh. The crying has tired her out.

I follow her into a large L-shaped lounge with heavy crimson velvet curtains that hide the windows. Large silver-framed photos stand neatly on top of a grand piano, which takes pride of place in the centre of the room. This is Esther's other life – her real life, not the shadowy one she lives in a drab two-star hotel.

I run my fingers over the piano keys. 'I didn't know you played the piano?'

'The kids played when they were younger, right up to grade six,' she says. Her eyes are still red from crying.

'And that's them, right? Your kids?' I point to the young man and woman posing in a silver photo frame.

She lifts the photo and brings it close to her face, as though trying to recognise the faces. The boy in the frame is young, with a thick head of dark curls and a full sensuous mouth that carries his father's sneer.

Esther's daughter is more like her – the same long hair and troubled expression in her deep-set eyes. They're both laughing at something. A private family joke, caught for ever inside a camera lens.

'Happy family, eh?' I turn to Esther and touch her cheek. It feels warm.

'Yes, those were happy times. But you know what Tolstoy says about happy families…' Her voice falters.

'Your son lives in America, right?' I ask. She's told me before about his ambitions and his top grades.

'The photo's quite old. Ollie's a lawyer in LA now, overworked and overpaid.'

'He must be a smart kid.' I think of Amar's report card, covered in Ds.

It feels strange talking about our children. We come to each other uprooted and unwrapped, freefalling from a nameless map, and now here I am looking at holiday snaps taken in restaurants, on beaches and ski slopes. They show a young, smiling Esther and Cedric holding hands, a couple happy to be together, except that Cedric seems to be always looking away from the camera, as though distracted by something more important, and Esther's smile always looks a little forced.

'Let's have a drink to calm us down,' Esther says. 'What a dreadful night it's been.' She removes her shoes and walks over to an art-deco style glass drinks trolley by the window. 'Some champagne… or shall we have something stronger? Whisky, maybe?'

I nod, and she lifts the heavy glass decanter and tips it expertly over two crystal tumblers.

We sit together on her brown leather chesterfield sofa, drinks in hand, ostensibly a cosy couple spending a night in, her head on my shoulder. Except it's not my house, and she's not my wife.

'What do you think Gupta will do next?' Esther asks. She absent-mindedly touches her pearls, but she doesn't look at them.

'I'm not sure,' I say, shaking my glass so the ice cubes jiggle. 'I've known Gupta a long time, but I don't quite know how his mind works.'

'I wish we'd come up with a better excuse. Something smarter.' Her head collapses back against the big squishy sofa cushions.

'He caught me by surprise,' I say. 'He knows I'm lying…'

I think of our college days in Bombay. He always had the knack of catching me out, bursting into my room when I was with a girl.

'Sorry, sorry,' he'd stammer and leave, but not before taking a good, long look.

'How do you do it, buddy?' he asked me once, eyes twinkling behind his glasses. 'I screw pictures in *Playboy*; you end up shagging the real stuff.' He is a jealous man.

My throat is tight and dry. 'Could I get some water, please?'

Esther gets up and goes into the kitchen. I hear cupboard doors open, shut, and the sound of running water. Ordinary sounds of an everyday home. If I shut my eyes I could pretend it's my everyday life.

She comes back and hands me a glass of water in a blue tumbler. It's expensive and heavy, not like the cheap Pyrex ones we have at home.

'It'll all be over once the family find out. They won't bear it. We'll be the laughing stock of our community. Can you imagine what your rabbi would say…?' My mind is busy spinning through different outcomes.

We look away from each other, into a future that has stopped including one another.

'Just kiss me,' Esther says. Her mouth trembles. 'Make me forget all that's happened tonight.' She raises her face, waiting for my kiss.

But I put down my drink and get up to leave. 'I don't feel comfortable here. This is Cedric's house. I keep expecting him to walk in any minute,' I say.

'He's far away in China, far, far away. He always is – and the house is mine, too; how many times do I have to tell you that?' she cries, her cheeks reddening with anger. 'Do you want a tour?' she says spitefully. 'We have a home cinema in the basement with Dolby surround sound.'

'Just be reasonable, Esther,' I say, placing a hand on her shoulder.

She downs her drink in one gulp and puts her hand on mine.

'We could watch a movie?' she says, softening slightly. 'A French film about doomed lovers, maybe? How about *Last Tango in Paris*?' She laughs.

'Have some water,' I say, giving her my glass.

'Let's drink some more whisky. And I like it neat.' Esther holds out her empty glass stubbornly. Reluctantly I top her up. She is determined to be drunk. I don't want a scene.

The walls of Cedric's house are closing in on me. I want to get away from the heavy drapery, the overstuffed furniture, the dead-eyed silver framed photos. I don't belong here. Meeting Gupta has changed everything.

* * *

Esther doesn't try and stop me. She leans against her front door, one bare foot rubbing against her ankle, the whisky glass pressed against her chest.

'When will I see you?' Her voice is shrill in the cold, damp night.

'Soon, very soon. Just go to bed and stop worrying,' I reply. 'Take a sleeping pill or something. I'll deal with Gupta. I promise.'

'PK… promise me this isn't the end?' she says, and before I know it she is running down the steps, still barefoot, catching hold of my hand. 'Maybe it's no bad thing if they find out. We'll be free then. We can be together,' she says, cupping my face in her hands, kissing my forehead, my cheeks, my chin.

'How can it be the end? We've only just begun,' I say. I'm talking to a child, soothing her fears. I remove her hand gently, prising away her fingers one by one, and head towards the car.

I drive around the empty Manchester streets until the weak light of the morning sun tells me it's time to return home.

Dear Lopa didi,

A strange thing happened. Gupta came to see me. He rang home. I told him he would find PK at the office. He won't be there, Gupta said, mysteriously. I told him he wasn't at home, either. He should know PK is a busy man. But Gupta wanted to talk to me. Let's meet for coffee, he said. I agreed, because maybe he was having problems with Usha. They have been married a long time and she is not the easiest. I was at my course, having coffee with my Polish friends when I saw Gupta walking into the cafeteria. He dresses so shabbily. PK looks like a Bollywood hero next to him. I wish Usha would polish his shoes and iron his shirts, but she is so lazy – more interested in collecting gold bangles for her daughter's wedding.

He took me to a corner table and made me buy him a coffee and carrot cake, and asked if I was happily married. The cheek of him. He told me to be careful. There were people who wanted to see my marriage break up. He told me to leave the course and stay at home. You should speak to Usha, he said. She will explain how to keep the fire alive. You mean sex, I said. I'm not afraid of using that word, and he blushed red to the tip of his nose. I didn't know Indians could go pink. I told him PK and I were too old for all that hanky-panky. We are in our fifties, not youngsters. That shut him up. Thankfully the bell rang and I went to my class. I don't think I will tell PK about this meeting. As it is he looks like a frightened ghost these days. His hair has grown more grey and he is drinking a lot. I wish he had joined the civil service in India or become an accountant. Running your own business has so many worries. You are lucky Jijaji has his brothers helping him. We are here all alone in this foreign land. All these worries keep me awake at night. Good news about Bubbly. The boy sounds smart. I really hope PK will let me come to Bombay for the wedding.

Geeta

26

HER OLD AGE WILL BE CROWDED WITH PEOPLE

I don't hear from Gupta. He doesn't phone or show up at the house. But one morning, soon after that fateful meeting, I wake up to find Geeta leaning over me, holding a cup of tea. She's wearing my old cardigan with the missing buttons. The beige colour makes her cheeks look grey and drawn. I'd told her to donate it to Oxfam, but she insists on holding on to it.

'You were shouting in your sleep,' she says, handing me the teacup. Her hands are unsteady and the tea spills on to the bed sheet.

'Did I say something stupid?' I'm worried I'd called out Esther's name.

'Some rubbish I didn't understand. Something about Cedric and Gupta,' Geeta says.

I peer at the bedside clock. 'It's still early,' I say.

'I was scared. I thought you were dying or having a heart attack,' she says in a worried voice. 'You've never done it before – talking in your sleep.'

'You're not getting rid of me so easily. I'm strong as an ox,' I say, patting my chest to show her my heart is pumping just fine.

Geeta goes to the window and draws open the curtains. It's another Manchester morning – dark and obscured by rain. We watch raindrops slide down the windowpane.

It's a Saturday. I've no work and no Esther to worry about. I could stay warm under the duvet, sip my tea, stare at the rain and pretend I'm on a holiday from myself.

Geeta stands by the window, looking out to somewhere far away. 'It almost feels like we're in Bombay today. Maybe I'll fry some pakoras and we can watch an old movie.' A small smile spreads across her lips. 'Remember when it rained non-stop for a week and we couldn't get out? The roads were flooded and the generators were down.'

'I remember. I bet Bombay still has those power cuts, too,' I say. 'If we were still there I bet we would often have to sit in the dark, playing cards till the lights come back on. You were always good at rummy, but I won every time we played.'

Geeta's smile becomes broader at the memory. 'I always let you win, like a good little Indian wife.' She breathes out deeply. 'The darkness in England is so different. I don't think I can ever get used to living here. Not in a hundred years.'

Geeta's dream is to see Amar grow up and get married. 'Then we'll have enough money to retire and go back to Bombay,' she always says, her eyes ablaze with determination.

'What if he falls in love with an English girl and wants to stay on?' I ask. It's a running joke between us.

But she doesn't treat it like one. 'Never, never,' she says, shaking her head. She is going to find Amar a nice, dutiful Gujarati girl – one without fancy ideas or aspirations, not like the Punjabi girls. Then we will go back home to Bombay – a triumphant return to the homeland.

There is a suitcase underneath our bed, specially kept for when we go back to Bombay. All of Geeta's best things are packed away in there – her Kanjeevaram silk saris, the ones she thinks are too good for Manchester, our wedding album, a silver-plated tea set, her M&S cashmere cardigans and twelve red lipsticks from Boots, tied together with a rubber band.

Sometimes, when she's watching an Indian film on TV, Geeta's eyes get a thirsty look in them. She gets up from the sofa and paces up and down, her arms hanging limply by her side, her eyes fixed on some point beyond the walls of her house. Her old age will be crowded with people. Sons, daughters, grandchildren, uncles and aunts, a permanent merry-go-round in a Bombay flat on Nepean Sea Road, where the sun always shines and the food never runs out. For Geeta, Manchester will always be a detour, not a final stop.

She comes back to bed, pushing away the duvet, her hands deep inside her cardigan pockets. The petticoat she sometimes wears at night rides up, showing her legs – legs that were shapely once, but are now just solid, covered with a dark sprinkling of hair she's not bothered to wax. But her ankles were still girlishly slim. Her feet are like a dancer's, long and narrow.

We lie side by side, our bodies rigid, untouching, like wooden marionettes in a display cabinet, our eyes fixed on the rain outside.

'You remember it rained on our wedding day?' Geeta says, her voice ending the silence. 'It was auspicious, your father said, but he had such a long face that day. My mother thought he was constipated.' She laughs.

'Rain is auspicious in a Hindu wedding,' Father had muttered, but his voice was unsure and his eyes were worried. His heart and his head weren't in the celebrations.

Mother had died a year earlier, and everything in the house was like a bell ringing out her absence. The armchair where she sat knitting on winter afternoons still carried the shape of her body, and the radio stayed tuned to her favourite station, the BBC World Service. There were just the two of us left behind, along with Ramu, our Bihari servant who threatened every month to go back to his village unless we increased his salary. We were left bewildered by Mother's death, unfit even to boil an egg, and so we caved in, increasing Ramu's salary until he earned as much as a babu in a Government ministry.

Father had been dreading the wedding festivities. He found being happy an effort, a habit that needed to be learnt. It was far easier to be sad and hold a grudge against his son and wife. Mother and I had always laughed at his petty rages. 'There he goes, putting the world to rights again,' Mother would say, shaking her head as she sat by the window, her hands busy at the Singer sewing machine, a pile of saris at her feet waiting to be embroidered.

'Why does he keep writing to the papers, Ma?' I couldn't understand his weekly letters complaining about burst sewage pipes and refuse collection in our neighbourhood.

'Your father is a good man, but he never learnt to live. Too scared to spread his wings, so all he can do is whine,' Mother told me. 'Make sure you learn to fly. Always approach life with a telescope, not a microscope.'

There they sit by our bedside – my dead parents talking to us on that rainy Manchester morning.

'Remember Uncle Hari and Aunty Bina?' I remind Geeta. 'Father begged them to come and help with our wedding. They stayed on for months.'

'Uncle Hari from Moradabad?' She giggles. 'You couldn't stand him. You refused to touch his feet after the wedding, and he got so mad.'

I hated my uncle. He had my father's mean mouth, and was little more than a small-town trader, selling brass utensils to pilgrims on their way to Haridwar. He died of a heart attack, just like my father – and both of them were on their way to a tea shop for their daily chai and gossip session.

His sons, my cousins, wrote to me, pleading for jobs in England. I wrote back saying they'd better stop dreaming and stick to Moradabad. I had no time for their slow, simple village ways, their annoying little tics, the way they sat on the sofa with their feet on the cushions or the noisy slurping as they drank their tea, tipping it first into the saucer to cool it. Their ways were not mine. They wouldn't have slotted into the English way of life.

I didn't find Geeta. Her father found me. I was waiting at the Shivaji bus stop for the next bus to the British Council. Instead of attending lectures, I hung around the Council, watching free reruns of *Casablanca* and *Dr Zhivago*, dreaming about meeting a girl who looked like Julie Christie. At six-foot tall, with broad shoulders and thick, wavy hair, I must have stood out among the puny local boys loitering at the bus stop.

Geeta never tired of telling everybody the story of how we first met. 'My father's car broke down – the tyre had a puncture, near Shivaji stadium. There was a crowd of people watching him, but no one came to help this old man; no one helped him lug the spare tyre out of the boot – until…' here Geeta would pause and point triumphantly at me. 'Until a handsome young man rushed from the bus stop, got down on his hands and knees, ruined his clothes and replaced the tyre.'

Her father was a big-hearted man who'd invested his money shrewdly. He gave me a Fiat Padmini, and promised me a colour TV for the bedroom in the wedding dowry. Geeta was his youngest daughter.

'She may not be very beautiful or brainy, but she has a kind heart,' he implored, folding his hands together. 'She'll be a Lakshmi and bring you good luck and fill your home with children.'

I had no time then for small, plain-looking girls with long, oily plaits. I craved glamour – girls who spoke English and had western-sounding names like Sabrina, Maya or Anoushka.

Geeta Patel, with her rounded shoulders and deep, dark eyes, wasn't meant to be a part of my life. But they were stubborn, father and daughter. They didn't give up on me. Geeta made friends with my friends, bought them tickets to the movies, treated them to kulfi on Chowpatty beach.

The night before the wedding, Father came to my room, leant nervously against the door and said, 'You don't have to go through with this marriage, you know. You can always return the car.'

'I'm not changing my mind,' I told him. I was young and I wanted a woman in my life. Geeta loved me. She didn't care that I had a second-class degree from a second-class college. 'At least you dream big,' is what she said when I told her I was going to build a future in the West. 'I won't be an IAS officer, but I will make you happy,' I promised her.

Geeta had a ready smile, and wore her sari wrapped tight and low around her waist, her belly button winking at me every time she moved.

'I want to marry her,' I insisted.

'She doesn't seem your type,' Father said, his eyes downcast, fixed on his Bata chappals. He thought he knew me better than I did.

'I don't have a type, Father,' I said. 'What's important is that she will look after me. She loves me and we'll have a big family.'

'Make sure you take good care of her,' he said, and left the room. On the wedding day, he dutifully slipped my mother's gold bangles on to Geeta's arm.

I've never told Geeta about my father's doubts. She still wears those gold bangles, even though they are tight on her plump wrists.

We both wanted children. Lots of children, right from the start. I wanted desperately to cancel out the silence that comes of being an only child by filling my house with the sound of running feet and voices clamouring to be fed or to play. 'We'll have two sons and two daughters,' I promised Geeta on our wedding night. 'Big, strong kids who'll know their place in the world.'

She'd giggled and nodded and said maybe three sons and two daughters would be better. Sons for our old age and daughters to spoil and cherish.

It didn't quite happen like that. Miscarriage followed miscarriage, and then along came Amar. All those dreams of a big family, and all we ended up with was Amar.

One day – I can't remember exactly when – I came home from a trade fair in Birmingham to find Mrs Ahmed pottering about the kitchen. Amar was sitting on the floor at her feet, playing with Lego pieces, the colourful plastic blocks scattered around him.

'Where's Geeta?' I asked Mrs Ahmed. She said she was resting after a hospital visit.

'She's had her tubes tied. She felt too tired to go through another labour,' she explained, pushing a plate of corn fritters, her speciality, towards me.

And this was how Geeta went behind my back and cheated me out of a large family.

'Why did you do it? I asked her.

'I'm tired. Very tired, PK,' she replied. She pursed her lips. 'I'm forty now, too old to be a new mother. It's best I look after the one we have, our darling bundle of joy, Amar.'

The talk of old days makes us feel tender and open. Geeta picks up an old photo album from her bedside table and together, our heads touching, we flick through the album. There was Geeta, head covered, slim like a pole in her gaudy red sari. Standing right beside her, almost a foot taller, was a young man with full lips and thick-lashed eyes. Instead of the traditional kurta, he wears a three-piece grey suit.

'Was that really me?' I ask.

'You were a proper film star, you were,' says Geeta. 'My friends were so jealous of me.'

Does Esther have days like this, I wonder, when she stays in bed with Cedric, holding hands under the duvet, talking about the old days and regretting the new ones?

Then I think of Gupta, and the whole misery of the evening when he caught me with Esther comes rushing back. He's going to bring my house down.

'Has Gupta been in touch?' I ask Geeta casually, getting out of bed. I stretch my arms, going through the motions of a man without a care in the world.

Geeta says no – why would he call? He's a busy accountant.

'He's a busybody, all right,' I say. She agrees.

Looking at the album has put her in a good mood; she's humming a song from an old film. She puts away the album and, squatting on the floor near the chest of drawers, starts matching up socks and folding my ties, my vests piled high on her lap like a baby being put to sleep.

Dear Lopa didi,

I wasn't going to post you this letter, but I've changed my mind. I'll send it to you. You will only laugh and say, Silly Geeta, still being homesick after all these years. Just shut up and put up. It's like a wave that comes and overwhelms me. Yesterday was such a day. It was a proper Manchester rainy day, and PK and I stayed in bed. Nothing romantic, but like good old friends swapping stories about Daddy and our marriage. The old days – are they always the gold days? Or maybe it's better to forget the pain. Sometimes I feel PK hasn't forgiven me for getting sterilised after Amar. You were angry too. I remember how you shouted at me over the phone. But three miscarriages was no joke, didi. Each time I would be filled with hope, and start knitting baby booties, buy a new cot and bottles, and then I would see the blood trickling down the toilet or be paralysed with cramps. My body was telling me to stop. God has blessed us with Amar. One day he will grow up into a smart young man and bring home a bride. Someone sweet and gentle like your Bubbly. God bless our children and keep them from harm.

Love,
Geeta

27

NEVER LET YOUR SHOES RUN FASTER THAN YOUR FEET

'I've heard rumours.' Margaret shakes her head and presses a tissue to her nose. She always gets a cold when there's bad news to deliver. I'm worried she's talking about Gupta – maybe he's Googled Esther Solomon and knows exactly who she is. He's made enquiries, and he's ready to drag my name through the dirt. I have two missed calls from him on my phone.

'It's Ali,' Margaret says. 'I've heard Cedric's shifting his production over to him. He came over last week and met Simon Philips, Solomon's purchasing manager. They've signed some sort of agreement.'

I reach for my cigarettes. 'How did you find out?'

Margaret clears her throat and blows her nose delicately. She studies her keyboard. 'It's all over the industry – *Drapers* even had a feature on it. Cedric is moving his knitwear production from Morocco to Bangladesh. The labour is much cheaper and there is less unrest. The Moroccans don't want to pump money into Jewish hands – some nonsense about Cedric's links with Israel.' She rolls her eyes. 'What a tribal world we live in.'

'Why didn't I know about this?' I ask. Ali was going to have his hands full with Cedric's account. He wouldn't have time for puny little orders from the likes of me.

'Your head is buried in sand these days, that's why,' she says. 'You don't turn up for meetings. You cancel appointments. You'd better get a grip on things, or there won't be much of a business left for Amar to take charge of.' She's right. 'Solomon is a sneaky little thing!' she goes on, lowering her voice. 'We could sue Ali for breach of contract, couldn't we, PK…?'

The room starts spinning. I grip the table to steady myself. My mouth is dry and my head feels heavy. I know Cedric has every right to screw me – it's Karma calling. It's my dead father laughing. It's my dead mother wailing. It's Geeta, Amar clutching at her breast, screaming that I've betrayed them.

'I deserve it,' I say, my head in my hands,

Margaret is by my side, shutting the door, pressing a glass of water into my hand. 'Don't worry, PK. It will be fine, it will be fine.' She stands over me, her ice-cool palm pressing against my forehead, the clean, starched smell of her clothes pulling me back into the world.

'How can it be fine? I want to kill that bastard Ali,' I snap. 'I had it coming.'

'Never let your shoes run faster than your feet, PK,' Margaret says. Her soothing voice becomes firm. 'I told you we shouldn't have put all our eggs in Ali's basket,' she says. 'We should've kept other suppliers on the back-burner. But you wouldn't listen, would you? That's the problem with you. Sometimes you can be too obstinate for your own good.'

So Ali has gone over to the other side. I need to make phone calls and enquiries about other suppliers and factories. The orders for next year are going to come through soon – I have to find a factory that can stitch the garments in time.

Margaret sees my face. Her voice becomes gentler. 'Don't worry, PK. We'll pull through this. Just like we've pulled through everything else.' She blows her nose.

Margaret is a wise, Scottish soul. She knows the business better than me. She understands when I am losing my grip on it all. I hired her when I was just starting out – she'd answered an advert in the *Textile Gazette* and came down from Glasgow for an interview. I had trouble getting her broad Scottish burr at first, and made her repeat everything twice. 'We're both outsiders, you and I,' she had said in the interview. 'We will tick along just fine. Hard work is grafted in my bones, just like in yours. We'll show the English what we are made of.' I liked her fighting spirit, and I employed her straight away.

'Is she pretty? Is she sexy?' Geeta asked when I got home. In the early days she still fretted over such things.

'As pretty as a pink and white mouse.' I said, and encircled Geeta's whippet-thin waist with my arm to reassure her. 'There's no need to worry. Ever.'

There had been one kiss, maybe ten, fifteen years back at our annual Christmas party. We'd just signed a big order with an Irish department store, and my head was dizzy with success. Margaret came up to congratulate me. Her blue dress lit up her eyes. I grabbed hold of her hand, nudged her outside on to the landing and gave her a kiss. Her eyes shut, her sad little breasts squashed against my jacket. Her mouth tasted of Baileys. She didn't wear that dress again.

* * *

I go home early, stopping at the Timperley library to borrow a book: *The Cultivation of the Home-Grown Mango Tree*, written in the 1920s by a James Melville. I picture him, Melville, rosy-cheeked, with a handlebar moustache and a red soldier's jacket, a bayonet swinging by his side. India would have destroyed him, the heat bleeding the colour out of his cheeks. I wonder which dusty, nameless village he lies buried in, a circus of flies swarming over his grave.

The librarian, stamping out the book, reads out the title and says in a loud, disbelieving voice, 'Surely, you're not thinking of growing one of them here? You'd be better off with an apple tree…'

'My mother loved mangoes,' I tell the librarian. The library is quiet and she clearly has time on her hands.

It's a simple explanation, but it dredges up so much. Every year my mother waited impatiently for the mango season to begin. I'd return home from school to find our flat abloom with their fragrance, and there would be my mother, eyes shining with joy, peeling them carefully in the kitchen, urging me to come and dip a slice of bread in its juice.

'Eat as many as you like,' she would say. 'These are Alphonsos, the king of mangoes.'

'It's a tropical plant,' says the librarian. 'How on earth will you get it to grow here?' She looks outside at the flat grey afternoon pressing against the library windows.

I lean over the counter and look her right in the eye. 'Look at us Indians. We are tropical, but we are flourishing here, aren't we?' It's a lame joke, and she smiles.

I know the mango tree in my garden isn't really a proper tree – more a sapling that I had sneaked in from Bombay, back in the days when airport customs turned a blind eye to the traffic of pickles and people flowing between the subcontinent and England. Every winter I shroud the plant with polythene, carefully watching for any signs of frost or disease. As the years passed, it grew an inch or two, once even sprouting what looked like a fruit, but which turned out to be a dud. But I didn't give up hope. When I look at it now I see the tree that it will become one day, with a huge, king-size trunk and branches that flare out in all directions, glossy golden mangoes hanging from every tip.

I'm almost home when Esther rings. We decide it's best we don't meet for some time.

'I want to find out what's going on in Gupta's head,' I tell her.

She asks if he is the type to snitch on his best friend.

'I don't know,' I say. 'He's funny like that. He'll think he is protecting Geeta, but what is cutting him up is that I am having sex with a beautiful woman like you.'

'Be careful,' she says. 'Don't push him into a corner.'

I tell her I will spend more time at home, do a bit of gardening and work on my mango tree. She says she'll find ways of killing time too. The rabbi wants her to organise a charity fashion show, and her daughter is visiting from Israel – maybe she'll find an online course, learn Italian or French. Her voice is flat as she describes the different ways in which she will try to be less lonely.

* * *

Geeta is home early, hunched over a computer that takes up most of the kitchen table. It's big and looks old-fashioned, like an early IBM machine. She's working on an Excel sheet for her course.

'How's it going?' I ask, touching the computer. 'Is this new?'

'I got a deal,' she says. 'PC World had a special offer. Computer and printer for only £499.'

'It's a bargain. I just hope it doesn't break down,' I say, and go outside into the garden. I fill up a watering can and open the mango book. I'm busy fretting over the brown blotches on the branches when Geeta comes out to find me. She looks cheerful.

'There's a new Shah Rukh Khan film out at the Odeon,' she says. 'Usha just called to say there are tickets available. It has good reviews.'

'What about your homework?' I ask.

She makes a face and says it can wait. 'The film is only showing until Friday.'

'Is Gupta going too, or is it just the wives?' I ask. Gupta and I still haven't spoken to each other since he caught me red-handed with Esther.

'Just the wives,' she replies. 'Usha is picking me up.'

I relax. At least I won't have to face Gupta's accusing eyes.

'What will you do?'

'I have a few work calls to make,' I say and add that Ali has been two-timing us at work.

Her face falls. She knows he's our main supplier. 'Speak to him. Tell him it is wrong. Has he stolen money too?'

'He has gone for something better,' I say.

'I'll cancel the film,' Geeta says. 'I'm not in the mood.'

'Don't be silly. Just go and get ready. The Guptas are so bloody punctual. They think they're English.'

'Amar's upstairs with Alice. They're busy with some school project,' she says, and hesitates, glancing up towards Amar's bedroom window, where the curtains are drawn.

'I don't really like him spending time with her,' I say.

'She has a good heart. She was so nice to Amar on his birthday when you weren't there, and she cheered him up, baking him a cake, making sure he went on all the rides.' There she goes again, reminding me again of my failures as a father.

* * *

I'm reading the book again when my mobile rings. It's Esther. I walk to the far end of the garden, near the beech hedge that divides our garden from Mr Peters'.

'Why are you calling?' I say. 'I'm at home.'

'Lara's not coming.' Esther sounds upset. 'She was meant to come this weekend, but she just rang up to say she can't.'

'I'm sorry,' I say. I know how much she's been looking forward to her daughter's arrival.

'Cedric's away too, and the evening's too long without anybody – no Lara, no nobody.' Esther's voice had a catch. 'Can't you sneak away? Have a quick glass of vino with me? I could do with a friendly shoulder.'

She's breathing heavily into the phone, and it suddenly strikes me that she's the same age as Geeta. Not a young girl finding love, but an old woman fighting for it. I am filled with sadness.

'I don't think that's a good idea,' I say. 'Gupta might be dropping by, and Geeta's all tense and irritable. I can't just get up and leave. It's too risky.' I glance back at the house. The walls seem painted with ears. Our bedroom light is on. Geeta's getting ready for the film.

'Since when have you become so practical?' Esther's voice rises. 'I thought you couldn't get enough of me.'

I walk further away from the house.

'I'll find us another hotel, somewhere safer. But let's not meet for a couple of weeks, until I'm sure about Gupta's intentions.'

There is a sudden noise behind me, and I hear the sound of approaching feet. I cut off the call.

It is Gupta, his hands deep in his pockets, his thin lips unsmiling. 'Long time no see, my friend,' he says.

I don't answer, and instead pretend to flick through the book. But it's dark, and I can't read the print any more.

Gupta crouches down by the tree, rubbing a single leaf between his fingers. 'No scent at all – smells like death. Like the funeral parlour,' he says, sniffing his fingers.

I can feel his eyes on me.

'I thought just the women were going to the film?' I ask.

'I decided to chaperone them.' He gives a dry laugh. 'Why don't you come too? It will take your mind off Esther Solomon.'

'I don't feel like going out tonight,' I say. I ignore his reference to Esther.

We make our way back to the house.

'She was pretty… a little middle-aged, maybe – but what eyes.' He strokes his chin, as though pulling at an imaginary beard. 'Mind you, I would have thought if you're going to have a midlife crisis you'd go for someone younger. You've always had good taste. The poor woman – I made her jump out of her skin.' He chuckles at the memory.

'Where's Usha?' I say, opening the lounge door. She loves our Italian settees and never gets tired of sinking her plump body into the soft suede cushions.

'I told her to wait in the car,' says Gupta. 'I wanted to be alone with you, to ask you about Esther. What's going on, PK? Please tell me it's only a one-night stand and I'll be OK with it.'

'What are you talking about?' Geeta says, entering the kitchen. Her favourite blue pashmina is draped around her shoulders, and she has put on red lipstick.

Gupta snorts in amusement, but he doesn't give me away. 'Just an old joke between friends,' he says. 'Now get in the car quickly. We're going to be late.'

He squeezes my arm as he leaves and whispers, 'Come to your senses soon.'

* * *

Amar, Alice and I sit at the kitchen table eating the food Geeta has left behind for us. Egg-fried rice, prawns and chips. Alice finishes the chips, drowning them in a thick gunk of ketchup and vinegar. I'm still distracted by what Gupta has said, and am weak with relief that he didn't blurt it all out to Geeta. Amar complains that Alice has eaten all the chips. She is double Amar's size; her big, broad shoulders dwarf his round plump ones.

'How old did you say you were again?' I ask. I open a bottle of wine to help me get through the evening. It's a New Zealand wine, Cloudy Bay, Esther's favourite.

'She's sixteen,' Amar chips in. I see the adoring way he looks at Alice, rushing to the sink to get her water and spreading the butter on her slice of bread. She mops up the ketchup with the bread. She has a set of small, yellow, uneven teeth.

'Are you repeating a year? You seem older than Amar,' I say.

Again, Amar answers for her. 'She moved mid-term, that's why, Dad. She'll soon catch up.'

Alice merely smiles and looked down at her plate. I find her slow and heavy, dangerous, like an animal.

'Mind if I have a sip?' She points to my wine glass. Her nails are long and painted pink.

'You're only sixteen,' I say.

'Dad, let her have a sip. It won't kill her,' Amar says, his eyes shining with devotion.

'My mum lets me drink at home,' Alice says. 'She gets through a bottle most weekends.' She giggles.

Amar giggles too. 'My dad drinks too. All the time.' He snorts, his double chin shaking. 'It pisses off Mum big time. You should see her screaming.'

These aren't his words. He's borrowed them from her. I frown at him. 'Mind your language, Amar.'

I get up from the table. I'm anxious for Esther and worried about what Gupta might say to Geeta on the way to the cinema.

The cuckoo clock chimes. 'What time are you meant to be home, anyway?' I ask Alice.

'I've got my own key. I can get in any time,' she answers, her tone defiant.

'We've not finished our painting yet, Dad,' Amar says. 'The paint will dry soon, then she can go home.'

Amar's button-round brown eyes look back at me, clear and innocent. He is still a kid, and I have an absurd desire to press his plump little face against my chest and weave my fingers through his hair.

* * *

I take the wine upstairs to my office, and call Esther to tell her about Gupta's visit.

'I hate that man!' she says. 'Our story is over, isn't it? What do you think is going to happen now? What will he do next? Is he going to ring Cedric? Is he going to tell my kids?' Her voice is hoarse.

There's a tinkle of glasses in the background, a sudden burst of laughter, like a pistol shot. She is out. She tells me she's in a wine bar on Deansgate having a drink on her own. 'I don't want to sit in an empty house. Maybe I'll pick up a man to go home with,' she says, and hangs up.

She's so different to the woman I'd seen at Mowbray Hall. And I'd done that to her – unravelled her peace, broken her home. Could I ever face the world again with clear eyes?

I call Ali next. It is early morning in Dacca, and his sleepy voice only answers the phone on the fourth ring. I ask him about Cedric Solomon. He pretends not to understand.

I repeat my question slowly. 'Are you taking on production of Solomon's line?'

The connection is bad, he whines – too much static – he can't hear me.

I ask him if the denim shorts for the next season are going to be shipped on time. I have the buyer from MK1 breathing down my neck.

'The factory is on strike again,' he says. 'I can't promise anything.'

The best I can do is sue him for breach of contract. And that will take years and lots of money. 'I'm going to email you a copy of our contract,' I shout down the line. 'You can't get away so easily.'

The line is bad, he says, again and again. There's nothing to do but slam the phone down and finish the wine.

Esther, Ali, Geeta, Gupta… I want them all dead and gone.

I stare at the pictures on the wall – the courtier gowns and party frocks are mocking me. I take Esther's postcard of the dancing horses down and tear it up.

Downstairs I can hear Amar's thin, needy voice calling for me. It grows more insistent, and I come down. He is too big to hoist himself up the ladder into my study.

'Dad, can you drop Alice home?' he says. 'You're not too drunk, are you? You can drive?'

'Can't she catch the bus?' I say. 'I'm busy right now.'

'It's really late, though, Dad. We can't let her wait at the bus stop alone.'

'Fine, fine, I'll drop her home,' I say, reluctantly. I unhook the car keys from the wall and put on my coat. The evening has been ruined anyway.

They're waiting for me at the front door. 'Aren't you coming along too?' I ask Amar, who hasn't got his coat on.

'I'm tired,' he says, beginning to say he's staying behind.

'Come along, lazy boots. You could do with some fresh air!' I say, cutting him short, pretending to give him a playful clip around the ear.

He steps back and his arms fly up to hide his head. 'Don't hit me', he whimpers. 'Don't hit me, please.'

My hands drop to my sides. 'I never hit you, Amar. Where'd you get that idea from?'

Alice is observing us keenly, her ugly lips curled into a smirk. 'Don't bully him,' Alice says. 'He'll be all right. He's a good lad.'

We get in the car, Alice in the front, a sulking Amar in the back. I take a good look at her as she gets into the car. She's a large girl, with big pink hands and short stubby fingers. The girls on my hemming floor have hands like those. They are working-class hands – so different to Esther's long slim fingers.

'I know it's a pain dropping me home, so thanks,' she says, pushing her hands inside the sleeves of her black fleece. It is thick and old, and her leggings have a tear near the ankle. Everything about her is dirty and damaged.

She shifts in her seat, trying to get more comfortable. Her large white thighs gleam palely beneath the thin material of her leggings.

'Fancy leather seats you got here,' she says, stroking the car seat with her hand. 'And you've got a personal number plate. You must be dead rich.' She has a lazy way of speaking, half chewing her words. Her eyes dart around like a rabbit's.

'It is a Mercedes SL7. Top of the range,' Amar pipes up from the back seat. 'But it's not new. It's second hand.'

'What's this school project you and Amar are doing?' I say, changing the subject.

'We went on a school trip to Wales.' She repeats the names like a parrot: Conwy Castle, Rhuddlan and some other castle that starts with an S.

Have I ever been to Wales, she wants to know. I tell her no, there are large bits of Britain I still haven't seen. Now it's too late. I always wanted to see more of the world, places with names that taste like a fruit on your tongue: Zanzibar, Peru, Tonga. I'm different to Geeta, whose world begins and ends with Bombay. I'm different to

Gupta, who gets out an A–Z map of Great Britain every summer and ticks off the places methodically – Salisbury Cathedral one year, Stonehenge the next. His ambition is to hire a camper van and 'do' Scotland before his kids get married.

'Right bore Wales was,' says Alice. 'But Amar and I sloped off and hid behind the walls.' She turns round and winks at Amar.

'It was naughty. Very naughty of us,' Amar giggles.

'That wasn't very smart of you,' I say. 'I want Amar to do well in his exams, do well in life, and this skiving won't help.'

'But he can't really do well, can he?' Her voice is innocent. 'You hit him in the head with a cricket ball.'

'It was an accident!' I shout. 'Amar knows it was an accident.'

* * *

We drive past Wythenshawe Hospital, on to a street with a large Woolworths and an Asda. It's unfamiliar territory – a place I wouldn't want to linger in after dark. Alice lives on a narrow road of terraced houses. There is an overturned pram in front of one, and two teenagers stand about, idly kicking a ball near a bus shelter where the glass has been smashed. Shards lie on the pavement like an anthill of icing sugar. They stare at my Mercedes. Alice winds down her window and waves to the boys, who stick two fingers up.

'England at its best,' I say to Alice, who doesn't get it.

'They've seen me in this posh car,' she says, her face pink with pride. 'We're here,' she says, and I pull up outside a white terraced house. There is a cat sitting on the front step.

'Come on in, Amar,' she says, getting out and bending over the cat. 'Hi, Brittany. Hi, doll.' She tickles the cat's neck. 'Mum's in – come inside and say hi,' she calls.

Her mum is in the front room watching television, her blue-stockinged feet propped on the coffee table, an ashtray piled high with cigarette butts at hand. She is wearing a blue nurse's uniform, and has a thin pink lipstick line for a mouth.

We sit down beside her on the red leather sofa. It has a torn armrest, and the foam stuffing juts out like Santa Claus' beard.

Alice disappears into the kitchen to make tea. Her mother is watching the television intently.

'What's your medical speciality?' I say, making small talk.

'I'm at the cancer place. The Nightingale Centre.' She tilts her chin in the direction of the window. 'Not far from here. I look after the stage-fours.' Seeing my confusion she adds, 'The ones on their last legs. I help them to the other side.' She gives a dry chuckle and changes the channel.

A game show is playing. 'Deal or no deal,' she says when I ask her what it is.

'My mum watches this,' Amar says. But the mother pays him no attention – her gaze is fixed on the screen.

'Nothing horrible about death,' she says, picking up our previous conversation, her eyes back on me. She switches off the television. 'Death is part of life. You just got to deal with it.'

How do I deal with death? I think of my mother, the long, lingering, musty smell of her death. The soiled sheets, the untouched bowls of puréed carrot and potato, the endless drone of her cassette playing devotional songs. I didn't deal with it. I survived it.

'So, you just moved to Manchester, I hear? You lived in Grimsby before, right?' I'm being polite. Our worlds couldn't be more different, I think, looking at the pile of *Hello* magazines on the floor, the little china cats on the mantelpiece and the television on the wall.

Her eyes narrow. 'Who told you I lived in Grimsby?' she asks. 'The school?'

'Amar mentioned something,' I say. 'And Miss Connor, the class teacher.'

'Why's she going about bad-mouthing me for?' She frowns and flicks some cigarette ash from her lap.

'She didn't say anything bad,' Amar pipes up. 'She likes Alice. She says it's good she's my friend.' He looks around for Alice, but she's nowhere to be seen.

The mum relaxes. 'Yeah, so we did. Lived in that shithole for more years than I care to count. Had to leave in a hurry, though.' She stops. She wants me to ask why.

I do.

'He was doing funny business with our Alice, he was – my ex-boyfriend, that is. I was working late shifts and came back one morning to see our Alice sobbing her heart out. Got the cops on to him bloody quick, but we had to leave. Left in the dead of night. He had a mean streak, Jim did. You wouldn't want to mess with him.' A smile suddenly twists her mouth, but the eyes stay watchful. 'I got one up on him, though. Restraining orders and all that.'

I get up. 'It's getting late. I've got an early start tomorrow.'

Amar gets up too, brushing away imaginary crumbs from his tracksuit. 'Where is Alice?' he whines. 'I want to say bye to her.'

'She'll be in the loo, most likely. Being sick,' the mother snorts. 'You got far to go?' she asks. 'Alice says you live in a big house, with a big car and gates.'

'I live in Timperley,' I reply, taking out my car keys. 'South Manchester.'

'Your lot have done all right in this country, haven't you? All the big houses, all the big cars. Money sprouts in your pocket like magic… while the rest of us, real English people, work our arses off… and…' she mutters something under her breath. She sits on the sofa scowling at me, a pathetic plastic watch pinned to her left breast pocket, her eyes accusing me, freezing me to where I stood. A poor immigrant fleecing the deserving.

'There's no secret to our success. We Indians are as real as you. We keep our head down and work hard,' I say, keeping my cool. I think of the unsold stock in my warehouse, the bank manager's call about mortgage repayments. Who am I kidding? The keys in my hand feel cold with my failure.

* * *

'You don't love me any more.'

I'm already in bed when Geeta says it. She's leaning against the bedroom door, her arms folded, pressed tight against her chest.

'Is this because of that Bollywood nonsense you've been watching?' I say. 'I'm married to you, aren't I? We love each other the Indian way – quietly, without fuss. The English are different – it's all loud kisses and slapping ass.'

'Prove it to me. Show me that you love me.' She comes near, the heavy drop of her breasts brushing against my wrists.

I make love to her that night. But I come too quickly and she doesn't come at all.

Lopa didi,

I hate the Guptas. They are trying to break up my marriage. We went to the Trafford Centre to watch the new Shah Rukh Khan movie. You must have seen it. He plays a cancer patient in New York. It's a love story. Anyway, instead of going to the cinema, the Guptas grab hold of my arms, one on each side, and said no, we're going to a coffee shop. It's the most horrible coffee there – no taste – but I had no choice. Usha ordered two almond croissants for us and then they started. Gupta asked if I had listened to his advice and given up the course. Was I being more attentive to PK? I needed to be careful about PK. He has been seen, he said. He's not invisible, I answered. Of course he'll be seen. Gupta started pulling his chin in that annoying way he has. He said, Geeta, try to understand. I saw your husband with another woman. It wasn't Margaret. I lost my appetite when he said this. I wanted to throw up. I told him he was lying. Told him he was jealous of PK. Usha butted in then, her mouth full of the almond croissant. But Geeta, she said, there is nothing to be jealous of any more. You were a big deal before, but not now. You know Patel and Sharma are in the same line of business, and they have managed to get their stock into House of Fraser and Peacocks. What could I say to that? I don't know where my husband supplies his clothes. I don't have the time to follow up on his every little worry.

But I remembered Harrods. We used to supply Harrods, I fought back. And that's the same as supplying the Queen. That shut them up. I think.

I got up and said in my most bossy voice, Enough is enough. I have faith in my husband. I trust him, so keep your tittle-tattle to yourself and drop me home. Thank you very much. We did not speak in the car, and I don't want to see them again. But I can't stop thinking of what they said. I have to protect my marriage for Amar's sake. He can't see us cracking apart like two broken dolls.

I will never post you this letter, didi – it would make you unhappy. But I had to unburden myself. Who else can I share this pain with? PK is a handsome man. I've always known there was danger in marrying someone so beautiful, but God has protected me till now. I hope our family remains intact. Please pray for me.

Yours,

Geeta.

28

A PAIR OF RED SHOES

Geeta doesn't keep up the computer course for long. I come home from work one day to find her lugging the computer into the garage. It took up too much time, she says. She was neglecting Amar, her only child.

'Look what I found,' she says, hesitating for a minute before handing me a scrunched roll of paper. 'It was in his bin.'

We unroll the paper together on the kitchen table, studying it and carefully hunting for clues about our child's secret life. The painting shows a girl, a naked girl, pink and unsmiling, arms spread out like Christ on his cross. The female bits – cut open like a gash – leer back at us. A crude drawing of a penis has been crossed out with a black felt pen.

Geeta turns away, her lip trembling. She picks up some scissors and starts cutting through the painting. I remember how I had done the same with the *Playboy* magazine I'd found in his room, a time which now feels like a lifetime ago.

'We can't ignore this like we ignored the cricket injury,' Geeta says. 'This is dirty stuff. Someone is polluting his mind.'

'I'll take him somewhere,' I say, ignoring her comment about the cricket injury. 'See a film and have a chat, maybe. See what's going on.' It's become a habit, how she blames everything on that one cricket ball arcing through the air that sunlit afternoon.

I call Gupta at work. He's busy, he says curtly.

'I'm only calling you because of Amar,' I say. 'You've had two kids, so you might be able to help…' I tell him about Amar's drawing.

'Are you still seeing Esther Solomon?' he says. His voice is stiff and annoyed.

'Forget her – it was just a one-night fling, like the girl you met at your Christmas party,' I say, bluffing my way out of it.

He lets out a long sigh. 'Phew! That's fine, then. I'll let you off. Does she have a sister?' He giggles. 'Tell me about Amar's drawing.' His tone is conciliatory. 'How about getting him a therapist? You know he's not been the same since your bloody careless—'

'We had him checked out – it was just a bruise!' I cut him off, shouting down the line. 'He's become sulky and secretive,' I continue.

'What do you expect?' Gupta replies. 'That's the price you pay for bringing up a kid in this country. Try spending some time with him – take him to the temple, talk to him in Hindi and teach him about our culture. And stop playing the romantic fool. It will come to no good.'

I cancel my meeting with Esther.

'Is Gupta blackmailing you? Has he told Greta?' she says, suspecting the worst. It's strange to hear her say their names.

I tell her he's a good friend. He wouldn't betray me. 'I told him you were just a one-night stand. That seemed to satisfy him. And it's Geeta, not Greta.'

'And is that all I mean to you?' she says.

'It's not about us this time.' I tell her about Amar's crude drawing. 'There was something disturbing about it. I need to spend more time with him. Maybe he's being bullied at school.'

'I wouldn't worry. It's just typical teenage boy stuff.' Her voice is dismissive.

'I've let him down before,' I say, thinking of his birthday. 'I'll have a chat with him. I'm taking him to the new James Bond film.'

'You'd rather spend time with James Bond than with me?'

'Don't be unreasonable, Esther, please.' I feel a headache coming on.

* * *

We hit the rush hour traffic, and by the time we reach the Trafford Centre the film has been running for half an hour.

Amar's eyes well up. His mouth turns down. 'I hate missing the beginning of films. You're always late, Dad. Always late for everything,' he says.

'Can you let us in? It's his birthday,' I lie to the girl at the booking office. She's young, seventeen at most, and is chewing gum.

'That's not true, Dad,' Amar pipes up. 'It's not my birthday. Stop lying.' He lurks behind me, the same self-conscious grin on his face he always wears when he knows strangers are observing him.

The girl yawns widely, and I see the well-chewed gum stuck to her molars. 'It's sold out,' she says, slamming down her window and flipping over a 'closed' sign.

We have two hours to kill before returning home, where Geeta will be waiting with a long list of questions, the television barking quietly in the corner.

'Let's have dinner instead, Amar, eh? What do you say? We'll catch the film over the weekend – bring Mum too.' I throw an arm around his shoulder. At fifteen, he's still a good head or two shorter than me. 'It'll save Mum cooking. What do you say?'

His eyes are filled with doubt. He hates surprises. We wander around the shopping centre looking for a place to eat. He drags his feet, his eyes dazzled by the shop window displays, and I tell him to stop hunching his shoulders and to walk straight.

'Hey,' I say, pointing to Pizza Express. 'Want to go to that posh pizza place?'

Amar claps his hands. He loves pizza, and in his eyes any place with a tablecloth is posh.

We sit beneath bunches of fake garlic and posters of Venetian gondoliers. It reminds me of the restaurant in Chester with its pictures of the Eiffel Tower. I try to think of things to say. If Amar was any other ordinary boy we could talk football, league fixtures and girls. But Amar doesn't work like this.

'How's school? This is an important year – you know that, don't you – GCSEs and all that…' My voice dries out.

Amar is bending low over his chocolate milkshake. His cheeks blow out as he sucks it through the straw.

'I've not missed any homework,' he says, sulkily.

'I saw your maths book. You didn't finish any equations. Do we need to get you another tutor?' I've not seen Haroon since the night of the altercation, but I assume he still turns up, swapping snacks and gossip with Geeta.

He shakes his head. He likes Haroon, he says. They play Lego together.

I press on. 'Is everything OK at school, Amar? You've not had a fight with anyone, have you? No one's bullying you?' I don't feel like naming Alice.

A tear falls down his cheek. 'There's a group of boys I don't like,' he says. 'They keep saying I'm a girl, always skipping games and wanting to be with Alice.'

'Ignore them. They're bullies,' I say. 'If it was me, I would have punched them to the ground, beaten the hell out of them, but…' I stop myself going further. 'I'll talk to the headmaster about moving you to another class. Just let me know if they carry on.'

He agrees and attacks his pizza, picking the olives off the top and depositing them in the ashtray like jewels to be discovered by the next customer.

His pizza finished, I see him eying mine. 'You've not touched yours – aren't you hungry, Dad?'

I push the plate towards him. I'm thinking of Esther, Gupta and the sordid mess that is my life. 'Have a slice and leave the rest. You don't want to become too plump. You won't get a girlfriend at this rate.'

Amar scowls. 'I don't want a girlfriend. I like Alice.' He takes a slice, and then another, taking quick bites.

'Is Alice your girlfriend?' I ask, smiling, indulging him, imagining them together, her hulking pink-white shape next to his round chubby-cheeked brownness.

He's embarrassed and says I am being silly, and then he softly says that she tried teaching him how to kiss. 'But I don't like kissing,' he says. 'It's yuck.' He screws up his face.

I tell him he will like it when the right girl comes along. 'Alice… she's messed up,' I say.

'She's not messed up! She is nice,' he says, placing his hand on mine. 'It's Mum who's messed up.'

I shift in my chair, bringing my face closer to his. His breath smells of tinned tomatoes. I'm surprised how his simple mind has tracked Geeta, pinned down her sadness, given it a name. What other secrets was he storing inside that head of his?

'She just starts crying for no reason and then runs upstairs…' he goes on. 'Actually, she walks upstairs,' he corrects himself. 'She's too fat to run.' He giggles, and picks up the dessert menu the waitress left behind. 'Can I have the brownie and ice cream?'

'You can't,' I say, shutting the menu. I call for the bill.

The old sullen look comes back on his face. 'You're never there – that's why she's crying, isn't it? Alice says you're having an affair or something. Your mobile's never on, you're never home on time and Mum's always got this long face on her. Why do you think I like having Alice around? You think I'm stupid, but I'm not.'

I hold his hand. 'Alice doesn't know a thing. Your mum is happy, and you're not stupid. You're special.'

He pushes away my hand. 'What does "special" mean? Miss Connor says I'm special, but then she doesn't pick me for the play or for the singing competition. Jo and Mark are always picked.'

'You're a late bloomer. Your time will come, just like my mango tree. One day you'll be big and strong and everyone will say, "Yes, he's special."'

Amar's expression changes. He wants to believe my words. 'Is that so, Dad?' he says.

'Let's get you that brownie and ice cream. I bet it's yummy.' A dessert will distract him and chase away the clouds of worry.

* * *

I smell Esther's perfume before I see her. She's in front of a shop window looking at some shoes, wearing her favourite Etro orange scarf. I hurry past her, nudging Amar forward so we wouldn't come face to face. But Amar spots a pair of bright red Nike trainers in the same shop window and slows down.

'Can I get those, Dad?' he says, pointing them out.

I read the price tag. 'Seventy-five quid! That's crazy. You don't even play football. What use are they to you?'

'I hate my old ones,' he says, not budging from the shop window. 'No one wears Clarks any more. I hate the Velcro straps. I look like a big nerd. That's what the boys say.'

'I thought I recognised that voice!' Esther says, turning around, her eyes lighting with pleasure. The scarf throws a tangerine-coloured glow across her face.

I catch hold of Amar's elbow, ready to steer him away. I see him through Esther's eyes – a pale, plump boy sprouting hairs on his chin, wearing a Disney sweatshirt with chocolate stains on it – and I feel ashamed for not insisting that he wear something smarter for our outing. 'Hi there!' I say, lifting a casual hand in greeting. 'What are you doing out so late?' I don't use her name.

She shrugs. 'Killing time, my dear mensch. It's what I do best. Cedric's extended his trip to Korea by another week, and you ditched me, so I'm a free bird.' She flaps her arms to show how free she is. Her handbag, which is looped through her arm, slips and falls on the floor.

Amar watches her, his mouth wide open. He bends down, picks up the bag and hands it to her. 'You've dropped your bag, missis.'

She extends her hand. 'Thank you, Amar. I get to meet the famous Amar Malik at last. How was James Bond? Did you enjoy the film?'

'We didn't see it,' Amar says, digging his hands deep in his pockets. At fifteen, he has the manners of a two-year-old. 'We had a pizza instead. I ate all the mushrooms. But I don't like olives.' His eyes go back to the trainers in the shop window.

'That's such a shame. And your daddy told me how much you love James Bond,' Esther says, kissing him on his cheek.

He steps back, rubbing his cheek. 'I don't like kissing.'

Esther laughs. 'I just love kissing. I could kiss all day long.' She pouts, giving me a wink.

'Dad, will you get me those trainers? Please?' Amar uses his special high-pitched wheedling voice that he saves for asking favours.

'Which shoes do you like?' Esther asks him.

'The red ones. They're Nike,' he says. 'But they cost a lot.'

'They're cool. I think you should get them.' She nods her head in approval.

'Daddy doesn't want to get them. He's so mean.'

'He's a mean man. A naughty man,' Esther agrees, jabbing her finger into my jacket, swaying just a little. She's been drinking. 'I'll get them for you, Amar. A belated birthday present. Eh? What do you say to that?' Esther says.

'How do you know about my birthday?' Amar watches her suspiciously.

She smiles recklessly. 'A little bird told me. And your naughty dad missed it too, didn't he? Make sure you give him a hard time.'

'You're not buying him any shoes,' I say firmly, placing my hand on Esther's arm to steady her. I lean in. 'You've been drinking. Go home. Please,' I whisper.

Esther ignores me. 'What size are you, Amar?'

Amar takes off his shoe, squints at the number inside and announces he's a seven.

'I really think you should go home,' I say to Esther. 'Don't drive. Get a cab.' I catch hold of Amar's hand, my nails digging into his palm, and start moving away.

'Call me tomorrow,' Esther shouts after us, holding a cupped hand to her ear, and disappears into the shop.

In the car on the way home Amar says it was sweet the way my friend wanted to buy him the trainers. He sighs in contented anticipation.

'She's not buying you anything. She was joking – just joking,' I say. 'Understand? Forget her, OK? She's not important. We won't talk about her at home and worry Mum. OK, Amar?' I look at him, but he's dozing, his mouth open and his eyes closed.

* * *

'Amar, how was the film? You liked it?' Geeta greets us at the door, rushing to take off Amar's jacket and gloves. Her eyes scan our faces for signs of shared father-son pleasure. 'Good outing, Amar? James Bond is very brave, no? Nice of Dad to take you and spend time with you. He's so busy,' she jabbers on.

'We didn't see the film,' Amar replies, suddenly wide awake. He throws himself down on the sofa and switches on the TV with a loud grunt, flicking through the channels until he reaches Nickelodeon.

'The film was sold out,' I explain, readying myself for Geeta's questions. The muscles at the back of my neck stiffen and my hands are clammy. I follow Geeta into the kitchen.

'How come you're late? What did you do instead?' she asks, stirring ground almonds into milk for Amar.

'We had a bite to eat. A pizza. Ham and mushroom. Amar polished off the whole thing, and then ate mine too…'

'We met Dad's friend. She's so nice, Mum,' Amar calls, his voice floating over from the sofa. 'A bird told her it was my birthday, and she wanted to buy me some new trainers, but Dad wouldn't let her.'

'Who did you meet?' Geeta asks casually. She drags the ironing board from behind the sideboard and picks up a pile of my shirts. The iron hisses in her hand.

'Just one of the girls from the office,' I say, and yawn loudly.

'A very nice friend, Mum. The shoes she wanted to buy me were seventy-five pounds,' Amar continues. 'I didn't know birds could talk, Mum.'

'So who is this friend you met today?' Geeta asks again in the bedroom. She sits on her side of the bed, her back to me, oiling her hair, massaging the scalp with both hands. It's her single beauty routine.

'I told you, she's not a friend. Just a woman from the office.'

Geeta is lost in thought. The fingers rubbing her scalp slow down and then stop moving. 'Margaret? Was it Margaret you met?' It's the only name she knows from the office.

'No, not her. Nobody you know. Nobody important. One of the new girls from the office.'

'And she wants to buy him shoes? Just like that, and worth seventy-five quid? Who does that? She's not his mother,' Geeta says, her tone disbelieving.

'He's making it up. You know how Amar is, always in cloud cuckoo land.' I make everything sound light and carefree, but feel my face burning beneath her gaze.

'Are you sure it wasn't Margaret? Maybe it was like a thank-you for giving her a job for so long?'

'It wasn't her. It's not important. Nothing to worry about,' I say. I don't know what else to add.

Geeta switches off the light and eases her heavy body into the bed, and suddenly groans.

I switch on the bedside lamp.

Her face contorts in pain. 'It's my back,' she says. 'I think I must have pulled a muscle or something.'

'It's all the bending down and ironing. It's killing your back. Maybe you should get a cleaner to come once a week? I don't know why we don't have one.'

'It costs money, that's why. The rate has gone up to seven pounds an hour. Someone in this family has to be sensible,' she replies. She lies curled in bed like a wounded animal, her mouth crooked and hurt.

'Turn over on your tummy. I'll give you a back rub,' I hear myself say.

'You will?' Her voice is unsure.

Gently, I raise her T-shirt. It's one of my old ones she wears to bed over her petticoat. Her back is so different to Esther's. It's tea-brown and smooth, without the scattering of pale freckles climbing up the spine. It is a back my hands aren't used to any more, the rolls of flesh just below the bra strap, or the tiny, dark mole that sits just beneath her left shoulder blade. I massage her for some time, my fingers tingling with numbness, taking care to be gentle, until she falls into an exhausted sleep. I pull the duvet over her and go outside.

The night sky is soaked with stars, and the moon is perched like an owl on a small silver cloud, glaring back at me with a cold, unforgiving stare. I stand beside my mango tree and touch the branches, which glitter with frost. I imagine Esther lurching drunkenly through the shopping mall, alone and abandoned, so different to the poised, glamorous woman who wanted a tour of Capability Brown's gardens. I think of Geeta's face, twisted in pain, and Amar's bewildered eyes when I refused to buy him the shoes. My sadness and deceit has infected everyone. The glow of my cigarette picks out a dark shape lying on the ground. I bend down to take a closer look. It's a dead sparrow. I wonder if I have become that bird, disoriented and lost.

Lopa didi,

It is true. There is a woman. Gupta was right. PK and Amar met her at the Trafford Centre. PK must have rung her and told her to meet them there. Maybe he wants to introduce Amar to her. If they get married, she will be his new stepmother. She sounds kind – at least, that's what Amar said – and she offered to buy him some expensive trainers. Maybe she was trying to win him over.

PK sprouted such rubbish, pretending this woman was a colleague. He thinks I'm an idiot. He was definitely lying. His voice became all posh and low, and he kept looking away.

Is she tall, fair and slim? I asked Amar about her looks, but the silly boy just kept saying she was nice. What does 'nice' even mean? The whole world is nice – Mr Peters is nice, the postman is nice – but this nice woman is going to destroy my family. I have to find out who she is. I have to tell her to stop her black magic. PK is like a child – it's so easy to flatter him. She must have gone on and on about his good looks. He is fifty-five, but still can't stop thinking he is some young man with his whole life ahead of him. Always dreaming such big dreams. Time to slow down and look after Amar. Make sure he grows up into an educated man with a proper job and wife. We will have grandchildren, and then, once he is nicely settled, we can go back home to Bombay, our heads held high. But this new woman won't let this happen. I have to stop her.

Didi, help me.

29

THE KINDNESS OF STRANGERS

'Cedric's working from home today,' Esther says. 'We can't be too long.'

I move my hand from her breast. 'What did you tell him?'

'I made an excuse,' she says. 'Something about a dentist and cavities.' She's worried, and her fingers are constantly tugging at her necklace – the pearl necklace I had given her.

She sees me looking at it. 'My husband thinks you've got good taste,' she says, laughing. She stops when she sees my face. 'It's a joke, my mensch. A joke! He liked the necklace – said he'd not seen it before. I said it was a self-gift. I bought it on a whim.'

I pull her closer, my hand tracing the outline of her mouth. 'Beautiful women like you have no business telling lies.'

'A beautiful woman caught in a bad kind of truth,' she replies.

The contours of her body press against mine. I kiss her mouth, which lies open, inviting. Her heart is a rapid drumbeat against my chest.

'What were you doing at the Trafford Centre?' I say, thinking of my narrow escape. 'Why the hell couldn't you have ignored us, pretended not to know me?' She avoids my eye. 'And you were acting so weird. Promising to get Amar those trainers. What's happened to you, Esther? We came home and all he could do was blab about his dad's nice friend to Geeta. Do you want to ruin everything?'

'It was a coincidence, I swear. I was just doing a bit of window shopping, and there you were. I felt sorry for your little boy,' she says. 'He wanted the shoes so badly.'

'You're a bad liar,' I say. 'I just hope you weren't mad enough to buy them for him.'

'I'm thirsty,' she says. 'Get me some water, please.'

I go to the bathroom, fill up a little plastic cup and take it back to her. She rests her head on my chest, her long hair hiding her eyes like a curtain.

'I am lonely. But is that what you think of me? I'm some kind of weird loony scaring little boys?'

'Don't be silly. I'm just terrified that we'll be discovered. We've had a narrow escape from Gupta.' I reach for her, my fingers searching for the soft, quiet darkness inside her.

She arches her back and closes her eyes, her body relaxing against mine. But making love doesn't come easy that day.

'Too many worries,' I say. 'We shouldn't have talked about Amar and Cedric.'

'It's never bothered us before,' she says with a sigh. 'Let's talk about happy things. Let's talk about the old days.'

'There are no old days between us, only new ones,' I say. 'I've only known you for a year. Can you share a history in such a short space of time?'

'History can be made in a day. You should know that,' she says. She tells me about the Mediterranean cruise her husband has booked for the coming summer. 'He's invited his sister and brother, the whole shebang.' She makes a face. She doesn't want to go. She wants to go to the Basle Art Fair instead. There is a rare Caravaggio coming on public display. 'You know who Caravaggio is, don't you?'

I have a vague idea. 'An Italian painter? I've not been to Venice, but there are some of his paintings in churches there, right?'

She pretends to clap. 'Bravo. You passed with flying colours. I can take you to the fair. You would love the sensuousness and texture of his paints.'

I shake my head and say that after the Marbella disaster we aren't going anywhere. 'How much is this cruise anyway?' I'm curious.

She doesn't know – all she knows is she needs to take long dresses for the evening.

'Packing will be a pain,' she sighs. Like most wealthy people, Esther can be both ignorant and helpless. It isn't her fault. She moves in such a world. Money is a facilitator of good things and not a prerequisite for existence. She is used to buying time, not using it. She tells me about the charity ball she is organising with the chief rabbi. 'Ten K per table,' she says. 'We're hoping to get Clinton as a speaker – fingers crossed.'

I tell her about having to lay off some more girls from the warehouse. 'They have no pride in their work. When I was their age, I used to put in fourteen solid hours a day, and for less than the minimum wage.'

She sits up abruptly, the bed sheet falling from her body, the two soft mounds of her breasts peeping like soldiers above a wall. 'Why are you always whining about money and work?' she says, angry. 'First it was the seventy-five-quid trainers. You didn't want to buy them for your only child? I mean, what the hell – don't you want to see him happy? And now all this talk about sacking girls… It's depressing.' Her face is alive with a type of emotion I've not seen on it before. 'I don't know why you men are always so tense about business. If there's a cash-flow problem I can always sort you out.' She sinks back on to the bed, as though drained of strength.

'I don't need your husband's money,' I reply coolly, collecting my things and getting dressed. 'Don't try to impress me with your money. Do you understand?'

I leave, shutting the door firmly behind me. Things have started to get this way between us more often – nothing loud or filthy, just nasty little words that linger for days like bruises.

* * *

Esther's words follow me to the house. It isn't the first time she's used her money as a window into a bright, new world. She paid for the hotel in Spain, and always wants to buy me gifts – Cartier lighters, expensive watches and pens. I refuse each time.

'You're not whistling today,' Geeta says when she sees me enter the kitchen with my head down. She's painting her toenails, her feet resting on a chair, tongue sticking out, her forehead puckered with effort.

'Nothing serious,' I say. 'Just office worries.'

She says she feels like coming to the office one day.

'But you hate coming to the office. You always say it makes you nervous.'

'I'd like to meet your new staff,' she says. 'Especially the one Amar was going on about. I'd like to talk to her.'

'You'll be wasting your time.' I pretend I don't know what she's talking about. 'They're a lazy bunch. I'll be sacking them soon.'

* * *

Just before going to bed I go outside to check on the mango tree. Fussing over it, teasing its branches, stroking its leaves makes me feel calmer.

Geeta comes out and stands next to me, drying her hands on a tea towel. Her toenails are pink and she's wearing a different tracksuit. The fabric, synthetic and cheap, clings to her body in all the wrong places. 'I noticed the branches were getting brown patches, so I went on the internet and ordered that pesticide you wanted. It'll come next week. It's from Shanghai. All the way from China.' Her voice is proud.

'That's great,' I say. 'The computing course wasn't such a waste of time – you managed to go online.' I touch her arm briefly to show I care. I get the feeling Geeta wants to say more, but she remains standing there, rubbing her neck with the tea towel, staring at the black sky.

'Remember how big the stars were in Bombay?' she says. 'You used to say you'd pluck them and string them around my neck like a diamond necklace.'

It starts to rain and we hurry indoors. Geeta goes over to the sideboard in the hall and shows me a brown cardboard box I'd not noticed before. It was delivered by DHL that morning, and was addressed to Amar, but she'd opened it. Why would Amar be sent a parcel? She opens it again. Inside is a pair of shiny red trainers. 'This is why I want to go to the office,' she says. 'I want to personally thank the girl who sent them.'

I check the sender information on the label. 'E. Solomon', nothing more. I look for a note inside, but there's nothing. 'Have you shown them to Amar?' I say, lifting out the shoes, turning them right and left, examining the soles, pretending it's perfectly normal for our son to be receiving shoes from strangers.

'Who is this E. Solomon?' she asks.

'I told you – a colleague.'

'You've never mentioned this name before. Is she new?'

'Where is Amar? Why hasn't he seen these?' I ask.

'He's gone bowling with Alice and some new friends,' says Geeta.

'But he's got exams soon, and he's so behind in maths. You shouldn't have let him go out,' I say. It's the easiest and most cowardly thing to do – deflect attention, shift the blame on to Geeta.

'What can I do?' Geeta says, her lip trembling. 'He gets bored at home. He wants to go out with his friends. He says they all go to parties. If only he had brothers and sisters to play with…' She covers her face with her hands.

I clumsily try to give her a hug, but she moves away, rubbing her red eyes with the tea towel. I grab my coat and say I'll bring Amar home.

30
THEY ARE MY FRIENDS

The streets are quiet and I reach Alice's home in no time. I ring the doorbell. A dark shape against the wall mews and slopes off into the night. I bang on the door. The light goes on in an upstairs room. A window opens and a cigarette tip emerges, shining like a torch.

'Who the fuck's that?' shouts Alice's mother.

'It's Amar's dad, come to pick him up,' I shout back. The window slams shut, and I hear heavy footsteps coming down the stairs.

Alice's mother opens the door, her bony body wrapped in a dressing gown printed with pink hearts. She scowls and says the kids have gone to the bowling arcade in Parrs Wood.

* * *

The arcade is next to a pub with a Union Jack bunting strung across the windows, fluttering feebly in the evening rain. A knot of men huddle outside, catching up over a last pint before they go home. I walk past them, instinctively quickening my pace, my head down, but nobody jeers or shouts 'Go home, Paki' as I fear.

The arcade is floodlit. Two black women in red T-shirts are sweeping fallen popcorn into grey bin liners. The bowling alleys are like runways waiting for an aircraft. Piped pop music floats aimlessly through the building.

Amar is standing by a pillar, drinking a Coke, slightly apart from a group of boys who are taking turns at knocking the skittles down. I watch him. His shoulders are hunched, his hair is pressed flat against his forehead and his jumper – his favourite blue one – is stretched tightly over the bulge of his tummy.

A boy comes up to him and says something. Amar shakes his head, but the boy keeps pulling at his sleeve. Amar goes up to the ramp and lifts the ball. He holds it carefully, as though it's as fragile as an egg. He turns it round and round, examining it, pressing it against his belly.

A girl sneaks up behind him. She has her back to me, but I recognise the bottle-bought yellow hair and the oversized black fleece. She knocks the ball from his hand and it rolls towards the skittles. Amar runs after it, skidding on the shiny surface before falling over heavily.

The other boys hoot with laughter. 'Wanker!' they shout. 'You big fat wanker!'

Alice claps her hands and joins in the laughter. Amar lies flat, sprawled on the floor, looking puzzled. He tries to get up, turning awkwardly on his side, his hands searching for something to hold on to. The friends are watching and laughing.

'Amar, Amar!' I call, running towards him. My strong arms help him up.

'Go home, baby, go home. Mummy will kiss it better!' Alice shouts. Mascara is streaked across her eyes like war paint.

* * *

The box with the new shoes inside is waiting for us on the kitchen counter.

'Dad, why did you come? We were having fun. Now Alice thinks I'm a right baby, all thanks to you,' Amar says.

'They're not your friends, Amar. They were bullying you.'

He doesn't answer. He just walks to the sink and clumsily drinks some water straight from the tap. His hand is shaking and his eyes slide away from me towards the fridge. 'I'm so hungry,' he says. 'All I had was a packet of crisps. The other boys had beer but I said no, Mum won't like it, so I only had Coke.'

He goes to the fridge and takes out a Tupperware of leftovers from dinner. He lifts the corners impatiently, but it's stiff and won't open easily. He yanks it again and the box falls, peanut rice splattering across the floor.

I hear the slap before I feel it in my fingers.

Amar rubs his cheek and looks at me in a slightly puzzled way. 'Why did you slap me? What have I done? I only wanted to eat something. I'm hungry. Sorry, it just slipped.'

'What have I done?' – I asked my father that same question the day he locked me out on the balcony. It was my school report that had upset him. The monsoon rain fell thick and hard, plastering my shirt to my back. Father's unreadable face stared back at me through the locked door.

I look down at my hands. How could I have hit my own child? My fingers are still throbbing with the violence of my action. I can't recognise myself any more. 'I'm sorry, I'm sorry,' I say, holding Amar close to me, pressing his face against my chest, my hands caressing his head. 'I was wrong to hit you. I'm sorry, my son.'

'It's OK, Dad. It's OK,' he whimpers. He stands stiffly inside my arms, shifting from one foot to the other the way boys do. His eyes spot the trainers in their box, and he pulls away, picks up the shoes, sniffing their shiny newness like a perfume. 'Are these for me? Did your friend send them?' His eyes shine with excitement. Sitting down, he quickly slips off his old shoes, squirming around until the new ones are snug on his feet. 'A little tight, Dad. But Mum can make them bigger. Your friend must like me.' He's forgotten the slap already.

'She's not a friend,' I reply. I'm suddenly tired of the lies I'm feeding my family day after day. What was Esther to me, anyway? I could picture her clearly in my head, the way she sat on the bed, crossing her slender ankles, a hand perpetually tucking her hair behind her ears, her blood-red lips inviting me in. But beyond that she remained a shadow. I was turning into a similar shadow, blurred, with no definition, except a howling need to be less alone.

* * *

'Did Amar like his new trainers?' Geeta asks me next morning.

'They're too tight. I'll return them,' I say casually.

She sits at the table, helping herself to a bowl of Bombay mix. I stare at her hand dipping in and out of the bowl. She can get through an entire packet in one sitting.

'Why don't you have something healthier, instead of this rubbish?'

'I like this rubbish,' she says. 'It's the right kind of rubbish. It makes me happy.' Her eyes sweep over my face and immediately look away, her expression closed, as though she's hiding something. 'I want to start a new course,' she says, 'a beautician course.' She wants to get a diploma in manicures and pedicures – she's saying something about gel nails and French manicures and ordering in bulk from a wholesaler near Ancoats. 'I can start a little business from home. Convert the garage, get a blow heater put in, put out some fancy magazines for the ladies to read, and you can get the fliers done at the office. Maybe your friend E. Solomon can help me print them.'

I make no reply.

'I said you can get the fliers printed in the office,' she repeats, rising from her chair and then sinking back down. 'You're not listening, are you? Aren't you going to say anything? You usually have a long list of why I shouldn't do things.' She waits. Little bits of Bombay mix cling to her top, like pale yellow gems.

'Go for it,' I say. My shoulders slump. The world is closing in.

Dear Lopa didi,

PK said you called a few times last week. You asked him why I had not sent you any letters. You asked why I had not phoned. I am not happy, didi – that's why I didn't feel like calling or writing. PK has found someone else. Her name is E. Solomon. This E. Solomon buys presents for our son and has the cheek to send it to our home. She has met Amar, and has turned my husband's heart upside down. He walks into the house as if he has just come from a funeral. No interest in anything except his mango tree. He is always outside in the garden, smoking away, talking to that stupid tree, which we both know will never grow in this cold climate.

I swallowed humble pie and met Gupta today. I lied to PK and said I was going to the dentist. We met in town. I've not been to the centre in ages. So many shiny skyscrapers, and a big department store called Selfridges has opened, too. It looked like Singapore. Gupta met me near his office at Spinningfields. He said he would treat me to lunch at Pizza Express. I couldn't eat a thing – I just had garlic bread and Coke. I paid the bill because he had left his wallet in the office drawer. He's such a stingy man. Anyway, I asked him point blank: Who is this E. Solomon? Since when did she start working with PK? Is she young? Is she Indian? She must be pretty. Gupta laughed so much that he started crying. My dear sister, he said – 'sister', he called me – your husband has gone mad. He has fallen for a rich Jewish businessman's wife. E. Solomon is Cedric Solomon's wife. Her name is Esther. But don't worry, it was just a one-night fling, that's what he told me.

Esther. I know her, didi. I met her once at a business dinner. She was my age and beautiful. But cold beautiful, not warm and friendly like us Indians. Maybe PK fell in love with her that day. She was wearing a beautiful gold brocade dress. It looked almost like a sari. Her husband had a mean mouth. She will never leave her husband, I told Gupta. Why would she?

Gupta was so sad – he kept shaking his head and saying PK always had a wandering eye, even at college. He promised he will speak to him and make him see sense.

I can't throw away twenty-seven years of marriage just like that. I'm going to put up a fight. What is your advice, didi? Call me as soon as you get this letter.

Geeta.

31

MR ATLAS

'I am bringing the well to the horse,' Gupta says, settling into a chair. 'The only way of getting hold of you these days is to drive the twenty bloody miles to your office and drop in unannounced.' He eases his thin, bony frame further into the chair and fishes out a toothpick from his front pocket, twiddling it between his thumb and index finger in a way that tells me he is ready for a long conversation.

'I've been busy,' I say. I've been meaning to call him and catch up over a drink.

He waves away my reply. 'Bullshit, PK. Come Thursday you'll be ringing me with an excuse – some crap about a sales meeting – when we both know the only meeting you'll be having is a horizontal one with Mrs Esther Solomon.' He chuckles. His eyes dart around the quiet office. He takes in the mute telephone, the dirty rain-smeared windows and the dozen clothing rails where unsold summer dresses sway on thin wire hangers in quiet shame. Crossing his arms, he sinks deeper into the chair. 'Where is your secretary?' he says.

Margaret is at home nursing a bout of flu.

'High time you called it a day, PK. Fifty-five is a good age to retire.'

'I'm busier than ever,' I reply, making a show of moving papers about on my desk.

My eyes float back to the computer screen. There is an email from Ali saying he is cancelling a trip to Manchester because of industrial action at the factory.

'The past months haven't been easy,' Gupta says.

I look up, surprised by this bit of news.

'The funeral parlour has been a pain in the backside. The business is run like a bloody Nigerian scam. They have no idea about facts or figures.' His voice is troubled. 'I keep passing that hotel of yours. It's quite a handy hideaway.'

'I don't know what you are talking about,' I say, drawing my chair closer to the desk and forcing myself to meet his stare.

'No need to act dumb, PK. That hotel with the ridiculous name.' He scratches his head, as though teasing out the name. 'The Didsbury Queen, that's it! I saw you both outside, clinging together like a pair of drowning rats. Esther Solomon. Pretending you were colleagues – bullshit! What do you take me for? One-night stand, my foot!' He takes the toothpick from his mouth, examines it and then wipes it on his trouser leg before carrying on. 'I've become friendly with the receptionist there – a West Indian fellow. I asked him if a middle-aged Indian man with a white bird ever use the rooms. Maybe a one-night stand. We're men, after all – our dicks are made of muscle, not marble. Oh yes, he said, they're regulars, he said – yes, "regulars", he called you – said you're always coming in with your dame.'

'Well, he's lying… must be someone else. We Indians all look the same,' I whisper. I hear my father's sour rasping breath in my ear, reminding me how I've failed him, dragged the family name in the mud.

Gupta gives a dry, painful laugh. 'You dirty dog!' He pauses, runs his tongue over his lips and moves his hands in the air, drawing the curves of a woman. 'I bet your Esther is a firecracker in bed. How does she compare to Geeta, eh? Less lumpy and dumpy, eh?' His voice is hoarse.

I walk around the desk and open the office door. 'You need to get back to work,' I say coldly.

Gupta slams the door shut. 'I'm not leaving until I get an answer. Are you or are you not screwing around?'

I grab hold of his shirt collar and my hands press down on his shoulders. 'Leave me alone,' I hiss. 'Have you been talking to Geeta? Playing the Good Samaritan?'

Gupta pushes my hands away and walks back to the chair, whirling it around, and sits down, facing me, his legs primly crossed like a woman. 'She seeks my advice sometimes. She is a worrier, your dear wife. She's worried about the trainers this "E. Solomon" has sent Amar. She's wondering how she'll repay her kindness. "Invite Esther home for dinner," I told her. "The English go weak at the knees over chicken tikka masala."' He chuckles again and fishes out a Kleenex from his pocket, carefully wiping his mouth.

'I can't stand people who go about poking their nose in other people's business,' I tell him. 'Just get up and leave, will you.'

'Don't take it the wrong way, PK. I'm only trying to help. I mean…' He rolls his eyes to show the absurdity of it all. 'I mean, fucking Cedric Solomon's wife in broad daylight – and thinking you can get away with it? That the world won't sit up and take notice? You think you're so superior to us all…' He pauses, searching for the right words. 'You can have your cake and eat it too. It's just not fair. Not fair. I want to report you to the police. You're spoiling our community's name.' His shrill voice rises until it seems to bounce off every wall.

His ridiculous plan to march me into a police station makes me smile. 'Is being in love crime? Since when?' I challenge him.

'Love?' He spits out the word. 'Love is not an old man's game.' He taps the side of his head and whistles. 'You're cuckoo. Plain cuckoo. You're a married man, for fuck's sake. And a bloody father. Have you even thought of what this will do to Amar? You know he's soft in the head. All thanks to you.' I see him anew, his sad, drooping eyes shining through the metal cage of his cheap spectacle frames, his hair thinning, his pot-bellied body soft in its ill-fitting BHS suit that smells of last night's cauliflower curry.

'You're a jealous bastard, Gupta. Thirty years of friendship, and that's really what you think about me?' I close my fists and open them again to show him the emptiness within them. 'Who gave you the loan to make the down payment on your house?' I remind him. 'Who paid for your wife's driving lessons when you got sacked from your first job? Have you forgotten all that?'

I remember it like it was yesterday. It was a Monday evening, and we were sitting down to dinner, back in the old home in Longsight. The radio was on, promising a week of showers and wind. Geeta groaned and said something about her sister's wonderful life in Bombay – the usual – while she was eating chickpeas out of a can in rainy Manchester. There was a knock at the door. Gupta and his wife stood shivering on the front step. We fed them biscuits and tea and dried their clothes.

'Usha and the kids need a place to stay. Only for a few months,' Gupta had whispered, downcast eyes studying the faded pink and blue rug hiding the scratched linoleum floor. He was moving to Birmingham for six months on a job, he said. They couldn't pay rent on two flats. We said yes straight away, no questions asked. I pushed the sofa against the wall to make space for his family, and Geeta brought down blankets and pillows. For six months I fed his wife and kids.

'Do you remember that day?' I ask.

He simply shrugs. 'You've always loved acting Mr Big, that's all,' he said. 'The kids have a name for you at home,' he giggles. 'They call you Mr Atlas. You think you are holding up the world, but damn it, you can't even hold on to your balls.'

In the end there is no drama, no blood, no brawl. My friendship with Gupta ends swiftly and quietly. He leaves without shaking my hand. I find his toothpick after he's gone, wrapped in tissue. I throw it – along with our thirty-year relationship – into the bin.

32

MENSCH

The call comes when we are on the lower ground floor of John Lewis, in the bed department. We're searching for a new mattress for Amar. His constant bed-wetting and restless tossing means that his mattress has gradually turned yellow and lumpy, carrying with it a permanent hospital whiff of Dettol.

The salesman, a young South Asian man with slicked-back hair and a prominent nose, follows us, arms behind his back, a pencil tucked behind his left ear, as Geeta pummels and sits on the various mattresses. She's trying out the fifth mattress, hitting it with her closed fist to test its resilience, when my mobile rings. I immediately recognise the number. It's Esther. But this is a Saturday, and she has no business calling me, so I ignore the ringing.

'How much is this?' Geeta asks the salesman in Hindi. The boy – the badge on his lapel says his name is Amin – looks confused, and gives her the price in English. Geeta ignores this, and continues talking in Hindi, saying the price is too high for what it was: a single mattress for a teenager – well, a child really. Maybe, she says, her voice hopeful, he could give us a special discount, seeing that we are all Indian?

Amin smiles thinly and replies that he doesn't 'speak Indian'; he is actually from Bradford, and his parents are from Mirpur, Kashmir. He pronounces 'Kashmir' like 'Cashmere'.

'Oh, you're Pakistani,' says Geeta, and her tone changes, becoming brisk, more businesslike. She turns to me and says she's seen something similar in Cheadle at the SweetDreamz Sleep at a fraction of the price.

I look at her blankly.

'You know it, PK,' she says, impatient at my slowness. 'Next to the Chinese restaurant. The one where Gupta had his party.'

I remember it, the dimly lit shop where mattresses are stacked on top of each other like inert corpses, their plastic covering torn and discoloured. 'It might have closed down,' I say. 'It looked a right state.'

The salesman listens to our conversation, and after a few minutes he clears his throat and asks if we are done. He has to attend to other customers.

'I'm not happy with your price, Amin, beta,' Geeta tries again. 'Can we speak to your manager? This mattress we are buying is for a child, not an adult.'

Amin is polite. The manager is on annual leave and everything in the store has a fixed price. 'Just lie down on it, Madam,' he says. 'The quality will be obvious. It's Vispring – top of the range.'

I tell Geeta to lie down on the mattress and get a better feel for the quality. She's doubtful.

My mobile beeps. This time it's a text. Two simple words.

'He knows.'

My legs are suddenly unsteady. He knows. I read the message again and again. She can't be talking about Gupta – that's hardly news. Can it be that Cedric…? Darkness presses against my eyelids, even though the shop is brightly lit. It's late afternoon and the shop is busy. Elderly couples and young mothers pushing strollers wander past us, eyes intent on their shopping lists, minds fixed on what they are seeking. No one even looks at us.

'Go on, try it out – this has to last Amar a long time,' I egg Geeta on, the mobile hot and heavy in my hand.

'It is a big purchase,' she agrees. 'Eight hundred pounds is a big deal.'

'I'll be back in a minute – I'm just going to the gents',' I say, leaving her just as she is hoisting herself on to the bed. Amin stands close by, arms outstretched, ready to help if she slips.

Once outside in the car park, I ring Esther.

'He knows,' Esther says, her voice audibly shaking. 'I need to see you right away. My head is in a spin.'

'You're not talking about Gupta? We already know he knows,' I say, dreading her reply.

'No! Not bloody Gupta! My husband has found out about us,' Esther replies. It is the first time she's referred to Cedric this way.

I have to sit down. I look around for my car. It's parked at the other end, near the exit – it's a little game I play to make Geeta walk a little further and exercise her legs more.

I feel giddy with relief and fear, and almost run to the car. The waiting is over. All the cards are on the table. All I have to do is pick the right one.

'We have to meet right away,' Esther says, and hangs up.

I slam my head against the steering wheel and feel my forehead break out in sweat. Tugging at my collar, I unbutton the top three buttons of my shirt, open the car door and quietly throw up on the dark grey tarmac of the car park.

I go back to find Geeta, and find her still perched on the bed, anxiously looking about for me. There's no sign of Amin. 'You were gone for ages. What happened?' she asks.

'Upset tummy.' I make a face. 'Must be those Hakka noodles.'

'I think we should buy this mattress,' Geeta says. 'After all, it's for our only son, and it will last until he is thirty. He'll be married by then, with his own home.' She smiles, her mind bounding into a golden future while I feel the bricks of our day-to-day life collapse around me.

* * *

Esther and I meet at a sandwich bar called Othello, not far from the hotel. Esther had laughed when we first drove past it, saying she never expected to find Shakespeare squeezed between the Hungry Mouth kebab shop and Poundland. It suddenly feels bold and foolish meeting her without the cover of darkness.

I sit opposite her, facing a poster of the Blue Mosque of Istanbul. A picture of a woman balancing a fruit basket on her head hangs next to it. We are the only customers.

'It's all rather biblical and primitive – not quite Starbucks,' Esther mutters, sliding into her chair. She seems different – more real, somehow, in her plain black jumper, her face pale and drawn in the daylight. I pick out the tiny freckles on the bridge of her nose that she normally hides under make-up. I notice her hands lying on the table. She's forgotten to put on her rings, and they seem bare and incomplete.

She watches me observing her. 'I must look a right state. I didn't even have time to put on my lipstick,' she says. 'It's been a mad, ugly rush.'

I tell her that her mouth is beautiful even without lipstick, and stroke her bottom lip with my thumb. The skin is dry.

'We're in a mess,' Esther says, placing her hand on mine. She lets out a long sigh.

The owner of the café, an old man with a shock of white hair and wooden prayer beads dangling over his blue jumper, shuffles over to take our order. I ask for a coffee. Esther wants peppermint tea.

'Do you have fresh mint?' She raises her voice a little as though talking to a deaf man.

He says the café only have teabags. 'They are English teabags,' he adds, as though testifying to their high quality.

Esther looks around, her eyes taking in the glass counter piled high with vanilla slices and sausage rolls, a yellow plastic triangle shouting 'wet floor' guarding the open toilet door. 'What a miserable dive,' she says, sighing. 'We seem to specialise in them, you and I.'

* * *

It had been an accident. A foolish accident. They'd gone to the rabbi's house for Shabbat, Esther says; they lit candles, passed around the kiddush cup, washed their hands and broke bread.

Cedric was in a good mood. He had heard rumours that he was going to be in the Queen's New Year Honours List.

'Can you imagine?' he said to the rabbi, stroking his chin. 'An East End boy who started out selling ladies' stockings on a market stall in Spitalfields rubbing shoulders with royalty. Not a bad way to end, eh – Sir Cedric.'

'It's your faith – that's what makes you shine,' the rabbi said, and Cedric nodded.

'Cedric's big on faith, and even bigger on donations,' Esther says. 'And the rabbi's a weasel – he knows how to get money out of people. You know, Cedric takes the prayer book, the siddur, with him on his business meetings… the same one he had when he was five years old. He's superstitious like that.'

'Most rich men are,' I say. 'They have too much to lose. I gave up on God long ago.'

'Don't ever say that,' Esther says, her voice fierce and her chin tilted defiantly.

I picture them at the rabbi's house, with their expensive clothes and finery, big-boned and elegant, outshining the modest front room and its possessions. They would have struggled to fit around the small rosewood table crammed with plates, glasses and piles of food. And all the while, the rabbi's wife would be fussing over them, her mouth pleated into a smile. 'Am I right? Is that how it was?' I ask.

Esther laughs. The sudden, carefree sound startles me. It is like someone setting off fireworks in a graveyard. 'You're so perceptive, my mensch,' she says, leaning forward and giving me a quick kiss on my forehead. 'It was exactly so. The rabbi's wife is a right bitch – everything about her stinks of failure.'

'How did Cedric find out?' I push her back to the topic at hand. I feel detached, sitting in the café listening to Esther telling me how our betrayal has finally caught up with us. It is like having a ringside seat for somebody else's misery.

She had gone to the bathroom, Esther explains, leaving her handbag behind on her chair, its zip open. Her mobile, lost somewhere inside the usual untidy tangle of lipsticks, cigarettes and loose change, had suddenly started to ring. Cedric answered it for her.

'It was probably some stupid telesales chap from Bangalore selling PPI,' Esther says. 'I mean, who else would ring on a Friday evening?' Her eyebrows are raised in the exaggerated, teacherly way she uses when exasperated by something.

Cedric dismissed the nuisance caller, and there was a lull in the conversation – the rabbi's wife had gone through to the kitchen, and the rabbi, a man of few words, was distracted by his chicken soup. Cedric absent-mindedly scrolled down through the recent calls, stopping at the entry for 'mensch'. Intrigued, he turned to the messages and read all our texts. The silly declarations of passion we sent to each other, the longings to meet, to be together, to make love. Frozen on that two-inch Nokia screen was the ridiculous love history of two middle-aged married people.

Esther came out of the bathroom, smoothing down her dress, ready with ideas for the next fund-raising drive.

'What are you staring at?' she asked Cedric. He was holding her mobile like a new toy he'd just discovered.

'Who is mensch?' he said. He looked at her.

* * *

'It was as simple and as stupid as that,' Esther says, her voice sounding distant. 'Cedric got up suddenly, saying he was unwell. The rabbi blamed the soup and his wife followed us to the car, wringing her hands and apologising in her whiny little voice, begging us to stay. And you know the first thing he did when we got home?' Her hair, gathered up in an untidy ponytail, comes loose, and she tugs at it and coils it again at the back of her head. 'He went to the lounge and emptied the entire whisky decanter into his glass and began drinking steadily. "No one does that to me. No one makes a fool of me," he kept repeating, and when the bottle was empty he went to the bedroom, stripped off, folding his clothes neatly, rolling up his tie, pressing down the shirt cuffs mechanically, like a Japanese woman doing origami. He even emptied the ashtray by his side of the bed. Once that was done, he got under the covers and promptly went to sleep.' She closes her eyes at the memory. 'It was brutal. Just brutal. His silence. Not one word about "Why did you have to do this to me, Esther? What happened to our marriage?" This morning he called Lara and Ollie. "Your old mother is having an affair," he told them. Next thing I know, he's out of the door, driving to work. What kind of husband is that?'

Her mouth dips unhappily. This was how she will look at sixty, I think – little lines of discontent criss-crossing her face like dried-out rivers on a map. The teabag floats in her untouched cup, little green flakes of mint clouding the water.

'Did you tell him it was me?' I ask. I want to see myself through his eyes.

'He got it out of me. He couldn't place you at first. "PK Malik… PK… who?" He kept repeating it like an idiot, and then he remembered. "That small-time Indian trader, Ben's sidekick? What does he do again? Run a market stall?"' Esther repeats Cedric's words parrot fashion and then, taking a deep breath, continues. 'He said he thought I would have gone for someone…' She chooses her words carefully. 'Someone bigger and wealthier.'

I shift in my chair. A Beatles song comes on. The owner of the café has switched on the radio. I recognise the tune. It's Geeta's favourite. 'Love, love me do…' she would sing along, giving it an Indian lilt as she manoeuvred Amar's pram through the Tesco aisles. I always try to correct her accent, but she shrugs and says the Beatles were vegetarian Hare Krishnas who did yoga, so they were semi-Indian anyway.

'What next? Did you ask him for a divorce?' I say.

'He said we'll talk when he's back from his trip to Russia. Our break-up can wait until he opens his next store.' Her shoulders become rounder, slumping down.

I take her hand. 'What do you think he'll do? Will he turn nasty? Are you sure you want to leave him for a loser? For "Ben's sidekick" – that's what he called me, right? Am I really worth it?' I ask.

Her fingers rest on my cheek. 'Have you forgotten everything, my mensch?'

'Don't call me "mensch" again, please,' I say. The word feels soiled now that Cedric has seen it. It has a cheap ring to it, like Christmas tinsel bought from a discount shop. It has lost its meaning.

The owner of the café is over by the counter, scratching his ear, listening in. I call him over. 'Can I have egg on toast and some beans, please?'

Esther frowns when she hears me order. How can I be hungry at a time like this? But there's a dull, hollow feeling at the pit of my stomach that needs to be filled.

'I've thought about it, and you know what? Cedric knowing is the best thing that could have happened to us,' she continues, leaning forward, her minty breath close to my face. 'At last we have a resolution – what were all those days and nights adding up to? We can do it, start afresh. It's our chance now. I don't know why I was so petrified of him finding out.' When Esther is angry she starts using new words. Her accent changes, becomes more BBC presenter-like. She sits up straighter. She looks more foreign.

I shut my eyes and Geeta and Amar are before me, arms outstretched, beseeching me to stay. I feel trapped by my responsibilities and my Indianness, by my father, who growls in my ear, 'You bastard, you've failed me again.'

'So what do you think we should do?' she asks, obviously wanting me to take the lead. To be the man who'll hold her hand and say 'Yes, let's go for it.' I don't want to meet her eye.

'Cedric will definitely file for divorce, but he can keep his millions. I don't care. And you can do the same – ask for a divorce. You're not getting much love out of Greta, anyway.' Her words come out in a rush. She carries on. 'We could go somewhere warm and sunny. Start afresh. I picked up some brochures the other day. There are some fabulous condos going for a song in Florida.' She stops, smiles nervously, waits for my reaction.

I try to imagine the new life she is painting. Florida is now our new dream destination, the place to play out our love games.

'Who is going to pay for this new existence? Buy this condo? It's not that easy, this starting a new life together,' I say. 'You keep forgetting Amar is still young. He's even younger in his head. There was this accident long ago – a cricket ball…' My vision becomes blurred as I hear myself saying these words. 'I hurt him, and I didn't do much about it. I can't just walk away from him. And then there's my business—'

She doesn't let me finish. 'Do you want to lose me? Have you forgotten what my friend Maratha said? "Grab life by the balls." Your business is going down the tubes anyway, and as for your Amar, he'll grow up and forget about you. Don't you understand that kids are survivors?'

'And what about Ollie and Lara? Are they as easily disposable as Amar? They won't forgive you. Their mum running off – and at our age, too. The world won't stop laughing.' I stroke her hair with my hand, trying to be kind. She has forgotten to retouch her roots. The strands of grey lost within the lush brown expanse seem like a reproach. And here she is, dreaming of starting afresh.

'Why are you dragging my kids into this?' she asks. 'This is my life, not theirs.'

'But you share your life with them,' I say. 'How come we never talk about them? I don't know a thing about your son.'

'Sometimes we end up loving our children out of duty and desperation, and they just hurt us,' she says.

I think of the way Geeta loves Amar. I remember the night Amar was hurt by the cricket ball. Amar's bedroom. The curtains drawn. The room heavy with the smell of incense and Tiger balm. Geeta crouching by his bed, her hands folded in prayer, face puffy with tears. She stayed up through the night, pressing a damp towel on

Amar's forehead, where the bruise shone with a dull, purple glitter. I think of my mother. The way she waited up for me night after night while I was out playing truant.

'My children won't have much to do with me,' Esther continues. She stares at her hands. Geeta has the same defeated look sometimes when she's just finished a pile of ironing and done the dishes. 'Ollie is a lawyer in LA. He advises the rich and famous on clever ways to break up.' Esther laughs and then corrects herself. 'Actually, he calls himself an "alienation-of-affection consultant". Maybe he could act for us? But he wouldn't be cheap! He's smart – I've seen him in action – just like his dad.' She makes her voice light-hearted, but her eyes remain dark and broody.

Is Amar like his dad? I wonder if he's inherited my gene for failure, whether it runs in the Malik blood, a slow, silent song of disappointment, handed down from father to son like a cursed gift. 'How often do you get to see him?' I ask.

'I went to visit him once, when he had just moved to LA. Stayed for a month, helped him settle down, bought him a sofa, pots and pans. His neighbour was Cameron Diaz. Just imagine – they share a podiatrist.' There's mother's pride on her face. 'I've not been back since. I wait for his call, but he's a busy man, just like his father, and I'm too proud to beg.'

'Proud? You're his mother, for God's sake.' I can't imagine Geeta ever asking Amar's permission to visit him. 'You don't need an invite from your child, surely, Esther? Just go when you want to go. His home is your home.'

'That's where we're different, PK,' she says, sounding different.

The sound of pots banging comes from the small kitchen at the back of the café. Esther wrinkles her nose as the smell of frying oil wafts over to our table. She continues.

'Maybe this open-door policy is part of your Indian culture, but in ours we don't just go barging in like that. We wait for a proper invite. The last I heard, Ollie was sharing with some Russian model. She wouldn't want me there, would she, an old hag like me?'

The eggs arrive on a flower-patterned plate. They look like plastic – the yolks, a sickly yellow, shimmer beneath a thin film of oil. The man hovers around, offering knives, forks and spoons.

'How can you even think of eating at a time like this?' Esther stabs the bread with the tip of her finger. 'Processed white bread!' She tut-tuts mechanically, as though scolding a child.

'Just give Ollie a ring,' I tell her. 'He'd love to see you.'

She shakes her head. 'Don't you want to know about Lara? My little girl?' she asks.

'I saw her photo in your house. She's pretty, like you.' I remember the slender features. 'It must be great having a daughter. I know my mother would've loved one.'

In the long, lingering days before her death, fed up of the bedsores and the pain, my mother had screamed out repeatedly for a daughter who would soothe her pain and sit by her side, massage her legs or rub coconut oil into her hair. I was no good to her in her final days, too busy playing cricket and acting smart with girls.

'Lara has her whole life ahead of her. She's young.' A different kind of sadness enters Esther's eyes.

Does she envy her daughter's youth, the possibilities that stretch ahead of her like a long, seemingly unending road? Esther wants to walk that road too, but it's too late for her. 'She comes home once a year, usually at Passover. She dropped out of school – didn't even finish her A levels. Said she wanted to get in touch with her roots. Make a difference. We tried to stop her, but…' She trails off, as though she's run out of time. It's a speech she's told before. 'Are you listening to me?' she says. She lights a cigarette. Her ponytail unravels and the long hair falls untidily over her face, hiding her eyes. She blows a smoke ring, stubs the cigarette out on her saucer and narrows her eyes. 'If I didn't know you so well, I'd swear you were thinking of excuses for me to hang on to this bullshit marriage.'

'Our kids will hate us,' I say.

'I'm thinking of my life now. I'm fifty-three. I want some freshness in my life before all this ends.' Her voice shakes as she slaps her face and runs her hands over her breasts and thighs.

I turn around to see if the café manager has seen her pantomime, but he's busy on his mobile, his back to us. Freshness in life – that's what I've been after, isn't it? And here she is, offering me just that. All I have to do is tell myself I've had enough of Manchester, enough of the business and enough of Geeta, and I can walk off into a new life.

'Just talk to Greta. She'll understand. Tell her you don't love her in the right way any more.'

'Is there a right way to love?' I ask, too tired to correct her. Geeta will always be Greta to her. But Geeta isn't Cedric. She doesn't have the soft cushion of money and power to fall back on. Geeta is fragile and alone in a foreign country.

'What's come over you? Don't you love me any more?' There is a catch in Esther's voice.

'I've got a son who needs looking after,' I say, surprised at myself.

'And what about us? What are you proposing we do? Keep fucking in filthy little dives until we both shrivel up and die?' Esther's mouth gapes like a wound. She stands, pulling down her jumper. The waistband of her black skirt cuts into her belly button. I have explored the dip of that belly button so many times, my fingers wandering gently down. Her handbag slowly swings from her arm like the pendulum of a clock that's losing time.

She leaves the café, slamming the door. There is no kiss, no lingering touch, no coming together of hand or heart. It feels like the beginning of the end.

The old man, a blue and white tea towel limp over his left shoulder, rushes after her, calling to ask if something is wrong.

'Leave her be,' I tell him. 'She's angry, that's all.'

He shakes his head and starts counting his prayer beads. 'We have a saying in my country,' he says. 'She is strong enough to walk away, but broken enough to look back.'

Esther doesn't look back.

33

MANGOES IN MANCHESTER

Amar's report card comes in the morning post, and he has a C grade in maths.

'A C… a C… I got a big fat C!' he sings, skipping around the kitchen, waving his report about like a kite. His short, plump body moves clumsily round the chairs and the table.

Geeta snatches the report, reads it once more, mouthing the grades carefully, and then goes over to her little makeshift temple on the window sill, bowing her head before the brass statue of Ganesh, her palms pressed together in thanks. She lights the incense stick and puts a red tilak on Amar's forehead.

'Ganeshji is blessing you,' she says, kissing the top of his head. 'We must buy your maths tutor a nice box of chocolates as a thank-you – and also a tie. Marks and Spencer sell some nice silk ties,' she says, looking at me for confirmation. I nod.

We celebrate together as a family. Amar's report card, propped against a ketchup bottle, takes pride of place at the centre of the kitchen table. Geeta cooks a big breakfast for us: her special omelettes with mushrooms and peas and a chocolate milkshake with chocolate sprinkles on top for Amar. 'A special treat for a special boy,' she says.

He says he's very hungry. 'It feels like Christmas, Mum.' he says, and grins as she piles his plate with more toast and beans.

'Do you think we should send him to art school?' Geeta says, turning to me. '"Amar shows exceptional promise in his use of colour and brush technique,"' she says, reciting the teacher's comments from memory.

'Let him pass his GCSEs first,' I say, putting down my fork. It's impossible to eat.

'Not hungry, Dad?' Amar's hand reaches for my plate. He's wearing his favourite blue Donald Duck T-shirt, and his arms are bare.

'What's that?' I say, catching hold of his wrist. There's a burnt mark on his skin – a small, puckered wound sitting on top of the plump padding of flesh.

He pulls back his hand, hiding it under the table. 'It's nothing, Dad. It was in Chemistry. We were doing an experiment and I was clumsy. I knocked over the Bunsen burner.' He starts to well up, but then his eyes brighten. 'But aren't you happy about my C in maths, Dad? A C!' He beams at me.

'Here, show me your arm,' Geeta says. She is standing behind me. If I tilted my chair, my head would rest upon the soft round mound of her stomach.

'I'm not showing you my arm,' Amar says, slouching forward so his arm dangles below the table, out of reach. 'Mum, why do you always make a drama out of everything?' He's speaking with his mouth full, and his voice comes out muffled.

I get up and empty my plate into the bin. I can hardly bear to look at them.

'What's wrong? You're not angry about his report card, are you?' says Geeta, following me. 'He got a D in English – at least he didn't fail this time. And the maths, that was something, wasn't it, getting a C?' Geeta is worried. 'Let's take him to Pizza Hut tonight. He would love—.'

'Shall we go for a walk? The sun is shining,' I say, interrupting her, and go towards the patio doors.

It is a typical Manchester morning. Tepid, pale light that passes for sunshine and the shudder of a chilling breeze among the trees. A white ribbon trails behind an aeroplane, threading the clouds as it passes high above the garden. I remember my promise to Amar about taking him to Disneyland Paris. Everything lies in ruins.

'I don't want to walk. You two go,' Amar says. He is still at the table, the arm with the burn tucked between his legs, while his other hand clutches his report card. 'But where will you go? Alice said a new coffee shop has opened in Altrincham. Why don't you walk to it? They sell nice blueberry muffins. I want two of them.'

But Geeta's knees are playing up and she doesn't want to walk that far. We go into the garden instead.

'You're turning into an old woman, Geeta. You need to start looking after yourself – go and see a doctor or a specialist about your knees.'

She dismisses my words. 'It's nothing serious. I've got these new shoes now – flitflops… fitflops or something. They're supposed to be good for back support.'

I glance at her feet, which are swaddled in thick, grey socks. The brown open-toed sandals make her feet look webbed, like a duck's.

'Anyway, doctors are a waste of time. I might try yoga. Didi was saying it's becoming very popular in Bombay – all her friends have the DVD of this Hollywood actress, Jane Fonda, who does yoga better than we Indians – just imagine…' she rambles on.

The dog next door is barking. The harsh, persistent sound bounces through the air, rising to meet the clouds above. I shut my eyes. I know I have to tell Geeta about Esther. Before Gupta does. Before Cedric does. Before the world encircles her and taunts her with its pity and scorn.

Geeta bends over the mango tree and strokes a thin branch tentatively and tenderly. The shadow of green rot has made the branch brittle. One sharp gust of breeze and it will snap, falling to bits. 'We should never have planted it here,' she sighs. 'Mangoes aren't meant for Manchester. It is sunny now, but just wait – it will start raining soon. It confuses everybody. Especially this little tree.' She pulls her shawl closer around her shoulder. 'Let's go inside. I'm cold,' she says, and starts walking back towards the house.

'There is something I have to tell you,' I say, catching hold of her hand.

'What is it…?' She stops. Her face suddenly shrinks, becomes smaller, while her eyes grow bigger and wider, the pupils dilated and brimming with tears.

I cannot bear to look at her. 'I have met someone,' I say, and let go of her hand.

34

YOU WILL ALWAYS BE MY LITTLE MUNCHKIN

Amar stands over Geeta, watching her. She is in bed, her face pressed against the pillow, hiding from the world. Her shoulders shake and her arms are limp, hanging down the side of the bed. From time to time Amar pats her head, only to quickly draw his hand back as though he's touched fire.

'Do you think we should ring Lopa masi? Tell her to fly over from Bombay?' He says, turning to me. The rain falls steadily outside the bedroom window. It sets the gutters flooding, and the windows screech with the sound of water slithering down. The curtains aren't drawn, and Amar yelps in surprise as a thick bolt of lightning tears through the sky, setting off car alarms. But it's quiet inside the house. The silence is broken only by Geeta's intermittent sobbing.

'Her name is Esther. Esther Solomon. I've been seeing her for almost a year,' I had confessed. It was a relief to release Esther's name into the air.

It didn't take Geeta long to place Esther's name. Her hand flew up to her mouth, as though to stifle a scream. 'It's true – Gupta was right! It is Esther Solomon. That tall foreign woman.... Cedric Solomon's wife? She sent those trainers, didn't she? And that golden dress... you thought I'd forgotten about that fabric. Everything makes sense now.' She paused for a moment before continuing. 'Gupta said it was just a fling, but now you're saying it's something more. She's destroyed our life!' Geeta shouted, raising her hand as if to hit me, and then turning on herself instead. She stood there slapping her face, and her shawl, slipping from her shoulder, gathered at her feet like a pool of blood.

Amar had been watching us from the kitchen, and ran out, shouting to Geeta. He pulled her inside and helped her up the stairs to our bedroom.

'What's going to happen, Dad?' he asks, frightened. 'Is Mum going to die?' He is a six-year-old again, holding his father's hand to cross the street.

'Everything will be all right, Amar. Don't worry – one way or the other we will get out of this mess,' I say.

But he doesn't believe me. He covers his face with his hands. His shoulders are shaking. I gather him in my arms, the whole sobbing clumsy weight of him.

But he pulls away, his face distorted in anger. 'You've made Mum cry. You are a bad man.'

* * *

The room is dark, except for the glow of my cigarette tip. We sit on the bed, our heads resting against the headboard, lost in our own kingdom of sorrow.

'Your father was right,' Geeta says. 'He warned me about you. He said you had twitchy feet and a restless heart. But I was taken in. I fell for your looks, and I'm paying the price. Why did I follow you here? For what reward? So that you can leave me for an English woman who can't even pronounce our names? What kind of sickness is this?' Her voice is weak and exhausted.

The numbers on the bedside clock stay frozen. We try to sleep.

I hear Geeta move beside me in the night, and, even though it's dark, I sense her eyes on me. I reach out across the bed for her arm, my fingers touching the warm inside skin of her wrist.

'I am sorry, but try to understand, Geeta. I was going nowhere, and then she came along,' I try to explain.

'But you *are* going somewhere,' Geeta protests, her voice excitable and irritated in turn. 'You're building up a business for Amar to take over. And once he's settled, we'll return to Bombay, return to happiness. I've got it all planned. Don't you see?' She sits up and flicks on the bedside lamp so I can see the future more clearly.

'Geeta, you are living in some kind of dream. The business is failing. The orders are drying up. We'll be lucky if it's still there in five years' time. And as for Amar…' I stop. How much more could I wound her?

'What about Amar?' She persists. 'What about our boy?'

'Amar's going nowhere.' As I say this, I have the sensation of someone pulling my head below water. Not pure, life-giving water, but water that smells like gunk, thick as molasses, that allows no room for escape.

'I don't believe it. Look at Chintu, Lopa didi's son – he's got into IIT, and he was just an average student at school. We must work together and help Amar.' There is passion in her voice.

I don't answer her.

'What's going to happen to us?' Geeta asks me. The mattress dips as her body turns towards me. I smell the coconut oil in her hair. She presses her face against my bare shoulder. Her forehead is burning.

'You've got a temperature,' I say, stroking her cheeks, which are damp with her tears. My hand slips inside the old T-shirt that she wears to bed. Her breasts sag down like two sad balloons losing air. I caress her belly, the silver streaks in her pubic hair. I kiss her between her legs and don't try to stop her tears from falling, and then I do what I've not done in a long, long time. I take her in my arms and become one with her. Our lovemaking that night is desperate and long. We come together as a man and wife, but there is a sense of doom in the air.

* * *

The television is mute. The washing machine is silent. A pile of clothes waits on the ironing board. Unhappiness prowls through the rooms like an uninvited guest.

I ring Esther and tell her I have given Geeta the news. I sit in the car with the engine idling, the windows frosty with the early-morning breath of winter.

'You actually told her?' Esther's voice dips and rises through the mouthpiece. 'The poor woman. How did she take it? What did she say?'

'She is destroyed,' I say.

'She will get over it. We women are survivors.' Her tone is practical and matter of fact.

'It will take time to untie everything,' I warn her, unsure of whether she understands the enormity of what I've done for her. I want her to acknowledge my sacrifice.

'You will find a way, my mensch,' she says. 'Maybe it is best you move out for a few days so she can start getting used to the idea.' The self-centeredness of love – it takes me by surprise.

I replay it all – the look on Geeta's face when I said I was ending our marriage, Amar's face, his hands, doubled into fists, pressing against his eyes, which were squeezed shut, his whining voice repeating again and again that I was leaving because of him. He slid down on to the floor, his legs drawn up, and slowly and silently a dark stain spread down the front of his tracksuit bottoms.

'You've never loved me, Dad. You can pretend all you want,' he said through his tears. Seeing the ketchup-red trainers, Esther's gift, on his feet, he wrenched them off, spat at them and threw them into the bin. I hated him, he said. He was a failure, a disappointment. It was all the Ds and Fs year after year that had broken my love. And now I was taking it out on his mum.

Geeta didn't speak up in my defence. She stayed in bed, a blanket drawn up to her chin, eyes staring at the ceiling, a hot water bottle pressing against her belly.

* * *

Two days have passed since I told Geeta the news, and she still refuses to come down or eat her food.

Her sister calls from Bombay. 'Is Geeta sick? Shall I come over? Or do you think it's just a virus?' Her tone is wary. She has never liked me.

I debate with myself about telling her – 'Yes, come over and try and repair your damaged sister. Try to mend her heart. You're her family.' Instead I just listen to her complain. It's her daughter's graduation and her house cleaner has called in sick.

'You know how Bombay is – the servants never stay put,' she says. 'It's a nightmare getting loyal staff these days.'

'Give my love to the kids,' I say, ending the conversation.

Veins appear on the side of Geeta's forehead, and she squints at the sunlight peeking through the window.

'Amar needs you, Geeta. Please – please be strong, for his sake, at least. You don't want him to do something stupid,' I beg her.

Amar, sitting at the foot of her bed, listens carefully, his tongue sticking out, thumbs punching buttons on his PlayStation.

'Get up, Mum. Get up. I want you to cook for me. I don't want to eat pizzas every day. I want you to look after me.'

Amar's pleas do the trick. Geeta forces herself out of the fog of misery and sets about making a home for him again. She does a big shop at Tesco, coming home with twenty-four toilet rolls and enough canned tuna and baked beans to last for months. 'I just don't want to run out of anything,' she says, talking to herself. Little beads of sweat dot her upper lip as she carries the bags from the car to the kitchen.

'You're acting as though I'm dead,' I say. 'I'm still around. I'm not giving up on you or Amar. Life is a mess, but we'll get through it, just like everybody else.' I help her stack the tins on the shelves in the garage.

'How do we stop the world from finding out?' Geeta says. 'Can you imagine the shame of it? What Indian man cheats on his wife? It will be front-page news in the *Timperley Messenger*. I won't be able to go to the temple again. And Gupta – can you imagine his face when he hears about this? He will grin and say, "I told you so!"'

She goes to the wall covered with our family pictures, her fingers running over the cheap, tawdry frames. She is thinking of the cricket match and the trip to Alton Towers and all the different ways in which I have let her down. I hear the loud, angry ticking of her mind. 'How did we end up like this?' she says. Her eyes, locked in the past, are as bewildered and lost as mine.

'I don't have any more answers,' I say. I sit down and put my head in my hands.

'How can you love her? You're not even married to her,' says Geeta. This is how her mind runs – neat little lines connect the heart to a family to a home. There is no room for detours or deviations in such a world.

'I do love her. In a different way,' I say. She makes me feel alive, I want to add. But how can I say that to my wife?

'You think you love her. But you don't. It's just an infatuation – a longing for something different. Let's go back home. You can get a job in Bombay.' Geeta's small voice is suddenly energetic. 'We'll buy a small flat in Bandra with a view of the sea. Amar can go to the American school, and you can start a new business. Maybe a call centre. I've heard there is money in that.' She holds my arm, shaking it, her eyes hopeful. 'Just think, PK – this will all be just a bad dream. You can join the CCI Club in Churchgate, start playing cricket again. We can visit my sister on Sundays. Get takeaways from Bademiya.' Her eyes are filled with dreams.

I shake my head. 'We can't go back, Geeta. We have left it too late. All these years in England, just to go back, tail between our legs. We'll be called failures. And India has changed. We won't recognise it any more. It's full of shiny shopping malls and five-star hotels. How will we fit in? Our old friends are scattered. They wouldn't know us if we passed them in the street. Even your old home has been demolished and turned into a twenty-storey office block.'

The truth is I belong here, in Manchester. I like the moodiness of each day, the constant play of sun and rain, the sun feeling like a gift when it finally peeps out. I have grown with this city, seen the old decrepit warehouses torn down, shimmering skyscrapers taking their place. I like driving down Princess Parkway on a spring day and seeing the daffodils on the verges. I like taking the metro to Old Trafford and being one with the energy of the young and old. There is a spark here that keeps me alive. No, there is no going back.

'I think I'll check into a hotel for a few days. Sort out my head,' I say.

* * *

Amar stands on the front step, leaning against the door, one bare foot rubbing against the other.

'Go inside,' I say. 'You will catch a cold, and that will be one more thing for your mum to get stressed about.' I put my overnighter in the boot, ready to drive away.

Amar comes over to the car, his bare feet leaving damp patches on the grey tarmac of the drive. I unwind my window and he sticks his head through and asks me to come back. 'I saw a Channel 4 documentary last week,' he says. 'It was all about how children can be intelligent in different ways. They don't always have to be good at numbers or science.' He surprises me, wisdom shining through from his muddled child's brain. Why have I not paid more attention before?

I jump out of the car and press his head against my chest. 'It has nothing to do with you, Amar.' I caress his cheek with my fingers. 'Mummy and Daddy are just having a little holiday from each other, that's all. Everything will be fine.'

His breath swims towards me in little clouds of cold air. It's a very cold morning, and the soft, dark hairs on his cheeks and chin stand up stiff like soldiers. He starts shivering in his thin tracksuit.

'This isn't about you, Amar,' I say, and pat his cheek.

'Can I come and see you?' he asks.

'I promise I will come around every day. It's like I'm going away to the office. I'm only down the road. I just need to clear my head. Stay away for a few days. You will always be my little munchkin.'

Munchkin? The word has slept inside me for years. It was my special name for Amar until he was ten. And then one day Geeta told me to call him by his proper name. Those baby names weren't good for his development.

'You are punishing Mum because of me. I know that,' Amar says. He runs back to the house. He runs awkwardly, his shoulders lopsided, dragging his heavy body like a great load. The front door shuts quietly behind him.

* * *

Room six at Didsbury Queen is being refurbished – there is damp in the walls – but room eleven at the back is free.

'It's smaller, but at least you won't be out of breath taking all those stairs,' Marvin says, counting the cash I hand him, holding the notes up to the light. 'Just to make sure, cos you're moving into a new room,' he explains, when I say he ought to trust me by now.

'It's only temporary,' I reply.

He sniggers. 'She finally threw you out, eh? What took your wife so long?' He grins, taking hold of my suitcase and swinging it into the new room. He pushes it under the bed with the scuffed heel of his shoe.

'It's only for a day or two, Marvin,' I repeat. 'I need to sort out a few things.'

He taps his crotch with his index finger. 'Get this in order, mister, and the rest will follow.' If only it were that simple.

I call Margaret as soon as I've settled in. I'm ashamed to tell her I am an absconding husband, so I pretend Geeta isn't well and I'll be working from home for a few days.

'Work is quiet,' she says. 'Take your time and look after Geeta. She needs you.'

It is the run-up to Christmas, and business isn't meant to be quiet. All over the city cash registers are ringing louder than the church bells. Trucks bearing festive frocks tear through the night, their headlights glaring. Wallets are being emptied as the world gets ready to cheer in another year – everywhere except in my warehouse, where the girls sit filing their nails, the phones mute, the order books shut and the sewing machines quietly rusting.

Dear Lopa didi,

Thank you for calling me so many times. Amar told me that you want to come and help me but there is graduation and servant issues. I understand – children must always come first. A lot has happened since we last spoke. PK has met someone else – a woman called Esther. I think I told you about her. He is in such a muddle, the poor man. I am angry with him, but more angry with her. How can a woman break up two families? So you know what I did? I called her. It was easy to get her number. PK is so careless with his mobile. She was saved under her own name. Men can be stupid.

We have met before, she said. Her voice was shaking when she recognised me. Greta, is that you, she said. Idiotic woman – she can't even say my name right. I told her to leave PK alone. You would have been proud of me, didi. I spoke firmly and loudly. Don't come near him, I warned her. Our marriage is not a house of cards, it is made of solid bricks. We have an autistic son and he needs his father, I said. Not 'special', 'autistic' – all these years we've never said the word aloud, but I used it that day to try to save my marriage. You are very beautiful, I said, you can choose someone else – please leave us alone. A proper lecture I gave her, and she listened quietly. Like a mouse. PK never told me your son's problems, she said. I'm so very sorry. It's not cancer, I said, and I don't want your pity.

Afterwards I went to the temple and prayed long and hard. I gave Panditji money to hold a special prayer for the family. PK has checked into a hotel, but he will be back. He has to understand his life is with us. No one else. There are no choices once you get married. Only one single road to walk on. So much is happening so fast. My head is in a spin.

Geeta

35

BETTER DAYS AHEAD

Room eleven looks out on a park. It isn't especially beautiful – a few graffiti-scrawled benches and a basketball backboard with the hoop missing. The dog owners of the neighbourhood use it as a public toilet, watching their pets empty their bowels on the bare flowerbeds. In the afternoon, schoolboys in shiny purple blazers lope in, fling their satchels on the woodchipped ground and chase each other round the swings, hollering out filthy names. They never sit on the swings, they just grab hold of the seat, twist it round and kick it as high as it will go. The schoolgirls are different. They sit apart on the benches, skirts hitched high up to their thigh, tapping on their phones and chewing gum.

I spend a lot of time looking out at the park, looking into my future, the room slowly filling with cigarette smoke. I think of old age. Old age that comes with dentures, insulin shots and arthritic knees. I'm frightened of walking towards the ugliness of old age. On days when this fear becomes fierce, I shut my eyes and think of a postcard I kept in the top right-hand drawer of my office desk. A mustard yellow beach bordered by an ink-blue ocean. A few coconut trees stand on the margins of the card, and a lone fisherman, scarcely bigger than a dot, throws his fishing net into the waters. I want to take my last breath in such a place.

The postcard is of Pondicherry. My father brought it back from a trip to a pharmaceutical factory when Pondicherry was still owned by the French. The factories made a profit and ran on time, unlike the Indian ones across the state border, where workers dozed through the heat playing cards under banyan trees.

I fell in love with the tranquillity of that image. I couldn't believe there were places in India where one could be alone without running into another person. 'I want to die there,' I'd announced, when I was only twelve.

'Stop talking bullshit,' Father said, clipping me around the ears. 'There's no holiday from life. You just keep studying.'

In my twelve-year-old eyes, the beach transformed into my mother's six-yard yellow silk sari, which was fringed by a border of dark blue. She wore it during the Ganpati puja that year, when, clapping our hands and chanting loudly, we trailed behind the six-foot pink and white statue of Lord Ganesh as it wound its way through the streets before being dumped into the warm, eager mouth of the Arabian Sea. It was the one time I saw my parents relax, my father clumsily trying to tie jasmine flowers into my mother's shiny plait. She lowered her eyes and smiled. Afterwards we ate pav bhaji in Chowpatty and pistachio kulfi at Rajesh Ice Cream Centre, opposite the railway station.

At the age of fifty-five, stranded in a dilapidated hotel, I pine for the stillness of that postcard.

Esther visits me. Her sad eyes skim over the pile of clothes on the chair, the open suitcase, the empty beer bottles lining the window sill like trophies from a war.

'I have made the leap,' I say. I wait for her reaction.

Small beads of perspiration sparkle on her forehead.

'We'll be happy, won't we?' I ask.

She eases my head on to her lap, stroking my forehead and my cheeks. 'You've lost weight, my mensch.' She sighs. 'This is no way to live. We must find you a flat – a proper flat with a decent bed and a cleaner.' She lifts the bed sheet and frowns at the yellowing frayed edges, picking at them till the thread comes loose.

I pull her close, hiding my face in the long, brown tangle of her hair. There's no longer a ticking clock, a running meter, a knock on the door to drag us back into our other lives. We are no longer thieves stealing time together.

* * *

I have a dream that night. It's a bright day and I am driving slowly over a road littered with dead birds. The sun dangles in the sky like a yellow lightbulb. The wheels of the car roll over the birds, over the soft mound of feathers. I hear the quiet crunch of their bones breaking. But I don't stop. I carry on driving, and then they're no longer birds, they've become Amar. Amar is lying spread-eagled on the road, and my car keeps moving, crushing his bones.

I sit up with a start. Saliva clings to the side of my mouth. The top of my head is raw, as though someone had swung a hammer to it.

'What's the matter, darling? I'm here. I'm here,' says Esther. She gets me a glass of water. 'Drink this. It will do you good.'

'I dreamt I killed Amar – ran over him with my car. I tried to stop, but the car kept moving.'

'Don't worry about it. It's only a nightmare. Amar's all right.'

I stare stupidly at her and pick up my watch, trying to read the time in the dark. 'I'm late. It's time to go home,' I say.

'You've left home,' Esther says, sitting next to me and lighting a cigarette. She hands it to me and lights another for herself.

It's still night outside. Not a single star shines through the half-broken blinds. The only sound is the rain, quietly purring through the gutters like a bedtime lullaby. This is it. There's no schedule, no errands, no running back home. I could be a vagabond or go missing. The future belongs to me. No Geeta to nag me, no Amar pleading with me to play with him. But erasing them has only left behind emptiness.

'Isn't this what you wanted, Esther? It's a big thing I've gone and done.'

She doesn't reply. She simply concentrates on smoking. Puff after puff of smoke blows out of her mouth, wreathing her head. Her nails are perfectly manicured. A new ring, shaped like a snake, is wrapped around her second finger. She walks naked to the window, lifts the sash and throws out her cigarette. She turns round and looks straight at me.

'Cedric won't agree to a divorce. It's to do with the structure of the company – something to do with share ownership or finance. He wants a fresh start. He wants to move to Hale, build a big house with a swimming pool.' She presses her knuckles against her cheek, starts weeping and then comes back, laying her head on my shoulder, her hair tickling my cheek. 'He won't set me free.'

'It's about the money, isn't it? The divorce will screw him, so he'd rather you screw around and turn a blind eye,' I say. 'I can't stand your bloody husband.' My impotent words ricochet around off the bare walls. I am no match for the Cedric Solomons of this world.

The joy has been sucked out of being with Esther. I feel emptied of love. She stays inside my arms, her hand massaging the back of my neck feverishly, as though rubbing out a stain. There is a door out of this misery, but I can't see it.

I hold her chin, tilting her head so her face catches the light from the lamp. She shuts her eyes, the long lashes sinking down like feathers. Her full mouth, rubbed clean of lipstick, sags down.

'What is going to become of us now? I've walked out on my family for you, and you're saying Cedric is ready to take you back?' I say, trying to pin her down.

'Not exactly "take me back",' she says, choosing her words carefully, weighing each one. He is ready to forgive me my little… fling.' She drags out the last word. 'A menopausal fling. That's what he thinks you are to me.' Her voice is little more than a whisper.

'You seem confused. What exactly do you want, Esther? You say he's happy for you to play around with me while I've gone and set my house on fire.' I push her away and stand up. 'Here, put on your dress.' I fling her dress at her.

'Help me,' she says, her arms raised like an obedient child waiting for her school uniform to be put on. It's a habit, this little ritual of ours – I pick up her bra, my hands closing around the warm, heavy weight of her breasts. She presses against me, teasing me until I feel hard with desire. But not tonight. The touch of her flesh leaves me cold.

She stands by the bed, fidgeting with the frilly cuffs of her sleeves. 'Your wife, Greta – she called me. God knows how she tracked me down. I nearly fell of my chair when I heard her. "This is PK's wife," she said. She told me to leave you alone, and then she told me about Amar. You never told me he's autistic. Come to think of it, there was something odd about him at the shoe shop.' She strokes her chin, as though deep in thought. 'Why haven't you taken him for ABA therapy? There is an Autism centre in New York. He can be cured. You know I could sort out the funding…'

I lift my hand to stop her from continuing. 'Geeta called you?' I can't quite believe it. I imagine her picking my mobile, searching for Esther's name, her eyes heavy, hooded with pain. I can just hear her telling Esther to leave me alone, her voice shrill, blaming Esther for everything. Such was Geeta's love – blind and loyal, like a dog's.

'Amar's not autistic, he's special,' I say. 'One day he will take over the business and do his painting on the side.'

She ropes her arms around me. 'Of course he's special. He's your son.'

I bow my head and think of Amar. The pinched look in his eyes, the way he gnaws away at his nails. 'What have we done to our children, Esther, you and I? We've abandoned them. I've been too hard on Amar and Geeta. I've not treated them right,' I say. 'How about Lara? Have you spoken to her?' Her son doesn't count. He's like Cedric – self-serving and smart.

'I'm going to Israel for a week to see Lara. Explain to her how messed up things are. Tell her about you. I need to see her. She's taken this quite badly,' Esther says. Her mouth trembles.

She reaches for her bag and takes out a compact, pursing her lips as she colours them with lipstick, like a child crayoning a picture, her mouth automatically forming a smile as she examines her reflection in the mirror. Like most beautiful women, she can't believe that her face or body will one day give up on her.

'How do you think this will end?' I say. I feel battered and bruised. 'I just don't have a clue.' It's like we're sleepwalking to an end.

'It will all fall into place. There will be better days ahead,' Esther says.

'And what about this mansion in Hale? "A fresh start", isn't that what he said? And what can I offer you? A miserable two-star hotel room with used condoms on the floor.'

It is time for Esther to leave. I walk her back to her car and we linger outside in the cold morning air. The days ahead won't be easy. She tells me to be strong while she's away in Israel. She starts her car and the engine drowns out my goodbye. I walk over to the funeral parlour to see if Gupta is still beavering away in one of the rooms. But the place is in darkness and a small sign in front of the door says 'business for sale'. Gupta has done his damage and moved on.

36

HE'S JUST A NORMAL BOY

These are ugly days, but I get used to them. I drop my washing at a local laundry and eat breakfast at Othello, where the owner recognises me and addresses me as 'brother'. A few days later, he hands me a loyalty card.

'For you and your wife,' he says, stamping the first circle proudly.

I ring home every evening, dutifully, like a doctor checking on his patients. Geeta reports on her day.

'The TV licence needs to be renewed – can you do it? And the washing machine has broken down, but I remember you taking out a guarantee.'

'It's upstairs in my office. I can come over and look for it,' I offer.

'Oh, don't worry,' she says. She climbs up to the attic, to my office, where she goes through the drawers until she finds the right folder. I picture her heaving herself up the rickety ladder, her weak knee burning with pain, her forehead perspiring. 'I had no idea you were so organised,' she says. 'There's a whole file devoted just to Amar. You've kept all my antenatal reports, even his first lock of hair.'

'I'll drop by to see Amar,' I tell her. 'Sort out the bills and other stuff.'

'Shall I make some biryani? I bought some fresh mince from Ravi today,' she says.

'Is Amar better? Why won't he talk to me?' I ask the same question every evening.

Geeta says he's been getting into fights at school. Miss Connor had rung her and told her he was picking on girls and younger kids.

'That's not like him. We need to speak to the school,' I say. Geeta agrees and says she'll make an appointment.

There is something else...' she hesitates. 'He's staying home quite a lot these days. The bed-wetting has increased, and he keeps complaining of headaches.' She sounds tired and broken. I've left behind a shipwreck.

* * *

I am back at office, trying to source a new supplier in Egypt. A mill outside Alexandria is ready to do business.

Margaret hands me the phone. 'It's Mr Brown,' she says, placing her hand over the receiver.

'Mr Brown?' I can't place the name.

'Amar's school – his headmaster,' she clarifies.

I'm glad he has called. I'll tell him to keep an eye on Amar and explain our family situation. But before I can say anything, Mr Brown says he wants me to 'drop in for a chat'.

'Is Amar in some kind of trouble?' I ask, and my heart slows its beat. Margaret is listening. The whole world is listening in.

There is a pause.

'These things are best discussed face to face. You and Mrs Malik should come in. We need to have a talk.' His voice is serious.

I leave work immediately, driving home to pick up Geeta, but she isn't there. I ring the Guptas. It's an instinct. Our friendship is over, but just like a tree that can't be uprooted, it will take years to clear up our shared history. Gupta still holds the spare key to our home and his name is the emergency contact on our passports.

His wife answers the phone. Her voice is cold. No, Geeta isn't with her, but I could try Rusholme. Far and Wide holds special deals on a Tuesday. 'Geeta loves a discount. Her marriage may be kaput, but she'll still go looking for bargains,' she sneers and puts the phone down.

* * *

I drive down Wilmslow Road to the supermarket, where the parking is free and the prices are cheaper than Tesco. The sun shines loud and bright, and a steady gaggle of students head past to the nearby university, satchels slapping against their legs, young faces strapped inside big, menacing headphones.

'What are you doing here?' Geeta says, dropping the aubergine she is holding. It slips from her hand and rolls into the gutter. Standing there in front of stalls piled high with papayas and guavas, chillies and coriander, the forgotten fruits of her childhood and youth, surrounded by women dressed in scarves and thin tunics and sandals that leave their toes open to the biting wind, she looks at home. 'What are you doing here?' she asks again, the shopping basket swinging awkwardly on her arm. 'How come you're not at work?'

'We have to go to Amar's school. The headmaster called. He wants to see us immediately.' I grab hold of her shopping bag and make for the car.

'He's had an accident,' she says. 'He's got hurt playing football or something. Everything is going wrong – first you leave… and now this.' She stuffs the corner of her shawl into her mouth and starts sobbing quietly.

* * *

I've been to the headmaster's office before, but I'm still impressed by the big desk, the row of framed certificates on the wall and the glass cabinet filled with silver trophies and cups, none of which Amar has brought home.

'He's just a normal boy.' Miss Connor's words come back to me as we sit facing Mr Brown.

Geeta clutches a handkerchief, which she twists and rolls around in her hand. 'Where's Amar? Is he all right?' Her voice rises, becomes hoarse.

Mr Brown raises a hand to calm her. 'I'm sure Amar's fine, Mrs Malik. But he's not in his classroom. He left after the first period.'

He consults a piece of paper on his desk. 'He is supposed to be doing maths right now.'

'He hates maths. He's rubbish at numbers, just like me,' Geeta explains. 'He must be in the library. Have you checked there? Maybe he is in the bathroom?'

The headmaster, his mouth unsmiling, shakes his head. 'It's not the first time he's skipped class.'

I pat Geeta's hand and tell her he's probably gone to the Trafford Centre. 'Being a typical teenager.' I glance at Mr Brown to see if he agrees with Amar being called a typical teenager, but he's frowning.

'This is a crucial year. His GCSEs are just around the corner. At this rate he will be retaking the year. And that's not typical,' he says, carefully pushing a glass paperweight from one corner of his desk to the other. The paperweight, a heavy globule of glass, holds a dead butterfly. A colourful, tropical butterfly, which has ended up lost and alone, like my mango tree, in Manchester.

When Geeta was pregnant with Amar, we decided our child would one day be a famous scientist trained at Oxford. 'He'll find a cure for Malaria,' Geeta said.

I said I didn't want any child of mine cutting patterns for ladies' skirts. 'Maybe he'll discover a new species of plant. Give his name to a constellation of stars.' We were big on dreams in those days, filled with pride that we'd produced a son and not been condemned to a childless life.

'There's also another problem…' Mr Brown removes his glasses and polishes the lenses before carrying on. 'One of the parents has voiced a serious concern.'

'What kind of concern?' I ask.

Geeta swivels in her chair, as though to get closer to the action. Her mouth is quivering.

'He hit a girl in his class. Alice,' Mr Brown clears his throat and glances at Geeta. 'He bit her arm,' he whispers. The gold pen in his hand hovers over the notepad like a fly. I notice he's left-handed, just like Gupta.

'There must have been some misunderstanding,' I say. 'Amar and Alice are best friends, and the situation at home is a bit tense at the moment.' I stop. I want to use the best formal language. 'My wife and I are having difficulties. Marital problems.' I stop again. I don't know how else to put it.

'I believe that was the reason for the fight,' Mr Brown says, his face empty of expression. 'Alice made some remark about your situation and Amar reacted violently. This behaviour is unacceptable – it's not in keeping with the school ethos.'

Geeta looks down at her clenched hands. 'We're trying to make things work,' she says, her head bowed in shame.

Mr Brown looks embarrassed. His cheeks turn pink. He leans forward and addresses Geeta, ignoring me. 'Please, Mrs Malik, this isn't the right place to discuss your personal situation. As I was saying, Alice has voiced a complaint.' He opens a drawer and pulls out a piece of paper. He lays it flat on the desk, smoothing down the corners with the palm of his hand. I can't make out the writing. He glances at it again before continuing. 'Mrs Jones, Alice's mother, has filed an official complaint. She said Alice came home crying with scratch marks and bruises on her arms.'

I saw Alice's mother in my mind, the thin mean line of her lips, her eyes flashing when she spoke about my big house. She held a grudge against those who did well in life, and this was her revenge.

'Mrs Jones is overreacting. It was probably just a little tiff.' I pause, clear my throat and continue, forcing my voice to sound confident. Full of power. 'You might not be aware, but Amar is on the spectrum. He might need specialist help. And he is not violent. He's just not the type. He's an artist. And a very good one too.' I finish feeling tired. I focus on the inkpot and brown blotting paper on the desk.

'We know that Amar may have learning difficulties, but that does not excuse his behaviour,' the headmaster says in a low voice. The gold signet ring on his little finger flashes as he scratches his right ear and thinks of his next move. 'I'll take into account what you've said about your family situation. I suggest you go home, find Amar, sit him down and have a chat with him. We could discuss therapy, perhaps. Some behavioural counselling will do him good. Some extra lessons after school.'

The meeting ends.

* * *

The school bell rings as we leave. Children pour out of classrooms, their voices loud and happy. It is break time. A few slow down and stare at us before dashing off to the playground.

I feel Geeta shrink beside me. She stops suddenly and points to a painting hanging near the reception desk, just by the main entrance. 'That's his,' she whispers, not daring to say Amar's name aloud.

We go nearer, and I read the caption: 'Amar Malik, Year 10. Runner-up in the Crayola Competition.'

'Did you know about this?' I ask Geeta.

'No idea,' she says.

He'd painted a playground scene in bright blues and yolky yellows. There are swings and seesaws and children holding hands and kicking balls. Two figures stand at the far corner of the painting, almost disappearing into the red striped border: a brown-skinned boy with his arm around a pink-coloured girl. Instead of mouths, he had drawn two hearts.

'The headmaster's got it all wrong,' I say to Geeta. 'Look at the painting. Amar and Alice are best friends. She's not the right sort, but she's still his friend.' I tell her we should go home. I'd talk to Amar. 'He'll be watching telly,' I say, my hand on Geeta's elbow, guiding her along. She's out of breath by the time we reach the car.

'He's been acting so strange,' she says. 'We should all go together to see a specialist or something. He's taken it badly, your moving into a hotel. You know he's stopped sleeping in his bed? He comes to my room every night. Wants me to sing him lullabies. Make him warm milk.' Her voice wavers, as though she's swallowing water. 'Maybe you should move back. For his sake.' She lets out a deep sigh. 'The doctors in London will be the best. They will all be English,' she carries on, falling back on old arguments.

'I'll Google some names today,' I say. 'There's bound to be someone good and not too costly. They can skin you alive, these specialists, you know.' It was easy before – I could pick up the phone and hire the best brains in the country. Malik Textiles packed a punch those days, and money was no object. But things are different now.

My mobile rings. I pull it out of my pocket and check the number. It's Esther. She's back from Israel.

'I'll call you later,' I say, and hang up.

'Who was that?' Geeta asks. 'Was it the school? Have they found him?' She sits erect in the seat, her hand tightly holding on to the seat belt, her eyes scanning the road, the crease in her forehead thick and dark like a scar.

'It's only the office. I'll ring them later,' I lie.

* * *

There are roadworks on Princess Parkway, and the traffic creeps along slowly in a single lane. I want to get home and tell Amar I'll make it up to him for all the birthdays and outings I've missed, that I'll buy him trainers in every colour of the rainbow.

Rain starts falling as we near home. Noisy grey drops the size of small pebbles fall and form a curtain. The only sound in the car is the swish-swish of the wipers and Geeta's heavy breathing. She's not said a word since my mobile rang. Her eyes are shut and her lips move in a silent prayer.

'Where is Amar? Where is he?' Geeta says, pressing her face against the car window, trying to pick out his bright blue anorak in the throng of people rushing home. She wants to hold special prayers at the temple. 'I'll book Panditji and invite all our friends,' she says, wiping her eyes with the sleeve of her sweater. 'It's that woman's evil eye,' she says. 'She's cursing our family. She's got it in for us.' She refuses to give Esther a name.

The rain stops as we pull up to our house, and the sun flashes out from behind the clouds.

'Things will turn all right. They always do,' I say, touching Geeta's knee, not believing a word I say.

37

I HOLD HIM LIKE A GIFT

The house is quiet. The post lies on the front step, and when I stoop to pick it up I notice a dead pigeon, its wings flecked with blood, lying near the hedge. I go over and gently kick it to one side. The dog from next door sneaks through the gap in the hedge and starts nosing it, his red slobbery tongue flicking all over the stiff grey body. Geeta claps her hands, shooing it away. Mr Peters hears her and comes to our gate, whistling for his dog.

Geeta says I should ask him if he knows any good therapists. He has a divorced daughter who is a GP. 'But without giving anything away,' she says, and goes inside to look for Amar.

I stroll over to Mr Peters, and we chat about the weather. 'The rain will be good for your mango tree,' he says, putting a leash on his dog. He says the same thing every time I see him.

I give my usual reply. 'If rain was the only thing needed, I'd have a forest of mango trees by now.'

The dog is straining at the leash, and Mr Peters says he's going for a walk.

'Pop in some time for a beer or something. Christmas is coming,' I say politely, forgetting for a moment that Amar has gone missing.

He nods and asks how my little boy is doing. 'Well, not so little any more,' he adds, laughing and nodding goodbye. I wonder if he means Amar is fat or that he's growing up.

Geeta comes to the front door and shouts out. 'Amar's not in his room. He's left his mobile on his bed,' she says.

'Maybe he's gone for a walk to clear his head,' I say.

She frowns. 'He isn't the type to go walking in the cold… or at all,' she says.

'Maybe he's gone to the corner shop to get some sweets,' I say. 'He does that sometimes. Anyway, I doubt he's just vanished, if that's what you're thinking.' I take out a cigarette. I go into the garden to check if he's hiding there. While I'm there I check on the mango tree to see if the new Chinese pesticide has worked. A single green bud trembles on the edge of a branch. I see this as a promise. The green bud is Amar. It's a sign – a new beginning. I decide I'm going to pull him out of school at sixteen and take him under my wing. I'll sell the warehouse, maybe even move to smaller premises, ditch Ali and start again. Forget women's clothing – I'll go into menswear. There's always demand for cheap, well-cut jackets. Amar will accompany me on buying trips, learn the tricks of the trade. To hell with his schooling, to hell with the world, I think, going back to the kitchen. I'm going to make him sharp – someone who can beat Cedric Solomon at his own game and teach him to call me a 'street trader'.

Geeta sits at the table, holding the telephone receiver in her hand. Her other hand grips Amar's mobile. 'It will be dark soon,' she says.

I put the kettle on and sit beside her. I want to tell her about my new plans, but she doesn't want to listen. She keeps turning her head towards the front door every time she hears a sound, and then she gets up and starts wiping the kitchen counters with the tea towel.

'Relax – you're worrying for no reason,' I say. 'He must have bumped into Alice. Maybe they've made up and gone for an ice cream or something, and he's just forgotten to call. You know how boys get.' I hide my own anxiety from her. I remember Amar's reproachful look as I left the house, the clumsy way he'd tried to hug me, his ice-cold cheeks, the touch of them. I pour the tea and give Geeta a cup.

She comes back to the table, slumps into her chair and holds her head in her hands, eyes far away, like searchlights looking for her son.

I mention the single green bud on the mango tree to distract her.

'So the pesticide worked. That is good,' she replies, her mouth still serious. 'I wasn't sure I'd ordered the correct one. Maybe I should order some more. But it wasn't cheap, coming all the way from China.'

I look at my watch. We've been back from Amar's school nearly an hour, but there's still no sign of him. It's not like him to disappear like that, and not on a day as cold as this. I tell Geeta I'll drive round to the shopping centre and check if he's there. I want to get away so I can call Esther and share with her the dreadfulness of my day.

I drive out into the growing darkness, which seems unending. I ring Esther. I tell her about our trip to Amar's school. 'We can't find him,' I say.

She senses the panic in my voice. 'Don't worry, my mensch. He's probably at a friend's house watching TV. My Ollie was the same – he'd disappear for hours and then come home at midnight asking if dinner was ready.'

'I'm not so sure,' I say. My mind is distracted.

The roads start to empty as commuters return home and settle into their nightly ritual of average dinners, mindless TV and bad sex. There is no lost boy loitering by the roadside or visible through the thin, metallic light of shops downing their shutters.

'Don't worry. He will be all right,' Esther insists. I try to believe her. Amar is timid and clingy. He can't have gone far.

I spot a shape slumped inside a bus shelter, propped up like a mannequin against the glass wall. 'I've got to go,' I say to Esther. 'I'll call you later.' I slow the car and park by the bus shelter and get out to take a closer look.

It isn't Amar. It's a thin, bedraggled tramp sitting in a drunken stupor, eyes half open, knees drawn against his chest. A discarded blanket lies by his side. His glazed eyes don't register me. I carefully drape the blanket around his shoulders so he'll have some protection against the night. 'I can't find my son,' I confide in him, and press a ten-pound note into his hand.

'Is he back?' I shout as soon as I enter the house. There's a clatter of pots and pans in the kitchen. Geeta seems more composed than when I left her. She's getting ready to prepare a meal. 'I've prayed,' she says, gesturing towards the little silver statue of Ganesh on the window sill. 'We're worrying for nothing. Ganeshji will protect him. He'll be back soon.' She makes her way over to the fridge. 'I'm making shepherd's pie,' she says. 'Amar loves it, and he'll be hungry when he comes back.'

'I can pick up a takeaway if you want,' I say. 'Save you the bother – and Amar loves his pizza.'

But Geeta says she wants to cook, and asks me to get the mince from the freezer in the garage. Every Friday she goes to the halal butcher in Rusholme and brings enough meat for a week. She stores it in the garage, out of sight – the sight of all the bones and flesh in the fridge makes her feel sick.

* * *

A strong stench of vomit hits my nose when I swing open the door into the garage. My first thought is that a squirrel has died, his body slowly decomposing behind Geeta's pickle jars and rice tins. I switch on the light, and my foot brushes against something soft.

It is Amar, lying curled up on the floor, his knees folded against his chest, his hands holding his belly. Thick green vomit covers the front of his tracksuit, zigzagging its way from his open mouth. His tongue sticks out, an alien blue, and his plump cheeks look collapsed, like tyres where the air has been let out.

'Amar! Amar!' I shout, trying to wake him up, and grab him under the armpits, trying to hoist him up, but he flops against my chest like a puppet whose strings have been snapped. I slap him twice. 'Wake up, Amar! What have you eaten? Say something, for God's sake! Talk to me.'

The world is upside down. My hearing becomes alert to faraway sounds – the distant crunch of tyres, the squeal of a cat – and I hear the beating of my heart. Even the rain becomes thunder, filling my ears till I feel I'm drowning.

'Wake up, son, wake up,' I whisper, feeling his forehead and his wrist for a pulse. Both are cold as ice. I gather him up in my arms, cradling his head in my lap, sitting on the cold concrete floor of the garage, the naked light bulb swinging above me, helpless in my aloneness.

'Geeta, Geeta!' I try to shout. 'Call the doctor! Our son is ill!' But my throat only makes a rasping noise, and has no sound or shape.

Amar's supine body lies in my arms. I gently close his eyes and wipe the sick from around his mouth with the back of my hand. I hold him in my arms like a precious gift I can't bear to part with.

There are footsteps and I hear Geeta saying the onions are burning. She comes in and sees me holding Amar, and her howl fills my ears, stabbing straight into my heart. Her legs buckle under her and she sinks to her knees, trying to pull Amar to her breast, but I won't let him go. She loses her balance and falls back against the wall.

'Amar's gone,' I say, not looking at her. I'm staring at the wall behind her, at the shelves stacked high with her pickle jars.

Her mouth makes a funny sound. 'You're lying!' she screams. 'You're a lying bastard!' Her tears hang from the tip of her nose like silver dewdrops.

I keep shaking my head, trying to tell her she is wrong.

'Call an ambulance!' she screams. 'Call a fucking ambulance!' She grabs my mobile from my pocket, fingers ripping at the seams, tearing the fabric. I hear her give the address and house number to the woman at the other end of the line. I imagine her to be a helpful woman – maybe even a mother. She'll understand our pain. She'll be kind.

'Geeta, Geeta, beg her to come quickly. Tell her he's our only child. Tell her it's not too late!' I hear myself roar, snatching the phone from her. 'Do you understand? This is an emergency! You have to save him. Come now!'

But the woman at the other end is muttering gibberish.

The mist clears and I start to understand her words. She's asking about Amar. 'How is my boy?' I wave the mobile towards Geeta. 'This woman is mad. She is asking how Amar is.'

'Tell her there's no blood,' Geeta says, 'only vomit, and he has wet himself. But he does that all the time. I felt something when I lifted him, and the smell was bad, so maybe he's done potty too.' She gives the information mechanically, as though she's reading the weather bulletin.

I cover the phone and watch her weeping, tears running down the side of her nose and on to her chin. 'They want to know if there's a gun or a knife somewhere. What do I tell them?'

I'm no help to Geeta. I just sit there holding my son in my arms, bearing his precious weight, unable to give him away.

Geeta crawls around on all fours, checking the garage for a knife. The knees of her cream trousers turn a filthy brown as she lifts everything and checks to see what was behind.

I see her holding up a bottle and turning it upside down. It's empty. I recognise its red label. It's the pesticide I'd made Geeta order from Shanghai.

It had arrived one morning as I was about to leave for work. I had joked with the DHL guy, saying it was my monthly fix of Viagra. And when I used it I was about to head to the garage to put it away when my mobile vibrated with a text from Esther saying she was waiting for me at the hotel. And so I'd shoved the carton under the kitchen sink and run off to meet her.

And all these months that deadly poison sat innocently between the bottle brushes and scouring pads, biding its time, waiting for Amar to find it. And Amar – little broken Amar – found it. I imagine him listlessly moving around the kitchen, opening drawers and cupboards, always on the hunt for a new snack or soft drink Geeta might have bought and hidden away as a future treat. His eyes would've spotted the bottle. What did he confuse it with? A new kind of juice? He must have twisted open the lid, sniffed the green liquid, squeezed his eyes shut and gulped it down in one go. Or did he drink it deliberately, fully knowing what it was, and then hiding himself in the garage to die in peace?

I take hold of Geeta's hand, but she pushes me away. She presses the bottle tight against her breast, her eyes fixed on Amar's still face.

The shrill siren of an ambulance comes nearer. The front door slams open and unknown voices fill the house.

'We're here!' Geeta shouts through her tears. 'We're in the garage!'

My mobile rings somewhere. It won't stop its ringing. But my hands are busy stroking Amar's cold cheek.

I see a pair of shoes. Practical black shoes with rubber soles. Someone is bending down, prising away my hands, pulling away Amar.

'Now, sir, please don't be an obstruction. Step aside, please.' Efficient voices are telling me how I should behave. Can't they see I'm holding my son?

I fold my hands in supplication. 'Please, I beg of you, save him,' I say, helplessly.

A stretcher appears and Amar is hoisted on to it. The footsteps retreat. Urgent voices speak in whispers. Somewhere an engine snarls into life and a siren sets up its wail.

'We should follow Amar – make sure he's OK,' I say to Geeta. 'Let's go. My keys. I need my car keys.' I'm fumbling through my trouser pockets for them, but they aren't there.

The mobile starts ringing again. Esther's name flashes across the screen. I let it ring and die out.

Geeta crawls towards me on all fours. She seems to have lost the ability to walk or speak. She huddles next to me and I put an arm around her to steady her. She's blinking rapidly. I have an overwhelming urge to pee. I give in. The urine trickles down the side of my leg and into my sock.

A draught of cold air blows in through the open garage door. We begin to shiver.

THE END

ACKNOWLEDGEMENTS

This novel has had a long journey. It first began as a PhD dissertation at the Centre for New Writing at the University of Manchester. I am grateful to my supervisor, the brilliant writer M.J. Hyland, for showing me what good writing can be, and for her faith and belief in my work.

This book wouldn't have seen the light of day without the passion and enthusiasm of Will Dady and Renard Press. Thank you, Will, for your support.

Thank you, above all, to my husband Raj and my children, Ravi and Sabrina, for being my biggest cheerleaders.